Fictions of Masculinity

Fictions of Masculinity

Crossing Cultures,
Crossing Sexualities

Edited by Peter F. Murphy

NEW YORK UNIVERSITY PRESS
New York and London

NEW YORK UNIVERSITY PRESS
New York and London

Library of Congress Cataloging-in-Publication Data
Fictions of masculinity : crossing cultures, crossing sexualities /
edited by Peter F. Murphy.
p. cm.
Includes bibliographical references and index.
ISBN 0-8147-5497-X—ISBN 0-8147-5498-8 (pbk.)
1. Masculinity (Psychology) in literature.   2. Literature,
Modern—20th century—History and criticism.   I. Murphy, Peter
Francis.
PN56.M316F53   1994   93-44104
809′.9352041—dc20

Manufactured in the United States of America

10   9   8   7   6   5   4   3   2   1

For

Paul Richmond,
David Brown, and Victor Chaltain.

   Dear friends
   who have tried,
   over the past twenty years,
   to keep me honest.

Man turns a little bit of soft, delicate and highly sensitive flesh into the factor which bestows power on him; he is blind to the warmth, the fragility and the hypersensitivity of his penis. . . . He does not see the softness of his glans, the fragility and extreme excitability of the frenum, the sensitivity of the shaft along the urethra, the rough tenderness of his scrotum. He tries, on the contrary, to desensitise the whole organ as best he can to give it the coldness and the hardness of metal. What he loses in enjoyment he hopes to compensate for in power; but if he gains an undeniable power symbol, what pleasure can he really feel with a weapon between his legs?

—EMMANUEL REYNAUD
Holy Virility: The Social Construction of Masculinity

Contents

x Contents

Acknowledgments

In many ways this book represents more than just another collection of literary criticism. Feminism, as the guiding principle behind all of these chapters, provides a radically new way to understand the dynamics of interpersonal relationships. As a political theory and as a personal practice, feminism requires us to examine the way we think, the way we work, the way we love.

Since the late sixties and early seventies, when feminism began to have a profound effect on my life and on my politics, many people have contributed to my ability to bring a feminist perspective into my scholarship. Whereas not all of the people who have contributed something to the production of this anthology may see themselves as feminists, many do. Of these, I want to thank in particular, Claire Kahane and Ellen DuBois: teachers, colleagues, critics, and friends. Without their continued demand of me to be more rigorous in my thinking, to write more precisely, and to look beyond what appears to be obvious, my work in the field of feminism and masculinity would have remained much less sophisticated. They are not, of course, responsible for any remaining short-sightedness on my part.

Other colleagues who have made invaluable contributions to the editing and overall production of this book are Neil Schmitz, Bruce Jackson, and Carole Southwood. Neil has been a close friend, an invaluable mentor, and a fellow traveler throughout my many years in Buffalo. For this book he was always available to help me determine which essays to give serious consideration and which to eliminate; he was also there when the job seemed too daunting or the tough decisions imponderable. Bruce Jackson, an extraordinary critic in his own right, helped me to hone my writing skills and to understand more fully the job of an editor. Carole Southwood encouraged me to believe in the project even when the evidence seemed clearly in opposition to such optimism. Her ability as an editor was unsurpassed; her continual insights and suggestions improved the overall quality of this anthology.

 For their support both of my scholarship and of my struggle to make feminism relevant to a critique of masculinity I want to thank Michael Kimmel and Thaïs Morgan. Michael has been a staunch supporter of this project since its inception several years ago, and Thaïs has been "the writer over my shoulder" since I began working with her on another project five years ago. Indeed, Thaïs has taught me more about writing than anyone else with whom I have worked over the course of my twenty-five years in the academy. Without both of their continued belief in this project I am not sure I would have made it to the end.

 Over the past two decades I have been fortunate to have many close friends, male and female, who have struggled to make feminism a significant, even determining, factor in their lives. These friends, friends for whom personal and political change has remained central, are important to me in many ways, and it is with great pleasure that I acknowledge them here: Mike Boughn, Billy Burton, Diane Christian, Art Efron, Gladys Fox, Charles Haynie, Peter Hirshman, Paul Hogan, Bob Keesey, Jennifer Lehmann, Yvonne Price, and Jon Welch.

 Two scholarly institutions in Buffalo, one old and one new, have assisted in the production of this book, and I want to thank them both: Talking Leaves Bookstore and Shuffaloff Press. And, although she will no doubt castigate me for mentioning her name in such a secondhand place as the acknowledgments, I will take the risk of thanking Susan Pearles whose support, love, and radical insights have contributed more to this work and to my life than any other singular experience.

 At a time when political correctness may tend to encourage an uncritical embrace of feminism, multiculturalism, and any number of other "isms," friends who are either not influenced by these theories or even opposed to them are difficult to find. Two of my male friends, neither of whom are in the academy, have, through their unwillingness to accept many of the academy's assumptions, contributed immeasurably to my own critical engagement with a feminist perspective. Firsthand experience of masculinity in the North Country of New York State provides challenges and insights that any number of graduate seminars may never begin to approach. I want to acknowledge the difficult questions and the relentless disbelief of two of my most important critics (and friends)—Richard Chaltain and Steven Bowman.

As academics, many of us know how difficult the completion of any published work can be even with the encouragement of the Chair or of the Dean. Here, too, I was fortunate to have the unparalleled support of my Dean, Thomas Rocco and my Associate Dean, Anne Bertholf. For their interest in and commitment to the completion of this book I owe many thanks. Without their understanding of the problems one faces when trying to write the last paragraph or the last word (or even the first paragraph, for that matter), the completion of this anthology would certainly have been that much more formidable.

Others at Empire State College contributed to the successful completion of this book, but I want to mention, in particular, Rosemary Ruper and Emily Riley. I am grateful also for the scholarly examples set by two historians, Nick Cushner and Bob Mac-Cameron. And for her computer wizardry, I thank Frieda Mendelsohn. For its financial contribution, which allowed me some much needed time off to complete the manuscript, I wish to acknowledge the SUNY Empire State College Foundation.

My graduate students at the Universidade Federal do Rio Grande do Sul in Porto Alegre, Brazil, where I was a Teaching Fulbright, forced me to clarify many of the ideas that inspired this collection. Even though we were involved in a seminar on "The Politics of Love," issues of male heterosexuality remained central to our discussions. Unwilling to accept my tendency toward generalization, these students solicited more lucid thinking and unambiguous characterization. Their contributions to this book, while subtle and indirect, have made it a better anthology.

I would be remiss if I did not thank Niko Pfund, my editor at New York University Press. Niko brings together a kindness and a rigor that is rare. Without his suggestions and observations this anthology would not have reached its present level of professionalism. In addition, some anonymous readers provided clear direction about strengths and weaknesses, and although I did not agree with all of their comments, their contributions were extremely helpful.

Most of the chapters in this collection are published here for the first time, but some have appeared previously. For permission to reprint the chapters by Habegger, Radavich, Murphy, Leverenz, and Dellamora I want to thank, respectively: G. K. Hall, *American Drama, Twentieth Century Literature, American Literary History* (Oxford University Press), and *Victorian Literature and Culture* (AMS Press). For permission to quote from individual works by authors examined in this collection I wish to acknowledge: Maxine Groffsky for quotes from Edmund White's unpublished essay, "Straight Woman, Gay Men"; John Hawkes for quotes from *The Passion Artist*; Penguin USA and The Provost and Scholars of King's College, Cambridge, for quotes from E. M. Forster's "Albergo Empedocle," in E. M. Forster, *The Life to Come and Other Stories*, ed. Oliver Stallybrass; Penguin USA for quotes from Richard Rodriguez, *Days of Obligation;* David R. Godine Publisher for quotes from Richard Rodriguez, *Hunger of Memory*; Random House for quotes from James Cain's *The Postman Always Rings Twice;* the author's Estate and their agents, Scott Meredith Literary Agency, for quotes from David Goodis, *Cassidy's Girl;* Grove/Atlantic Monthly Press for quotes from John Rechy, *The Sexual Outlaw*, copyright © 1977, by John Rechy; and John Burgee, Architects, for permission to reprint the photograph of the model of the AT&T Building.

Fictions of Masculinity

Introduction: Literature and Masculinity

Peter F. Murphy

This collection is inspired by the realization that masculinity, like femininity, is a fictional construction. Myths of masculinity have been perpetuated in literature, art, popular culture, and the politics of our daily lives. This anthology focuses on the role literature has played in reinforcing the assumptions about masculinity and, at times, helping to establish the norm of manhood. These chapters also attempt to identify other images, other roles, other options for men and masculinity.

Women writing about women dominate contemporary work on gender. Men have been far more willing to discuss female sexuality than their own; at the same time, many of the more radical and challenging analyses of male sexuality have come from women.[1] When men consider the issue of female sexuality they often speak from assumptions of security about their own unexamined masculinity. In the introduction to *Speaking of Gender* (1989), Elaine Showalter maintains that "for men to discuss masculinity [is] already to diminish or threaten their own manliness" (7). One idea behind the chapters in this book rests on the belief that men have to interrogate their own sexuality if there is to be a revision of masculinity.

As a set of rhetorical constructions (fictions), masculinity involves diverse and continually changing sexualities. This anthology examines the deep structure of masculine codes in fiction and asks the question "Who are the men in modern literature?"

1

Studying the tropes of Western masculinity and the force of the dominant values, the authors synthesize insights from feminism, psychoanalysis, poststructuralism, and new historicism to explain how male sexuality is influenced by and reflected in fictional representations.

By examining images of masculinity in modern literature, the chapters explore traditional and nontraditional roles of men in society and in personal relationships. The authors inspect the representation of men in literature—the fiction of manhood—and they attempt to unravel the assumptions behind this imagination. And they speculate on possibilities for creating a new image of masculinity by identifying what literature has to say about changing these social roles.

Much feminist literary criticism suggests that misogynist literature benefits men. This book seeks to identify ways in which literature victimizes men as well as women. An analysis of the misandric[2] nature of literature is long overdue.

The recent proliferation of books on men and feminism suggests that a multitude of voices is beginning to chip away at men's traditional silences about their sexuality. Writings by men on masculinity go back at least fifteen years and, in the case of literary criticism, over three decades to the publication of Leslie Fiedler's *Love and Death in the American Novel* (1960). Fiedler's focus on the ways in which masculinity was constituted over two hundred years of American literature informed much critical thinking about men's roles in fiction and resonates throughout several of the chapters in this anthology.

For Fiedler, several recurrent themes dominate the literary construction of manhood. From the novels of Charles Brockden Brown to those of William Faulkner and, more recently, John Updike, men's struggle to avoid women has been a dominant theme. Escape and flight, manifest in bachelorhood and male camaraderie, represent appropriate means to eschew women.

At the same time, though, physical impotence and spiritual failure characterize many men in American fiction. Men as cowards with a lack of moral firmness, stupid men and alcoholics, and men who die when most needed are the men who victimize

women in American literature. Such are the roles American literature provides. What remains most baffling is "why men, too,
should have accepted this travesty on their nature and role in life;
but they did, in fact, accept it, even repeating [it] in their own
books" (Fiedler 1960, 90). How this complicity on the part of male
authors manifests itself in negative constructions of masculinity
in literature informs several of the chapters here.

More recent material on masculinity, especially that published
in the United States, emerges out of pop psychology and relies on,
at best, a liberal analysis of men's social and sexual roles. Robert
Bly's best-seller, *Iron John* (1990), exemplifies this perspective,
although his hostility to women and his reliance on such classic
primitivist metaphors for masculinity as king, soldier, and warrior presents a more poignantly reactionary position than did
his precursors.

Beginning with the early classics of the American men's movement[3] the focus has been on "the psychological hang ups of an
apparently timeless hyper-competitive and dominance-seeking
masculinity [which urges] men to get their heads straight" (Hoch
1979, 30). An exception to this approach is Jon Snodgrass's pio-
neering anthology, *For Men against Sexism* (1977), which established an early forum to discuss the relationship between feminism and masculinity. Focusing on patriarchy as the system of
male power and privilege, the essays in Snodgrass's collection
document and analyze men's opposition to sexism. Even today,
though, many activists in the American men's movement ignore
the effects of large social systems on men and male personality.
British and French writers, on the other hand, have presented a
radical, even socialist, perspective.[4]

Over the past fifteen years several British publications have
focused on the social and historical construction of masculinity,
culminating recently in the publication of two major book series.[5]
From a review of the theoretical debates and political forces that
have worked to define sexuality during the past two centuries to a
concern with issues of identity, desire, and choice, these works
have argued for a historical and cultural understanding of sexuality.[6] Sexuality, then, must be viewed in the context of the struc-

tures of language and culture. This insight provides a broad framework out of which can emerge a deconstruction of literary representations of masculinity.

By tracing dominant Western conceptions of masculinity from the Bible to the present, a radical psychoanalytic reading might focus on men's internalization of masculinity. Paul Hoch (1979), for example, argues that the distorted social roles allotted to women and men in our society have similar social and cultural causes. Hoch claims culture has taught us that just as women are supposed to be both innocent and sexy, men are supposed to be both "white hero" and "black beast."

Myths about male sexuality have informed men's lives over the past two centuries and focus, frequently, on the relationship between a man and his body. Man's obsession with his penis as a symbol of power, an instrument of appropriation, and a weapon, exemplifies this relationship,[7] a relationship that resonates throughout modern literature.[8] But, as Reynaud's (1983) epigraph to this book makes clear, if a man gains "an undeniable power symbol, what pleasure can he really feel with a weapon between his legs?" (42).

Because many men are forced to comply with macho standards of performance, standards frequently reinforced in modern literature, they experience their power and sexuality as heavy burdens. By adopting a model of sexuality and social relations that is neither hierarchical nor exploitative, men can begin to construct alternative relationships among themselves as well as with women. Though men still have many more risks to take and much more to say about male sexuality, these chapters provide a forum in which literature becomes the basis for a close scrutiny of male sexuality. The chapters try to address ways in which literature provides insights or models for what these relationships might be like.

Except for Fiedler (and a few others) men have just begun to articulate a critical analysis of masculinity in contemporary culture and in modern literature.[9] More recent, and sometimes more radical, books have been written by sociologists, psychologists, and historians, not literary or cultural critics. Sociologists have focused on the relationship between power and masculinity with particular emphasis on the relations of power within which men's domination and women's oppression exist. They look at the worlds of men at work and at play, in politics and in science, and they examine the changing roles of men in American history and society. John Stoltenberg's *Refusing to Be a Man* (1989), for example, probes the social fiction of manhood and identifies a political and ethical construction based on sexual injustice.[10]

In the United States gay studies dominate much of the work on masculinity. Here too, though, critical analyses have been done by historians, sociologists, and psychologists, not literary critics. With the exception of James Levin's *The Gay Novel* (1983) and David Bergman's *Gaiety Transfigured* (1991), some of the most important work on homosexuality has been written by historians.[11] British sociologists have analyzed the resistance to dominant heterosexual assumptions about sexuality in the context of political organization and the possibility of alternative moralities and life-styles.[12]

As with the American men's movement in general, pop psychology has dominated writings on homosexuality, though a radical psychological perspective has informed some of the more important works in gay studies. Guy Hocquenghem, for example, develops a critique of psychoanalysis relying on Lacan, Deleuze, and Guattari and centers on the debate over "the transhistoricity of the Phallus" (31).[13]

Only recently, with David Bergman's ground-breaking book, *Gaiety Transfigured: Gay Self-Representation in American Literature* (1991), has a long overdue contribution to gay literary criticism arrived.[14] Bergman makes clear that his book should not be seen as a history of gay American literature, a history that he believes will not be written for quite some time. Even while acknowledging the difficulty of compiling such a critical history, Bergman maintains that for many gay people "homosexuality . . . is a literary construction. Gay men learned to speak about their sexuality in a rhetoric of despair and degradation" (6–7). This reliance on literary representation for a gay identity had a particularly profound effect on gay youth.

As the chapters in this anthology demonstrate, masculinity in general and male sexuality in particular cannot be understood as static, ahistorical, or essential. Literary representations of manhood have both relied on dominant cultural assumptions about masculinity and exposed the untenability of those assumptions. Whereas several of the chapters contribute to the critical work being done in gay studies of literature (e.g., David Bergman, Rafael Pérez-Torres, Jim Elledge, and Richard Dellamora), others confront the seeming one-dimensionality of male heterosexual behavior (e.g., David Radavich, David Leverenz, Christopher Metress, and Peter Murphy). The subtitles under which they are organized should make clear the fluidity of any gender categories; many of the chapters that cross cultures also cross sexualities, and vice versa. Crossing sexualities cannot include only those chapters about homosexuality; Radavich on Mamet and Murphy on Hawkes, for example, examine the complexity of male heterosexuality. Crossing cultures may not rely only on chapters examining nonwhite societies. Dellamora and Bergman on British men, and Leonard Duroche and Peter Schwenger on aspects of the German and/or Eastern European experience explore the dynamics of male sexuality, not just gay or straight, Western or nonwestern. Any differentiation remains problematic. The distinctions used here have relied primarily on an attempt to establish useful categories, not to create comprehensive or ineradicable classifications.

Leverenz's effort to link, rhetorically, the construction of masculinity to the stages of U.S. capitalism provides a broad historical context in which to read and interpret the many and varied works of literature examined in the other chapters. Radavich's chapter on David Mamet, whose plays realistically portray normative straight male society, gives a focal point for many of the other chapters as well. Each approaches that core from eccentric and even radical viewpoints (e.g., Nazi Germany, phenomenology, prostitution, male violence, homosexuality, and transvestism).

Leverenz reads the cultural poetics of manhood in texts by Cooper, Norris, London, Wister and Burroughs. In this way, the chapter traces the motif of a beast-man hero, from Cooper's "Hawkeye" and Frederick Jackson Turner's Andrew Jackson at the end of the "Frontier" essay, to the increasingly patrician male (Teddy Roosevelt, Tarzan, Bruce Wayne) who descends into the animal/underworld/underclass to redeem powerless middle-class capitalist civilization from its unmanliness. His historical framing of various narratives that depict the fantasmatic incorporation by men of both a primal violence and a cultivated code of honor or civility suggests some reasons for the peculiarly American obsession with powerlessness and manliness, despite an obviously empowered and dominant middle class.

Radavich analyzes Mamet's single-minded quest for lasting, fulfilling male friendship protected from the threats of women and masculine vulnerability on the one hand and the destabilizing pursuit of power and domination on the other. Mamet's concerns about masculinity take on a particularly intense resonance in the latter part of the twentieth century, as the traditional bastions of male companionship have increasingly been called into question. A desire for dominance, usually between men of unequal rank or age, battles with an equally strong desire for loyalty and acceptance, resulting in hard-won, intense, fundamentally unstable intimacy established in the absence of women. The duality of this conception results in a darkly comic artistic vision suited to a society in transition, moving from the comfortable economies of empire to the new, less stable realities of shared power and enterprise.

Murphy's chapter on *The Passion Artist* pursues the darkly comic vision of John Hawkes. Focusing on the impact feminism has had on this important postmodern male novelist, Murphy resists much Hawkes criticism that sees his fiction as just more misogynist male pornography. The novel explores the sexual awakening of Konrad Vost by examining the relationship between masculinity and femininity. By elucidating the fantasies, doubts, manifestations, and transformations of male heterosexuality in the context of a world besieged by hatred, fear, and shame, the novel conveys the male protagonist's sexual awakening from the artist of dead passion to an "artist . . . of the willed erotic union" (Hawkes 1978, 181). This long and brutal voyage culminates in Vost's acceptance of his role as a man, due in no small part to his experience of what it is like to be a woman.

In a similar fashion, Metress counters the more traditional reading of hard-boiled detective fiction, which sees the male characters as complete and heroic men at successful play in the fields of male desire. By focusing on the American *roman noir* of Wool-rich, Thompson, and Goodis, Metress examines a genre that offers a chilling contrast to the sometimes unsteady but ultimately reassuring images of honorable masculinity inscribed in the worlds of Hammet, Chandler, Spillane, and MacDonald. The novelists of this suggestively deviant strain, according to Metress, give us "complete men untarnished by and unafraid of physical and sexual challenges to their masculinity. . . . Such writers people their novels with fragmented men stained by an absurdly tragic past and tormented by emasculating landscapes of frustration and paranoia." Goodis, for example, not only gives us images of men without power but men without desire for power. Working out of a hard-boiled tradition that encourages above all else an assertive phallocentric poetics of masculine integrity, Goodis gives us instead a world where self-erasure offers the only hope of survival in a rude and absurdly antagonistic universe.

Transition, change, and emergence characterize the fictional masculinities examined throughout this book. A close weaving of text and context allows Dellamora to make important points about Forster's position at a moment of emergence, at a moment when possibilities for a discourse about masculinity are being redefined. He concentrates on the ways the successful prosecution of Oscar Wilde affected male homosexuals of that period and, in particular, the severity of this impact on Forster. Examining "Albergo Empedocle" (1903), Forster's first published short story, Dellamora focuses on the "heterosexual contract" and identifies ways in which this story "conveys the tone-deafness of its young men to the possibility of female alterity." For Dellamora, this deafness "may owe not so much to Forster's personal blindness . . . but rather to the structure of heterosexual interchange that defines woman."

Extending the work initiated in his previous essay on "The Masculine Mode" (1989) and in his book-long study, *Phallic Critiques* (1984), Schwenger examines how men write and, in particular, how they write in relation to the father. Beginning with the looming figure of Kafka's father, Schwenger's chapter moves to the larger figure of the Father in Freud's *Totem and Taboo*—the father whose murder is supposed to have originated the forms of culture as expiation. Schwenger then turns to Donald Barthelme's *The Dead Father*, which uses both these predecessors in a novel whose parodic postmodern strategies undermine the father's power and indicate the possibility of a culture beyond patriarchy.

In a chapter concerned also with discourse and writing, Alfred Habegger analyzes the soldiers' language in Stephen Crane's *The Red Badge of Courage* and explicates the relationship between the idea of loose talk and the representations of spoken language. Habegger examines ways in which "this inarticulateness, so pervasive and obvious in Crane's narrative, has to do with much more than an illusory realism of speech. Crane is also saying something about the social and moral constraints on expression." Crane's dialogue frequently "shows that unrestrained speech brings a risk of combat and inadvertent self-ostracism." Commenting on the frequency with which soldiers are wounded in the head in Crane's novel, and how often these injuries are linked to the capacity to speak, his reading draws out an insight into the larger cultural compulsions that render the process of masculine maturation one that is cognate with a heightening of discursive incapacity.

Duroche examines the conflicting male narrators that come to bear on an adolescent during the period of National Socialism—what it was like to grow up as a man in Nazi Germany. Duroche's analysis of *Katz und Maus* fits nicely beside Habegger's reading because it too tries to gain a purchase on the logic of modern masculinity by seeing it as inducing a necessary disturbance of communication. Indeed, Duroche's chapter is invaluable for its effort to think about the questions of masculinity raised in Grass's text in terms of the ways in which patriarchal language itself implies a compulsory narrative of "masculinity."

In his chapter on J. R. Ackerley's memoirs and autobiographical fiction, Bergman continues his examination of the power of gay literature to structure identity, complementing Schwenger's piece on the importance of the father. In Ackerley's works the recurring figure of the Ideal Friend epitomizes a tradition of gay literary representation going back at least to Homer. As Ackerley envisions the Ideal Friend, he is ostensibly heterosexual, but reserves a place in his affections and sexual responses for a single homosexual man—Ackerley himself. He is rough, lower class, and without intellectual or artistic pretensions—in short, Ackerley's seeming opposite. Yet a closer examination of Ackerley's work, particularly *My Father and Myself,* indicates that the Ideal Friend, like Ackerley himself, is modeled after his father and constitutes the working out of a reverse Oedipal relationship.

Pérez-Torres's piece on Rechy contributes to the discourse on homosexuality discussed by Dellamora and Bergman. He argues that the construction of a rebellious sexual other in *The Sexual Outlaw* reproduces many of the same repressive heterosexual social attitudes against which Rechy's novel speaks. Bringing Bakhtin and Guattari to bear on this text, Pérez-Torres offers insights into the effects of de- and reterritorialization. By rendering some of the complications of Rechy's gendered position in relation to his politics, the chapter exposes some of the contradictions and conflicts evident in notions of critical alterity.

Frank O'Hara's unwillingness to make explicit his homosexuality, coupled with an apolitical (though, at times, seemingly conservative) attitude toward the rapidly changing American society of the 1950s and 1960s, introduces another complex gay experience. Frank O'Hara's forty-four love poems chronicling his relationship with Vincent Warren must be understood, Elledge argues, as more than simply love poems. O'Hara's tendency to disguise, obscure, and even ignore the genders of the poems' lovers is examined in the broader context of O'Hara's selective openness about his homosexuality. The significance of O'Hara's "fear of reprisal by a homophobic society, a disinterest in homosexuality as theme or content in poetry, and a disregard for politics in general" informs Elledge's reading of the "Warren series." Seeing this sequence of poems as examples of how the lack of gender identification in love poetry strengthens the poetry, Elledge argues that the reader's attention becomes focused on matters that transcend gender: "Specifically, O'Hara investigates love, its intricacies, ironies and paradoxes."

Suzanne Kehde, Miriam Cooke, and Martin Danahay analyze some examples of the representation of masculinity in non-Western literature. Kehde's chapter draws together ideas from postcolonial theory and some of the current work being done around the questions of sexuality. Recognizing the importance of the imaginary in femininity and in the construction of masculine subjectivity, she emphasizes the political implication of gender construction. For Kehde, Hwang's play debunks traditional Western ideas of masculinity, femininity, and the rationale for the colonial enterprise by showing how these imbricated notions underlie the male fantasy most completely projected in Puccini's famous opera. *M. Butterfly* deconstructs not only *Madame Butterfly*, but also Lacan's theory of the totalitarian domination of the phallus by showing how belief in masculinist mythology can so cloud the judgment that a man may live for twenty years without noticing that his lover isn't a woman, with disastrous consequences for his material practice. *The Quiet American* exposes, also, the discourses of gender and colonialism. Unlike Hwang's play, though, Greene's novel provides no critique of gender stereotypes and little of imperialist assumptions. Indeed, Greene fails to acknowledge that there might be some connection between them.

By examining the early novels of Naguib Mahfouz, the Egyptian Nobel Laureate, Cooke uncovers the dynamics of gender construction in his treatment of Arab "neopatriarchy." She focuses particularly on the relationship between male protagonists and prostitutes in a neopatriarchal society. Like Kehde's chapter, this one keeps femininity in the discussion of masculinity (in the figure of the female prostitute), and also recognizes a broad political context. Danahay examines ways in which Rodriguez's poetics reflect and respond to the predominant white male construction of masculinity; Rodriguez both incorporates this culturally dominant representation and transcends it. Danahay complexifies the solidity of the public/private split that Rodriguez seems to want to repress and reads Richard Rodriguez's autobiography as a bildungsroman attentive to the processes of acquiring the social status of masculinity. His reading explores these processes in terms of the distinctive ways they are affected by the cultural marginality of those who choose between a "macho" masculinity that is resistant to competence in English as the language of the dominant social order, and a "feminization" through education that gains one access to a degree of power within that social order.

Individually and collectively, the chapters included here contribute to what Elaine Showalter refers to as "the genuine addition of gender as a 'central problem in every text' read and taught, 'whatever the era and whoever the author' " (1989, 11). In this way, the authors and I hope to problematize masculinity in ways not unlike the early impact of feminist theory on literary constructions of femininity.

Notes

1. Indeed, even in the emerging field of "feminism and literary constructions of manhood" women have edited two of the more important books. See Laura Claridge and Elizabeth Langland, *Out of Bounds: Male Writers and Gender(ed) Criticism* (1990); and Thaïs Morgan, *Men Writing the Feminine: Literature, Theory, and the Question of Gender* (1994).
2. Misandric is used here as an antonym for misogynist, meaning not so much a hatred of men as a negative representation of masculinity. Needless to say, though, the misogynist and misandric representations of gender are not necessarily mutually exclusive. Literature frequently incorporates negative representations of both women and men.
3. See, for example, Warren Farrell (1974), Marc Fasteau (1975), and Jack Nichols (1975).
4. For a more detailed review of how much more radical British men's studies work is than American, see Peter F. Murphy (1989).
5. Three works stand out as central to a radical examination of masculinity: Jeffrey Weeks's *Sexuality and Its Discontents* (1985); Paul Hoch's *White Hero Black Beast: Racism, Sexism and the Mask of Masculinity* (1979); and Emmanuel Reynaud's *Holy Virility: The Social Construction of Masculinity* (1983). Weeks has published several studies of sexuality ranging from an overview of gay politics from the nineteenth century to the present (*Coming Out*, 1977) to a chronicling of the regulation of sexuality since 1800 (*Sex, Politics and Society*, 1981). Both book series are being published by Routledge and Chapman: Jeff Hearn's Critical Studies on Men and Masculinities, and Victor Seidler's Male Orders. See also the books by Rowena Chapman and Jonathan Rutherford, eds. (1988); Andy Metcalf and Martin Humphries (1985); David Morgan (1992); David Porter, ed. (1992); Michael Roper and John Tosh, eds. (1991); Jonathan Rutherford (1992); and Victor Seidler (1989, 1991a, 1991b).
6. See, in particular, Jeffrey Weeks's *Sexuality and Its Discontents* (1985).

7. See Emmanuel Reynaud (1983).
8. Fiedler (1960) points out that Faulkner tended to portray "the hysterical masculine protest of his time in the image of the maimed male, revenging himself on woman who has maimed him with the first instrument that comes to hand, a weapon in place of the phallus" (346–47). Gilbert and Gubar (1988), in the first volume of their projected three-volume study, *No Man's Land*, comment on how literary representations of the penis frequently present it as "a therapeutic instrument in the domestication of desire, [which] was always on the verge of turning into the penis as pistol" (48); "not only has the penis now been redefined as a weapon, it has been defined as a weapon whose aggressive onslaughts women ought to want" (113–14).
9. *Men in Feminism* (1987), edited by Alice Jardine and Paul Smith, represents an early example of this effort. A provocative anthology of contemporary feminist thinkers, this collection provides a major contribution to the articulation of a male feminist theory. The ideas presented in this book should help men who are involved with feminism to apply that critical theory to their own lives as men and as teachers, especially teachers of literature. By calling for men to assume "the responsibility of speaking their own bodies" with the realization that men "still have everything to say 'about' [their] sexuality" (37), Paul Smith begins to counter the concern of many feminist critics who "worried that male critics would appropriate, penetrate, or exploit feminist discourse for professional advantage without accepting the risks and challenges of investigating masculinity, or analyzing their own critical practice" (Showalter 1989, 7).

   Though a relative dearth of books on men's roles in fiction still exists, at least a half-dozen new texts have been published over the past decade. Alfred Habegger's *Gender, Fantasy, and Realism in American Literature* (1982) focuses on the novels of Henry James and William Dean Howells. Peter Schwenger's *Phallic Critiques* (1984) looks at masculinity in twentieth-century literature (e.g., Mailer, Hemingway, Mishima). Three relatively new and important books include: Wayne Koestenbaum's *Double Talk: The Erotics of Male Literary Collaboration* (1989), David Leverenz's *Manhood and the American Renaissance* (1989), and Richard Dellamora's *Masculine Desire: The Sexual Politics of Victorian Aestheticism* (1990). Koestenbaum examines literary collaboration between male authors, Leverenz focuses on nineteenth-century American literature, and Dellamora analyzes the cultural construction of masculinity in nineteenth-century British literature. Joseph A. Boone and Michael Cadden's *Engendering Men: The Question of Male Feminist Criticism* (1990), examines literature spanning the past four hundred years. As the title suggests, this is a collection of essays by male critics that attempts to begin the task of retheorizing the male position in our culture. The essays examine poetry, fiction, the Broadway stage, film and television, and broader cultural and psychoanalytic texts.

10. For a sociological perspective see Arthur Brittan (1989) and Michael Kaufman (1987). For a historian's view see Mark Gerzon (1982), E. Anthony Rotundo (1993), and Peter N. Stearns (1979). At least three other publications on men and masculinity should be mentioned. Mark Carnes and Clyde Griffen's new anthology *Meanings for Manhood: Constructions of Masculinity in Victorian America* (1990), is a collection of essays by historians that includes "Middle-Class Men and the Solace of Fraternal Ritual," "Suburban Men and Masculine Domesticity, 1870–1915," and "On Men's History and Women's History." Harry Brod's anthology, *The Making of Masculinities: The New Men's Studies* (1987) exemplifies the recent development of men's studies programs. Including essays from diverse disciplines, this collection assumes the relevance and desirability of men's studies programs, rather than posing such academic alternatives as a critical consideration. And, Arthur and Marilouise Kroker's new anthology, *The Hysterical Male: New Feminist Theory* (1991), "traces out the logic of imminent reversibility in received patriarchal discourses in psychoanalysis, art, theory and culture. . . . What results is an intense, provocative and creative theorization of feminism under the failing sign of the unitary male subject" (xiv). These three books add an important dimension to historical, social, and cultural considerations of masculinity.

11. See Jonathan Katz's (1976) documentary history of lesbians and gay men in the United States, John D'Emilio's (1983) historical overview of the political struggles and social movements instrumental in the emergence of contemporary American gay culture, and John Boswell's (1980) comprehensive study of attitudes toward homosexuality from the beginning of the Christian era to the fourteenth century, which represent some of the more important works in gay history published during the past twenty years.

12. See the Gay Left Collective's *Homosexuality, Power, and Politics* (1980), for a collection of essays examining "the ways in which power has shaped . . . notions of homosexuality and resulted in a sustained sexual oppression" (7).

13. See Guy Hocquenghem's examination of *Homosexual Desire* (1978), which emerges from a major concern with language, psychoanalysis, and Marxism.

14. See also James Levin's *The Gay Novel* (1983), in which he used "the characters in the novels [he examines] as models of what attitudes were towards homosexuality and how this affected the lives of those who were homosexually oriented" (2). Limiting his field to those

novels in which the character is aware of his homosexuality, Levin's book is as much a social history of homosexuality as it is a work of literary criticism. Mark Lilly's *Gay Men's Literature in the Twentieth Century* (1993) is also of relevance here.

Works Cited

Bergman, David. *Gaiety Transfigured: Gay Self-Representation in American Literature.* Madison, WI: University of Wisconsin Press, 1991.

Bly, Robert. *Iron John.* New York: Addison-Wesley, 1990.

Boone, Joseph A., and Michael Cadden, eds. *Engendering Men: The Question of Male Feminist Criticism.* New York: Routledge, 1990.

Boswell, John. *Christianity, Social Tolerance and Homosexuality.* Chicago: University of Chicago Press, 1980.

Brittan, Arthur. *Masculinity and Power.* London: Basil Blackwell, 1989.

Brod, Harry, ed. *The Making of Masculinities: The New Men's Studies.* London: Allen and Unwin, 1987.

Carnes, Mark C., and Clyde Griffen, eds. *Meanings for Manhood: Constructions of Masculinity in Victorian America.* Chicago: University of Chicago Press, 1990.

Chapman, Rowena, and Jonathan Rutherford, eds. *Male Order: Unwrapping Masculinity.* New York: Routledge, 1988.

Claridge, Laura, and Elizabeth Langland, eds. *Out of Bounds: Male Writers and Gender(ed) Criticism.* Amherst, MA: University of Massachusetts Press, 1990.

Dellamora, Richard. *Masculine Desire: The Sexual Politics of Victorian Aestheticism.* Chapel Hill, NC: North Carolina Univ. Press, 1990.

D'Emilio, John. *Sexual Politics, Sexual Communities: The Making of a Homosexual Minority in the United States, 1940–1970.* Chicago: University of Chicago Press, 1983.

Farrell, Warren. *The Liberated Man: Beyond Masculinity: Freeing Men and Their Relationships with Women.* New York: Random House, 1974.

Fasteau, Marc. *The Male Machine.* New York: Dell, 1975.

Fiedler, Leslie. *Love and Death in the American Novel.* New York: Stein and Day, 1960.

Gay Left Collective, ed. *Homosexuality, Power, and Politics.* London: Allison and Busby, 1980.

Gerzon, Mark. *A Choice of Heroes: The Changing Face of American Manhood.* New York: Houghton Mifflin, 1982.

Gilbert, Sandra M., and Susan Gubar. *No Man's Land: The Place of the Woman Writer in the Twentieth Century, vol. 1, The War of the Words.* New Haven, CT: Yale Univ. Press, 1988.

Habegger, Alfred. *Gender, Fantasy, and Realism in American Literature.* New York: Columbia Univ. Press, 1982.

Hawkes, John. *The Passion Artist.* New York: Harper and Row, 1978.

Hoch, Paul. *White Hero Black Beast: Racism, Sexism and the Mask of Masculinity.* London: Pluto Press, 1979.

Hocquenghem, Guy. *Homosexual Desire.* London: Allison and Busby, 1978.

Jardine, Alice, and Paul Smith, eds. *Men in Feminism.* New York: Methuen, 1987.

Katz, Jonathan. *Gay American History: Lesbians and Gay Men in the U.S.A.* New York: Avon Books, 1976.

Kaufman, Michael, ed. *Beyond Patriarchy: Essays by Men on Pleasure, Power and Change.* New York: Oxford Univ. Press, 1987.

Koestenbaum, Wayne. *Double Talk: The Erotics of Male Literary Collaboration.* New York: Routledge, 1989.

Kroker, Arthur, and Marilouise Kroker, eds. *The Hysterical Male: New Feminist Theory.* New York: St. Martin's Press, 1991.

Leverenz, David. *Manhood and the American Renaissance.* Ithaca, NY: Cornell Univ. Press, 1989.

Levin, James. *The Gay Novel: The Male Homosexual Image in America.* New York: Irvington Publishers, 1983.

Lilly, Mark. *Gay Men's Literature in the Twentieth Century.* New York: New York University Press, 1993.

Metcalf, Andy, and Martin Humphries, eds. *The Sexuality of Men.* London: Pluto Press, 1985.

Morgan, David. H. J. *Discovering Men.* New York: Routledge, 1992.

Morgan, Thaïs, ed. *Men Writing the Feminine: Literature, Theory, and the Question of Gender.* Albany, NY: SUNY Press, 1994.

Murphy, Peter F. "Toward a Feminist Masculinity." *Feminist Studies* 15, no. 2 (Summer 1989): 351–61.

Nichols, Jack. *Men's Liberation: A New Definition of Masculinity.* New York: Penguin, 1975.

Porter, David. ed. *Between Men and Feminism.* New York: Routledge, 1992.

Reynaud, Emmanuel. *Holy Virility: The Social Construction of Masculinity.* London: Pluto Press, 1983.

Roper, Michael, and John Tosh, eds. *Manful Assertions: Masculinities in Britain since 1800.* New York: Routledge, 1991.

Rotundo, E. Anthony. *American Manhood: Transformations in Masculinity from the Revolution to the Modern Era.* New York: Basic Books, 1993.

Rutherford, Jonathan. *Men's Silences: Predicaments in Masculinity.* New York: Routledge, 1992.

Schwenger, Peter. "The Masculine Mode." In *Speaking of Gender*, edited by Elaine Showalter. New York: Routledge, 1989.

———. *Phallic Critiques: Masculinity and Twentieth Century Literature.* New York: Routledge and Kegan Paul, 1984.

Seidler, Victor J. *Recreating Sexual Politics: Men, Feminism and Politics.* London: Routledge, 1991a.

———. *Rediscovering Masculinity: Reason, Language and Sexuality.* New York: Routledge, 1989.

———, ed. *The Achilles Heel Reader.* London: Routledge, 1991b.

Showalter, Elaine. "Introduction: The Rise of Gender." In *Speaking of Gender*, 1–13. New York: Routledge, 1989.

Snodgrass, Jon, ed. *For Men against Sexism.* Albion, CA: Times Change Press, 1977.

Stearns, Peter N. *Be a Man! Males in Modern Society.* New York: Holmes and Meier, 1979.

Stoltenberg, John. *Refusing to Be a Man: Essays on Sex and Justice.* Portland, OR: Breintenbush Books, 1989.

Weeks, Jeffrey. *Coming Out: Homosexual Politics in Britain from the Nineteenth Century to the Present.* London: Quartet Books, 1977.

———. *Sex, Politics, and Society: The Regulation of Sexuality since 1800.* London: Longman, 1981.

———. *Sexuality and Its Discontents: Meanings, Myths and Modern Sexualities.* London: Routledge, 1985.

I

Fictions of (American) Masculinities:
A Historical Overview

1

The Last Real Man in America: From Natty Bumppo to Batman

David Leverenz

In the summer of 1989, one of the glossiest men's magazines appeared with a picture of Sean Connery on the cover. Dressed in a creamy ivory tuxedo, standing with arms folded against a beige background, visible only to the waist, he embodied elegance, sensuality, and virility. The caption proclaimed him "The Last Real Man in America."

Why should the Last Real Man in America be a British actor? The taunting ambiguity implies that no American can claim true manliness anymore; to see it at all is to see it vanishing. Only a working-class Scotsman who secured his international image as James Bond, an Englishman equally skilled in civility and violence, can temporarily import virility to American shores. Yet the pleasurable visual framing of his face as white on white on beige seems curiously reassuring. Connery represents the last, best hope, the master of everything not quite seen, dark, and below the belt. He can protect a civilized, yet effete Us from a barbaric though enviably violent Them.

The July cover of *Gentleman's Quarterly* slipped from my mind until late August, when I was standing in a check-out line at a Florida supermarket and noticed the September cover of *Celebrity Plus*, a decidedly downscale fan magazine. This cover featured Harrison Ford in a woodsy setting, with a yellow blurb announcing, "Rare Interview! The 'Last' Real Man."[1] Faced with such a flagrant intertextual rip-off, I began wondering: In what other country could variations on that come-on sell magazines? To ask the question exposes the strange mixture of bravado, anxiety, and nostalgia in the motif. Male readers in more traditionally patriarchal cultures might well feel insulted. Why did I feel a bit wistful, even teased? The motif has a beleaguered quality to it, as if urban, yuppie, corporate, feminist America had become intrinsically emasculating.

It was the summer of 1989 when Batman, the Last Real Man in Gotham City, galvanized the highest short-term gross in movie history by dramatizing a double myth of man-making. To save hapless bourgeois cosmopolitans from their high-tech powerlessness, Bruce Wayne becomes half beast and descends into the underclass, a downward mobility that also gives steel and grit to his aristocratic boyishness. The year before, another sweetly bumbling Bruce Wayne patrician had managed to step into Ronald Reagan's manly image and position by banishing what a *Newsweek* cover story had labelled "The Wimp Factor" with two brilliantly chosen counterimages. Willie Horton, the underclass rapist, evoked the powerlessness of middle-class voters as well as the spinelessness of liberal officials. With a more subliminal audacity, George Bush secured his mythic transformation into an electable manly image by choosing Robin as his running mate. The war with Iraq confirmed that new image so completely that cartoonist Pat Oliphant "temporarily retired" George Bush's purse.[2] Collectively, the war enacted a drama of national remasculinization in which "humiliating" Saddam Hussein avenged the still festering humiliation of Vietnam.

From spring through summer 1991, the number one best-seller was *Iron John: A Book about Men*. Robert Bly's book speaks to many midlife American men who look into themselves and find mostly rubbery adaptations. The movement Bly has inspired depends less on a recoil against feminists than on a widespread need to struggle beyond workplace-generated norms for fathering and male friendships. Many men want to feel both "wild" and strong yet emotionally open and vulnerable with other men, beyond the capitalist constraints enforcing competitiveness, mobility, and self-control. Astutely repackaging psychoanalytic confessions in Native American patriarchal trappings, Bly's movement offers Indian tribal ceremonies as initiation rites and mentoring support groups for remasculinization, in ways quite continuous with turn-of-the-century middle-class lodge rituals. Under this patriarchal cover, as Mark Carnes has argued for Masonic ceremonies, men can express their hidden nurturing side as well as their anger and grief about inadequate fathering, without feeling feminized or weak.[3]

The first Last Real Man in America, Cooper's Natty Bumppo, dramatizes a similar white flight from civilized unmanliness to Native American traditions of patriarchal comradeship. Especially in *The Last of the Mohicans* (1826), the novel-romance that established Natty's image as heroic frontiersman, an elegiac nostalgia suffuses Cooper's portraits of red and white heroes alike. As a variety of critics have demonstrated, Cooper simultaneously replicates and displaces expansionist conflicts by subsuming a collective story of manifest destiny in an elegy for primitive manly character.[4] Fleeing civilization and progress, "Hawkeye" or "La Longue Carabine"—almost his only names here—finds his soulmate in Chingachgook, the first "gook" to inhabit the enduring white myth of the self-subordinating man of color. When the reader meets Natty and Chingachgook, however, the two characters are vehemently arguing over why white people have any right to take the Indians' land.

At first Natty claims that the whites are just doing what the Indians used to do to each other. But it does seem unfair, he acknowledges to himself, that white men have bullets. Worse, modern white men no longer publicly shame the "cowardly" and acclaim the brave; they "write in books" instead of telling their deeds in their villages, Natty says in disbelief, and they spend their "days among the women, in learning the names of black marks," instead of hearing the deeds of the fathers and feeling "a pride in striving to outdo them" (35). Eventually the two friends agree to blame the whole problem on the Dutch, who gave the Indians firewater (37). But the solution seems patently inadequate to the tensions raised by the protracted argument. Or rather, the solution allows them to feel that their friendship can evade history, much as Natty frequently proclaims his uncontaminated white identity, "a man without a cross," while plunging further and further into crossover liminal realms of mixture.[5] At the end, when Chingachgook's son Uncas dies and the father himself ironically becomes the Last of the Mohicans, the "self-command" of both grieving friends gives way to bowed heads and "scalding tears" (414). Childless, facing death, and bonded with natural manly feeling, the two embody a double elegy for a vanishing patriarchal simplicity inexorably giving way to the settlements. Why would Cooper write a book to mourn the passing of a manliness that scorns the womanish writing of books? Because he and his civilized male readers could condescend to this "Natural Bumpkin" yet long for the manliness that Natty Bumppo represents.

Ostensibly devising a paternalistic narration to harmonize civilized and savage life with principles of moral conduct, as the 1850 preface to the *Leatherstocking Tales* sententiously claims, Cooper fortunately brings stress-points and contradictions out into the open. He reserves his most pointed mockery for the maladapted transplant from high civilization, David Gamut, the musician in the wilderness. On the frontier, where traditional class status seemingly yields to a hierarchy of natural manliness, psalm-singing David Gamut begins at the bottom. He can't even manage his mare. The hapless male musician has been a contrasting foil in various Real Man myths since the time of Hercules, who as a boy knocked his music teacher dead with his lyre. It was an accident, as the Greek myth tells it; the little lad just didn't know his own strength. Benvenuto Cellini begins his swaggering autobiography by recounting how he pleaded, fought, and fled from his doting father, who so desperately wanted Benvenuto to play the flute. The most recent American version of this myth comes from *Trump: The Art of the Deal:*

Even in elementary school, I was a very assertive, aggressive kid. In the second grade I actually gave a teacher a black eye—I punched my music teacher because I didn't think he knew anything about music and I almost got expelled. I'm not proud of that, but [!] it's clear evidence that even early on I had a tendency to stand up and make my opinions known in a very forceful way. The difference now is that I like to use my brain instead of my fists.[6]

At least Cooper presents David Gamut with amused respect for his civilized "gifts." Moreover, by the end of *Last of the Mohicans* David Gamut has ascended the scale of manliness. He demonstrates fortitude and integrity where other men display villainy and cowardice. He also helps to harmonize their beleaguered group, much as Cooper's narrative seeks to blend civilized and savage virtues through a traditionally patriarchal rhetoric of mutual respect and honor.

Like any conception of manhood, an emphasis on honor functions ideologically, which is to say, as a social fiction constructed by empowered constituencies to extend their power, yet felt as a natural and universal law. It shames individual deviance to protect the group, making men more fearful of losing the respect of other men than of losing their lives in battle. Cooper vividly dramatizes a ritual of public, tribal shaming in contrasting the stoic self-command of Uncas with the abject behavior of Reed-that-bends, both captured by the Hurons. Soon the Huron chief acknowledges the unflinching, manly stranger as someone who has "proved yourself a man" (286). Shortly thereafter, the father of Reed-that-bends publicly disowns his son, in the "bitter triumph" of a lonely "stoicism" over a father's "anguish" (293). If Chingachgook, Colonel Munro, and the aged Tamenund cannot protect their children or their people from kidnapping and carnage, they take solace in their rigid adherence to a traditional manly code of honor and shame.

If manhood is not forever, its seemingly ageless durability has less to do with testosterone than with social constructions of male shaming to protect the social unit.[7] In that respect, capitalism's great change has been to destabilize small-scale patriarchy, in which rituals of honoring and shaming depend on a long-term, knowable audience for their effectiveness. Natty Bumppo's characterization preserves traditions of patriarchal honor yet exposes their flimsiness by presenting him as a man of fixed integrity who is always on the move, forever estranged from stable community. Writing for an audience of strangers in an emerging mass market,

Cooper depicts Natty as an embodiment of patriarchal honor without the patriarchy, entrepreneurial mobility without the entrepreneur. An incipient clash between two social constructions of identity yields to an idealization of cross-color male chumship in an ahistorical mode. Yet Cooper taunts civilized readers with a vague sense of the shamefulness inherent in the white march westward—not, paradoxically, the guilt from exercising oppressive power but the shame from accommodating to a large-scale nation-state. There domestic intimacy and career advancement have superseded a manliness that already starts to take on the status of a compensatory simplification—a myth of mourning the fathers, not of emulating them.

Baffled by what he hears of the settlements, Natty wonders if it could be true that these new ways of living offer something "which binds man to woman closer than the father is tied to the son" (315). Urbane readers could indulge his naïveté yet feel the twinge of loss. How silly: Natty feels neither sexual desire nor delight in home companionship. How sad: no civilized white man feels the fabric of father-son bonds as Natty does. Once again Cooper forces his readers into contradictions evaded by Natty's portable manliness. His hero seems unnaturally asexual, yet more natural than men of the settlements, many of whom found their homes defined by their women and the marketplace defined by their competitive aloneness, without communal or paternal anchors.

That rhetoric, too, bespeaks a sentimental mystification. The instant success of *Last of the Mohicans* depended in part on Cooper's ability to recast emerging power relations as elegiac nostalgia. Fatherly yet childish, the Indians are vanishing to the cultural museum of literature by their own choice and accord. Besides, according to the implicit fantasy, so long as lower-class vagrants like Natty help to dispossess the Red Men for the better sort, some of his best friends can be Indians, and he can call his readers women or bookish or even married. Cooper's double elegy for patriarchal manhood, red and white, veils a postpatriarchal set of power relations based initially on class and racial dominance, and driven ultimately by capitalist modes of circulation that unsettle all modes of collective, stable identity except those based on the nuclear family and specialized skills in the corporate work-place.[8]

In Shakespeare's day, "pioneer" meant the basest manual laborers in the army, the men who dug trenches and mines. At the onset of his frenzy, Othello tells Iago,

> I had been happy if the general camp,
> Pioneers and all, had tasted her sweet body,
> So I had nothing known.
>
> (III, iii, 342–44)

Something of that baseness carries over to Cooper's portrait of his garrulous, illiterate hero. Yet a new myth of manly heroism also begins to emerge in Natty, situated as he is midway between preindustrial hierarchies of the honorable versus the base and a new, more diffusely fluid circulation of entrepreneurial middle-class energies.

As Kenneth Cmiel's *Democratic Eloquence* emphasizes, traditions of "character" could not hold against a democratization that blurred the boundaries separating genteel from vulgar, high from low. A new "middling culture" mixed formal and folksy speech to redefine proper public language and self-presentation. Along with a pervasive push for upward mobility came a premodernist sense of role-playing, offering "numerous identities . . . a multitude of expressive choices." Other historians, notably Stuart M. Blumin, analyze the paradox of a new middle class whose male members experience identity as competitive individualism, with class consciousness applied only to those at the top and bottom.[9]

If middle-class male constructions of "self" become linked to roles and competitive upward mobility in an increasingly professionalized workplace, "class" becomes either a genteel self-refashioning or a depth into which no capitalist climber must fall. Horatio Alger's most successful novel, *Ragged Dick* (1868), presents a Bowery urchin who rises to middle-class respectability not simply by pluck, luck, and entrepreneurial industry but also by continually telling tall tales about himself. He extravagantly fictionalizes his classy connections to play linguistic dress-up. Ragged Dick knows he will be capitalized by his genteel mentors only as he embraces both the speculative mobility of voice and the Protestant work ethic produced by capitalism.

In that context, a new myth of manly heroism takes on the self-divisions and psychic mobility fostered by a marketplace beyond small-scale ideological controls. An avenging hero, half animal and half human, fusing beast and patrician, descends into an evil underclass to save a helpless bourgeois civilization. From Tarzan to Batman, the mass-market myth expresses the paradox of a collectively empowered middle class in which men feel personally powerless, unmanly, or unreal except as they compete in the workplace. Simultaneously, the mass-market myth appeals to a fantasy of working-class remasculinization through often sadistic violence, diffusely directed against black men, gay men, and women.

The paradox has its contradictory sources in the Jacksonian era, when both Cooper's works and the Davy Crockett tales begin to exploit the beast-man motif, though without the later patrician incorporation. In Carroll Smith-Rosenberg's analysis, the Davy Crockett stories voice a widespread sense of being "powerless in the face of massive and unremitting social transformation." Challenging but not overthrowing the bourgeois struggle for legitimacy, Crockett's adventures represent several kinds of liminality: male and female adolescence, a society in transition from patriarchal communities to industrial capitalism, and crossovers between dominant and marginal groups. The tall tales of young, violent males taking on the bestiality of their animal or subhuman opponents celebrate individual freedom and personal control while dehistoricizing capitalist forces of change and inverting bourgeois heterosexuality.[10] Dramas of incessant personal dominance and humiliation seek to recast these dynamics in the preindustrial interpretive framework of honor and shaming.

In *The Last of the Mohicans*, Cooper edges Natty toward beast-man status, especially in the last third of the story, where Natty infiltrates an Indian village by dressing up as a bear. There, however, Cooper does almost nothing with the tensions latent in such a crossover. Fifteen years later, in *The Deerslayer* (1841), Cooper at last plunges toward the new myth, as readers learn for the first time how Natty got that strange animal name of "Hawkeye."[11]

In Chapter 7, Natty becomes a man by killing his first Indian. Instead of taking a scalp, Natty takes a new name as his trophy, a name bestowed on him by his victim. Behaving with traditional honor, Natty had refrained from shooting the Indian unfairly. But honor can't protect him against a "savage" whose body betrays his sneaky bestiality: his eyes rage like a "volcano," his nostrils dilate "like those of some wild beast" (108). Fortunately, just as the Indian crouches like a "tiger" in the bushes to shoot, Natty senses danger, whirls, cocks his rifle, aims, and fires, all before the Indian's tightening finger quite pulls the trigger. This is the kind of woodsmanship that Mark Twain so gloriously debunks in "Fenimore Cooper's Literary Offenses."

The mythic transformation begins after the shooting. Prone though still conscious, the victim watches Natty "as the fallen bird regards the fowler," while the lad feels "melancholy" as he stands over the "black" eyes of the "riptyle" (110–11). Then the Indian dies like a man. With "stoicism," "firmness," and "high innate courtesy," the Indian raises his hand to "tap the young man on his breast." The red man's dying words rechristen the white man: "eye sartain—finger lightning—aim, death—great warrior soon. No Deerslayer—Hawkeye—Hawkeye—Hawkeye. Shake hand" (113–14).

One could argue that this mutual mythic transformation relieves white readers of guilt for the pleasures of Indian killing. While a red man threatens, the narrative depicts him as a snaky beast. After he ceases to be dangerous, he becomes a man so that he can bless the suitably depressed killer with a new identity: Deerslayer becomes Manslayer. But the naming goes the other way, from Deerslayer to Hawkeye. A bird's soaring, predatory quickness dignifies and sharpens Natty's rightful yet brutal dominance. Here is a new myth of American manhood in the making: to be civilized and savage in one composite, self-divided transformation. The myth dramatizes a potential for downward mobility on the liminal frontier, to save the manhood of upwardly mobile men in the settlements.[12]

By the turn of the century, the new myth shapes a multitude of texts, from Turner's frontier thesis (1893) to Frank Norris's *McTeague* (1899) and Jack London's *Call of the Wild* (1903). Norris's tale of brute-man's downward mobility from petty bourgeois aspirations to theft and murder has grotesque violence to women at the center of McTeague's descent. If the dentist's hapless ambitions can be blamed on his mother and his wife, who goad him out of his natural niche as a miner to compete in a profession requiring intelligence and dexterity, McTeague takes his "apelike" revenge by killing his wife after nearly biting her fingers off. Throughout, Norris's patronizingly self-conscious genteel narration simultaneously relishes McTeague's brutality while exposing McTeague as a figure of urban powerlessness, helpless against complexity, rivals, or his own desires. Lashing out whenever he is made to "feel small," this Last Real Man in America ends his life as a comic butt, handcuffed to a pursuer's corpse in the desert, where he stares stupidly at a bird cage. Incapable of the self-transformations and poses by which "the Other Dentist" achieves success, McTeague represents a cautionary tale of the brute inherent in all real men, and the monstrous desires that have to be masked in the upward march to genteel decorum.[13]

For Jack London, the Last Real Man in America is a dog who turns into a wolf. London's *Call of the Wild* mocks the silliness of self-absorbed, hysterical Mercedes, the only woman who ventures onto the arctic tundra, especially when she tries to talk about theater and art. As she vanishes into an ice hole, the narrative all but says good riddance. Buck's allegorical manliness also survives his chumship with John Thornton, who saves and cherishes Buck with a "genuine passionate love" (74) climaxing in an ecstasy of penetration and talking dirty, from which the onlookers discreetly withdraw.[14] But Thornton, too, is only human, with a capitalist lust for gold, and therefore powerless when confronted by the arctic underclass, the subhuman Yeehats. In avenging Thornton's death and tasting human blood for the first time, Buck enacts Deerslayer's rite of initiation with a hint of comic reversal: the dog "had killed man, the noblest game of all" (98). Now he can fulfill the "pride" of his downwardly mobile call of the wild by taking over the leadership of a wolf pack.[15]

In human society, however, Buck too is powerless. As the first sentence declares, "Buck did not read the newspapers." He cannot understand why he is being bought and sold. The arbitrary buying and selling of Buck, which structures the plot, takes on meanings beyond his comprehension, yet obvious to those who can read:

Men need to carry the news, men want to find gold. Unlike Norris, London unambivalently contrasts Buck's natural leadership with the degeneracy of such men. Nevertheless, ideal manliness thrives in Buck only because he becomes less and less human, more and more wild, while his admiring narrator—like Cooper—writes a "wild" book about him for boy-men readers who feel trapped in their maturation and long for exotic virility.

Like tales of musician-bashing, the beast-man myth is as old as the dawn of story-telling. Its transformation into late nineteenth-century myths of vanishing American manhood also draws on age-old myths of a hero's descent into the underworld and on the cross-cultural bourgeois myth of an aristocratic hero who makes himself inhuman in order to become superhuman (e.g., the Count of Monte Cristo). Ultimately, as Victoria Kahn suggests for Machiavelli's rhetorical finale in *The Prince*, where manly *virtù* beats womanly Fortuna into submission, all myths of manliness may seek allegorical stabilization to ward off the perception that "the individual is not at all in control of his behavior."[16]

The special American quality lies in the new myth's exaggerated emphasis on frontier liminality, in the contradictory class mobilities, and in the incipient note of mourning. Why would upwardly mobile readers relish downwardly mobile heroes? The answer may lie in the narrative voices so divided between class loyalty and gender urgency. Those tensions bespeak a world in which both class and gender were starting to feel like nostalgic props.

To read Frederick Jackson Turner's "The Significance of the Frontier in American History" in the context I'm sketching here exposes his fascination with redemptive manly savagery and belligerence. For Turner, the frontier is "the meeting point between savagery and civilization," and therefore a crucible for "rapid and effective Americanization." Stripping a man of his European manners, the frontier "takes him from the railroad car and puts him in the birch canoe. . . . Before long he has gone to planting Indian corn and plowing with a sharp stick; he shouts the war cry and takes the scalp in orthodox Indian fashion. In short, at the frontier the environment is at first too strong for the man." Unlike Cooper, Turner relishes the prospect of such assimilation. The strong man "transforms the wilderness" only after the wilderness has transformed him. A hybrid, both savage and civilized, he is no longer ridden by class-linked, European manners; "here is a new product that is American" (463).[17]

Not until 1920, when Turner at last expanded his brief essay into a book, do the gender issues become flamboyantly manifest. Climaxing his vision of the frontier as a natural factory for manufacturing American manhood, Turner all but lets out a war whoop when the New World produces Andrew Jackson. Outrageously casting Thomas Jefferson as a frontier prophet, "the John the Baptist of democracy," Turner presents Jackson as democracy's incarnation, explicitly "Moses" and implicitly Christ. Above all, Jackson stands forth as the First Real Man in America. Why? Because when Jackson tried to speak on the floor of the Senate, his rage blocked his words. Turner exultingly quotes Jefferson, without a hint of Jefferson's patrician recoil: "When I was President of the Senate he was a Senator, and he could never speak on account of the rashness of his feelings. I have seen him attempt it repeatedly and as often choke with rage" (471).

What Ishmael finds both appalling and fascinating in Ahab, Turner celebrates in Jackson without reservation.

At last the frontier in the person of its typical man had found a place in the Government. This six-foot backwoodsman, with blue eyes that could blaze on occasion, this choleric, impetuous, self-willed Scotch-Irish leader of men, this expert duelist, and ready fighter, this embodiment of the tenacious, vehement, personal West, was in politics to stay. . . . The men of the Western World turned their backs upon the Atlantic Ocean, and with a grim energy and self-reliance began to build up a society free from the dominance of ancient forms. (471–72)

To be aggressive, rebellious, enraged, uncivilized: this is what the frontier could do for the European clones on the East Coast, still in thrall to a foreign tyranny of manners.

If Turner's bull-in-the-china-shop image of manliness empowered his own assault on an overbearing Eastern establishment, it also empowered the emerging profession of American history.[18] Just as with Norris and London, however, a diffuse sense of civilized powerlessness lurks at the margins of his text. He reemphasizes at the end that the frontier is closed now; the days of democratic man-making seem to be over. Now, to challenge the new "manufacturing aristocracy," he finds not frontier fire-eaters but only inequality, poverty, and labor unions. Turner's muted ending evokes a baffled Lone Ranger surrounded by Marxists and pluto-crats. As he concludes, the frontier has been a safety valve, post-poning the conflict between capital and labor: "But the sanative influences of the free spaces of the West were destined to amelio-rate labor's condition, to afford new hopes and new faith to pio-neer democracy, and to postpone the problem" (473).

As if waiting in the wings to seize the image of bully-boy patri-cian leading the nation away from class conflicts toward a re-newal of collective virility on international frontiers, the man who most successfully exploited the emerging myth of the cross-class beast-man was Theodore Roosevelt, not Eugene V. Debs.[19] Roose-velt epitomized manly zest for the new imperial nation in part because of his jaunty energy, but also because his image brought together both aspects of the new myth: the top rung of the ladder of social aspiration and the gladiatorial animal arena sensed at the bottom. In what other advanced industrial country could a former president, an asthmatic child of old money, make a serious run for his country's top office under the banner of "The Bull Moose Party"?[20] Later in 1912, after Roosevelt's quixotic drive for national leadership failed, he accepted the solace of another presidency, from the American Historical Association, as fitting reward for his various books about manliness on the Western frontier.

Like Turner, Roosevelt both celebrates and mourns the frontier as a crucible of man-making whose time has passed. *Ranch Life and the Hunting-Trail* (1888), for instance, begins with an epigraph from Browning: "Oh, our manhood's prime vigor! . . ." The book depicts the "daring and adventurousness" of stockmen (7) and the reckless, "defiant self-confidence" of cowboys (9) in Cooper-like terms, as "a primitive stage of existence," which is now "doomed, and can hardly outlast the century" (24).[21] Here "civilization seems as remote as if we were living in an age long past. The whole existence is patriarchal in character: it is the life of men who live in the open, . . . who call no man master" (6). Written self-consciously to Easterners, the book carefully differentiates among the exotic frontier types while warning that the West "is no place for men who lack the ruder, coarser virtues and physical qualities, no matter how intellectual or how refined and delicate their sensibilities" (10). For those who can take it, the frontier brings out mutual honor and self-respect—not "the emasculated, milk-and-water moralities" but "the stern, manly qualities that are invaluable to a nation" (56). Cowboys are "much better fellows and pleasanter companions" than men on small farms, Roosevelt declares, "nor are the mechanics and workmen of a great city to be mentioned in the same breath" (10).

Roosevelt had an immense personal impact on the two writers who inaugurated the most enduring twentieth-century myths of American manliness. In Owen Wister's *The Virginian* (1902), dedicated to Roosevelt, an urbane Eastern narrator quickly discovers that the ungrammatical but self-possessed hero from old Virginia (never named) embodies the essence of true gentlemanliness and bravery. Wister had been a David Gamut in the making. A *summa cum laude* graduate in music from Harvard who had played privately for Franz Liszt on the European tour preparing him as an opera composer, he suffered his first nervous breakdown in 1884, and went to Wyoming at the suggestion of his doctor, the ubiquitous S. Weir Mitchell. Over the next two decades, Wister and his friend Frederic Remington together created the myth of the cowboy, at the moment of the cowboy's obsolescence. Both men cherished Roosevelt's example and friendship.[22] In the second edition of *The Virginian* (1911), Wister's "Rededication" hails Roosevelt as an inspiring "benefactor" who brought "sincerity" back to public men after "nigh half-a-century of shirking and evasion." Earlier, as president, Roosevelt had specifically praised exactly what Wister had intended in crafting his cowboy myth: *The Virginian* fused frontier democracy with chivalric aristocracy, joining gentlemanly ideals of honor and rhetorical wit with frontier ideals of manliness.[23]

As Wister's first preface acknowledges, however, his book is an elegy for a rough nobility that must inevitably fade, in the transition to what has become "a shapeless state . . . of men and manners" (xi). Beyond the domestic comedy, in which the hero's "rhetorical aplomb" brings schoolteacher Molly Stark Wood to accept his patriarchal dominance despite his lower social status, Wister's enduring contribution has been the genre of the American western, where the plot culminates in a face-to-face shoot-out between good and evil. That drama has shaped and simplified national self-perceptions from the Virginian versus Trampas to General Schwarzkopf versus Saddam Hussein. Giving closure to the recurrent saga of triumph and humiliation, a man of honor who is also a man of violence stands tall and alone against the darkening sky, as elegiac counterpoint to the sunset of self-reliance and the rise of the corporate state.

Perhaps not surprisingly, the writer who codified the Last Real Man myth by fusing beast with patrician had been rejected by Roosevelt's Rough Riders. Published in 1912, the year of the Bull Moose Party, Edgar Rice Burroughs's *Tarzan of the Apes* presents a benignly self-divided hero.[24] Tarzan, or Lord Greystoke, an orphan child of British aristocrats who is raised by African apes, enacts the age-old drive of dominance over other males—but only as an ape. When his equally age-old gentlemanly instincts are aroused, he turns chivalric, especially with Jane, who shares his double self. In the novel's most mythic moment, having saved Jane from Terkoz, an ape-ravisher, Tarzan first "did what no red-blooded man needs lessons in doing. He took his woman in his arms and smothered her upturned, panting lips with kisses." Jane's primal self responds; her civilized self recoils. So "Tarzan of the Apes did just what his first ancestor would have done. He took his woman in his arms and carried her into the jungle" (156–57).

As Marianna Torgovnick emphasizes, however, Tarzan immediately feels great confusion about what a man ought to do. Should he rape, as Terkoz would? Yet he is a man, not an ape; how should a Real Man act?[25] Having carried her off against her (civilized) will, Tarzan resolves to "act as he imagined the men in the books would have acted" (166). These are the books in his parents' cabin that he is teaching himself to read, though as yet he can speak not a word. Giving Jane a locket, "like some courtier of old . . . the hall-mark of his aristocratic birth" (168), he sleeps outside her bower to make her feel protected from him as well as by him. By the end of the book, when Tarzan first speaks to her, he is bilingual and can drive a car.[26]

Burroughs's myth transforms Cooper's Hawkeye to a Rooseveltian pince-nez strong man. Tarzan the aristocrat lets another man claim Jane in marriage, because no gentleman would think of asking a lady to break a promise, while Tarzan the ape posts this terse warning on his parents' cabin door:

> THIS IS THE HOUSE OF TARZAN, THE
> KILLER OF BEASTS AND MANY BLACK MEN.
> DO NOT HARM THE THINGS WHICH ARE
> TARZAN'S. TARZAN WATCHES.
> TARZAN OF THE APES. (103)

No one notices Tarzan's casual equation of beasts and blacks, or his presumption of property rights, Eric Cheyfitz comments. What everybody wants to know is his name, which means "White Skin." Only mother-love is exempted from the novel's pervasive racism. African blacks represent an evil worse than apes, except perhaps on the generically male side. Equally brutish are the ship's low-class mutineers.[27] If Tarzan's character divides Natty Bumppo's harmony of civilized and savage gifts, the plot fulfills almost every civilized white fantasy of class and race domination.

So, more desperately, does *Batman*'s plot, which begins with Batman fighting urban muggers and ends with the hero on a tower fighting first a black man and then the Joker, his trickster double, the "artist of homicide." In *Batman*, human powerlessness is everywhere. Cooper's patriarchal controls vanish in the first scene, as Daddy takes his family down the wrong street toward urban danger, much as Tarzan's father led his family into African violence. Neither these fathers nor the city fathers can stop the seeping evil represented by "Axis Chemicals" and the Joker. "Axis," of course, brings to mind the World War incipient in these depressionlike scenes. Anton Furst's sets not only evoke the awed helplessness induced by Nazi architecture but also call attention to themselves *as* sets, making moviegoers half aware of their own presence as dwarfed spectators. Everyone sits in the dark, watching the flickering lights, wondering where the sun went, and passively awaiting the next random spectacle of mutilation.

Only a superhero could save this civilization of victims. After the Joker challenges Batman via the TV screen to a "mano-a-mano" combat, he dispenses money and poison gas to the greedy, faceless, depression era masses, along with cynical words about the uselessness of their ordinary lives. Enacting again and again the only drama he knows, he exposes everyone's loss of face. He disfigures the women he dominates, he turns underworld rivals into skulls, and he defaces himself with his ceaselessly inhuman smile, the inverse of the Batman symbol. Nor can Lord Greystoke's aristocratic instincts serve Bruce Wayne as a source of chivalric power. Stripped of his dress-up costume, the hero seems all too human and adolescent, to the initial disgust of Batman fans who expected a version of the *Dark Knight* comic book.

Here, in fact, the moviemakers may have been more attuned to their mass-market audience than sophisticated reviewers have allowed. If "Me Tarzan, you Jane" is Tarzan of the movies, simplifying Lord Greystoke's double self into a Noble Savage primitivism, Burroughs's novel voices a contradictory fusion of savage violence with a comedy of manners. This double drama of man-making mixes brutal dominance and humiliation with civilized self-control. From a very different perspective, the postmodernist uses of psychoanalytic doubling and gender crossover in Frank Miller's *Batman: The Dark Knight Returns* and Alan Moore's *Batman: The Killing Joke* (both of which influenced the movie) jettison the contradictory myth, replacing it with a Noble Deconstructionist.

In the adult comics, a battered, aging Bruce Wayne desperately tries to ward off the contemporary chameleonism, cynicism, and even psychosis that the Joker gleefully welcomes. "You had a Bad Day once, am I right?"[28] says Joker to Batman. "Why else would you dress up like a flying rat?" Everyone has been driven crazy; it's even crazier to pretend that it makes sense to keep on struggling. Where these comic books dramatize the story of an agonized, midlife consciousness on the verge of self-deconstruction in a world unravelling toward relentless urban violence and moral nihilism, the movie draws on similar images of futility while telling the story of a young near-Fauntleroy, whose salvational mission redeems the world, assuages his pain, and makes him a man.

Like Sherman McCoy in Tom Wolfe's *Bonfire of the Vanities* (1987), another rich boy-man who yearns to be "King of the Jun-

gle" and "Master of the Universe," Bruce Wayne seems to have it
all yet doesn't even know how to manage his first date with Vicki
Vale. Their comic awkwardness at opposite ends of his enormous
dining room table resolves into speedy downward mobility to the
butler's kitchen, where they can get to know each other like kids
on a sleepover. Wolfe's cynical narration has no such endearing
touches. Readers meet Sherman McCoy on his knees, trying to
put a leash on his dachshund before walking to his mistress's
apartment. Over 600 pages later, unleashing the Bernhard Goetz
inside himself, the real McCoy feels a climactic rush that comes
not from sex, not from money, but only from punching a tall black
man in the solar plexus. "You cold-cocked him!" a friend says,
astonished (651–52). Vitalized at last, McCoy wants to do it
"again" and *"again"* (656). While the people around him wonder
if he has become a "lunatic," he shows his teeth and "let out a
short harsh red laugh" as the band of demonstrators retreats
"down the marble halls." [29] With that bestial surge, the book ends.
This is the urban context for *Batman*'s more cross-class appeal.
Both plots offer what Richard Slotkin has called the frontier fantasy of "regeneration through violence" as a restoration of manliness, overcoming diffuse fears of urban powerlessness and deper-
sonalization lurking below the ostensible fears of random
muggings. [30]

Bruce Wayne's double drama of man-making occurs at the level
of cosmopolitan gender stereotypes as well as beast-man myth.
The Gatsbylike boy-man becomes a Real Man, in human terms,
when he visits Vicki Vale to tell her his half-human identity. Angry
because she thinks he has stood her up on a date, she starts to
voice her outrage. "Shut up," he explains, and pushes her down
on the couch. Accepting that move without a murmur, the Pulitzer
Prize-winning photographer waits expectantly. Ahhhh, viewers
should feel; we can relax. He *is* a real man after all. He *can* carry
her off into the jungle, or the Bat Cave. Besides, it is a typically
feminine trivialization to reduce all the horrors of what the Joker
tried to do to Vicki in the Museum to being stood up on a date.
Part of the scene's comedy, as Bruce reverts to inarticulate stum-
bling in his attempt to tell her about himself, is Vicki's immediate
inference that he must be gay. But viewers now know better: the

anxious rich kid will be a gentleman of force, the last one, not another lost or vicious urbanite, of whatever sexual persuasion.

Thereafter, despite Vicki Vale's fast-track city career, their dialogue updates *Tarzan*'s traditionally gendered comedy of manners while the plot enacts sadistic fantasies of man-making and humiliation. In Vicki's apartment as in the Bat Cave, it is much more important for a man to talk about his work than for a woman to talk about her feelings. When Vicki at last insists on bringing up Love, Bruce-Batman responds with an almost parodic imitation of the credo, "Later—a man's got to do what a man's got to do." From then on, Vicki becomes a marginal inconvenience and support for Batman's work identity. She never seems annoyed that he stole her potentially prize-winning photographs of him. Instead, she plays the traditional helpmeet, who lies a little about her weight and shows courage to aid his career. At the very end, Vicki does the ultimate, self-degrading sacrifice to help her man triumph. She goes down on the Joker, slowly and unmistakably sliding down his body and off the screen, to divert his attention.

As beast-patrician and fair young damsel are chauffeured away into their snug seclusion, one could imagine a feminist ending. Vicki Vale will return to her career with exclusive Batman photos, win a second Pulitzer Prize, and move on up to become the first female anchor of a prime time news show. Meanwhile, Bruce Wayne will have retired from his dangerous, adventurist, and unpaying job to become a contented house husband, managing the friendly servants who do the child care, the laundry, and the dishes.

On balance, however, it seems more likely that Vicki Vale's voluptuous presence as faithful sidekick functions primarily to remove the threat of homosexuality from the Batman myth, not to awaken hopes of a feminist swerve.[31] Several years before the movie was made, Batman fans responded to a poll by vigorously demanding that Robin be dumped. He seemed too wimpy and twerpy; some used gay-baiting terms. Yet much of the movie's power comes from its playing with the adolescent ambiguities in Michael Keaton's role. He *could* have become a Robin, or a homosexual, or an effete impotent snob, or a faceless husband to a strong career woman. Instead, he resolutely masculinizes himself in a world that seems hell bent on robbing every man of a father and virility. The fact of Kim Basinger's casting looms larger than her stereotypic gendering to empower the hero as yet another Last Real Man in America.

I draw six conclusions from this sketch of a changing myth. First, ideologies of manhood have functioned primarily in relation to the gaze of male peers and male authority. By suppressing complex feelings often involving women, such ideologies produce good workers, competitors, and fighters in the public sphere. Here several of Eve Kosofsky Sedgwick's arguments are to the point. In *Between Men* and *Epistemology of the Closet* she argues that "homosocial desire" builds on homophobia and misogyny to perpetuate patriarchal oppressions. Ultimately, the construction of public maleness as a privileged category to serve the social unit fosters a male preoccupation with measuring self-worth in the eyes of one's workplace peers. What Sedgwick takes to be the generating issue, an increasingly phobic and paranoid (hetero)sexual self-construction of maleness in the last century, seems to me a prime consequence of capitalism's early construction of the workplace as the exclusively gendered site for public rewards.

In theory, the workplace could be gender neutral. In practice, as Daniel Gilmore concludes in *Manhood in the Making,* a society's preoccupation with manhood "directly correlates with male-role stress," especially "when men are conditioned to fight." Gilmore intriguingly suggests that both male codes of combative or stoic assertiveness and female codes of self-sacrifice have to be learned, but that men need ritual and ideological socialization because they are more "atomistic," whereas women are "normally under the control of men," especially in precapitalist societies.[32] In capitalism, too, fathering and competition play roles at least as central in male self-construction as any forms of sexual desire or ambivalence about mothering, in large part because competitiveness drives the energy of any market economy.

What changes is how the respect of one's peers and authority is constituted. In preindustrial, small-scale societies, whether in Native American villages or Greek and Italian city-states, manhood connotes honor, fatherhood, citizenship, sexual prowess, and bravery in battle as well as pride of craftsmanship and primacy as family provider. In modern economies—especially in the United States where, as Alfred Chandler argues, capitalism has taken an exceptionally competitive form—patriarchy has given way to a more amorphous mixture of collaboration, rivalry, and role-playing to give upward mobility in the professionalized marketplace.[33] The evolving beast-patrician myth of man-making incorporates a mid-nineteenth-century image of entrepreneurial individualism with turn-of-the-century class extremes to stabilize a violent yet hypercivilized compensatory fantasy.

Second, the myth has become both more homophobic and more ambiguously playful about sexual identity. Not one of Cooper's contemporary readers would have dreamed of calling for a Kim Basinger to replace Chingachgook, though it's fun to imagine what Natty would do. Cooper half tried once, and egregiously failed, in *The Pathfinder* (1840). On the other hand, *Batman*'s social comedy flirts with Bruce Wayne's potential gayness, while his animal cross-dressing evokes Mark Seltzer's label for Jack London's heroes, "Men in Furs."[34] *Batman*'s disappointing sequel comfortably incorporates a strong, daring, and angry animal-woman (Catwoman), while erasing the more dangerous homoerotic energies playing at the margins of Batman's self-construction. What's missing is any disruptive, doubled charge between Batman and the Penguin. Taken together, the two movies confirm Sedgwick's basic insight about violent homosocial bonding across the body of a woman, perhaps with the additional covert pleasure of aristocratic and brute males coupling inside one heroic, isolated, guarded yet vulnerable male body.

Third, the myth continues to idealize, marginalize, and mutilate women. Though Jane and Vicki Vale are a good deal more respectably sexy than shrinking Alice Dunham or intrepid Judith Hutter in *The Deerslayer*, women continue to function in these narratives as adjuncts to a man's remasculinization, providing emotional supports and physical targets.

Fourth, the incipient theme of effete, feminized urbanity in Cooper becomes an explicit rejection of high society manners in Turner and Jack London, an attempt at amalgamation in Wister and Burroughs, then a cross-class dramatization of civilized powerlessness in *Batman*. In that sense, "woman" may be a token signifier for a larger, stranger issue, present also in *Tarzan* and *McTeague*, where spirited modern heroines become helpless victims: Why should the power of bourgeois civilization breed such fantasies of middle-class male powerlessness?

In *Epistemology of the Closet*, Sedgwick provocatively emphasizes "the production and deployment, especially in contemporary U.S. society, of an extraordinarily high level of self-pity in nongay men." She attributes this to an incipient panic about the "incoherences implicit in modern male *hetero*sexuality." More diffusely, pervasive fantasies of abusing and victimizing women can be legitimated by male fantasies of "maudlin" self-pity, as if to scapegoat one's own sense of victimization.[35] Here again, however, gender panic may be more symptom than source. A middle-class man's sense of being powerless or unreal, or incoherent at the edges of his gender construction, can be produced by a workplace-fostered obsessionality in which the safest way to feel embodied desire is to hyperventilate about homosocial achievement or dominance.

Fifth, I see three stages in the progression of the new myth. In the "Hawkeye" stage, Natty's lateral mobility and chumship with Chingachgook complement a nostalgic mourning for precapitalist patriarchy and a covert fantasy that frontier bumpkins can rid the civilized world of Indians. In the turn-of-the-century stage, McTeague, Buck, and Turner's Andrew Jackson dramatize a downward mobility from lower-class status into savagery to redeem and/or shock effete Eastern gentility. Norris seems to have written *McTeague* as a manly riposte to the feminized tea-party "realism" of Howells's *The Rise of Silas Lapham* (1885).[36] A relish for violence to women surfaces in Norris, London, and Burroughs, becoming a fascination with grotesque mutilations in *Batman*. In the third, post-Teddy Roosevelt stage, the hero seems comfortably (Tarzan) or uncomfortably (Bruce Wayne) divided between an old-money class identity and a role as bestial avenger, while urban civilization seems faceless and impotent. Here upper-class status seems stereotypically inadequate to empower masculine privilege.

Sixth, and finally, an ambivalence about the powers of the female body saps the strength yet girds up the loins of these Last Real Men. As he leads his pack after a rabbit, Buck feels "an ecstasy" of blood-lust, "a complete forgetfulness that one is alive," like an inspired "artist" or a "war-mad" soldier, "sounding the deeps of his nature, . . . going back into the womb of Time. He was mastered by the sheer surging of life, the tidal wave of being" (*Call of the Wild*, 49). Ape-man McTeague feels insensibly reborn in his manliness as he reaches the mountains, where Mother Nature is not "cozy, intimate, small, and homelike, like a good-natured housewife"—or the woman he has murdered—but "a vast, unconquered brute of the Pliocene epoch, savage, sullen, and magnificently indifferent to man" (212–13). With a simpler dichotomizing, Batman becomes invulnerable in his womblike Batmobile and Bat Cave, though instantly vulnerable in his all-too-fragile and phallic Batplane, shot down by a single blast from Joker's ridiculously long toy gun.

Here manliness seems regenerated not by violence but by umbilical connection. Perhaps, to apply Mark Carnes's argument about overtly patriarchal lodge rituals again, the macho masks hide and license a male maternalism: Tarzan feeds, shelters, and holds Jane just as Kala mothered him.[37] Or perhaps the womb-surge is even more basic. If Tarzan makes inarticulate sounds and howls in ecstasy while his blood pounds like a tidal wave, if Batman feels like sleeping upside down before careening toward the moon, it's not that a nice young gentleman has suddenly got rape and murder on his mind. The Last Real Man in America is just having his period.

Such fantasies empower women only tangentially and metaphorically. They legitimate male violence with a traditional sex role polarity: Within every animal-man hides a Good Mother. The claim belies the ugliness always latent in the Real Man myth. For me that darkness became most visible in a $10 batman shirt, a spin-off from the first movie: Not the Michael Keaton boy-man who plays protective urban terrorist, but Batman for the skinhead market. Under the blood-orange moon, his teeth gleam over dark, random corpses. By his left foot lies a prone, sallow body whose spiked Mohawk haircut clearly brands him as a dying Indian or street gang member, with a gun pointing aimlessly upward behind his shoulder. By his right foot, with a manacled arm reaching up Batman's cloak in a curious gesture—a prisoner? a slave? a homoerotic invitation?—lies a burr-head black man. Other scattered bodies and a litter of guns, knives, chains, and eerily disconnected limbs sprawl about his feet, evoking an American landscape filled with skulls and crossbones, urban muggers, and frontier violence. Above it all, collapsing American history into an image of the beast-man, stands Batman-Dracula, Master of the Universe and vampire bat, about to drink their blood. Here is the psychic landscape lurking below Sean Connery's white-on-white cover of *Gentleman's Quarterly*.

The skinhead Batman glories in the racist violence on which the myth of the Last Real Man in America has fed, from Cooper's Indian wars to Buck's killing of the Yeehats to Tarzan's killings of African blacks. Part of the myth's pleasure lies in what James Bond called the hero's "license to kill," a license helping to make the myth so serviceable in the international arena. A more basic pleasure lies in the ritualistic arena of mano-a-mano rivalry, where women and other complex states of being are out of sight and out of mind.

The myth of a Last Real Man depends on its equal and opposite myth, that of a subhuman underclass, to generate ceaseless dramas of dominance and humiliation. These ahistorical dramas of self-empowering express and evade both the felt facelessness of upwardly mobile men in the settlements and the diffuse resentments of the immobilized. So long as corporate capitalism structures male identity primarily through role-playing and workplace competition, the craving for Real Man myths will continue despite the entry of women into management positions. In a world where Sherman McCoys at the top and their fast-lane counterparts at the bottom measure worth only as supremacy in the cash flow game, the men at the top will talk of "hemorrhaging money" (*Bonfire*, 330) whereas the men at the bottom hemorrhage violence. Batman embodies an intimate circulation of old money and new blood.

But capitalism's opening beyond small-scale patriarchal stabilizings to diversified international markets, like academia's opening to multicultural constituencies, encourages the circulation and exchange of more heterogeneous energies. A currently intractable impasse between capitalism's production of material abundance and its production of a useless urban underclass fosters much of the anxious urgency invested in the ideology of upward mobility. If you are not rising, as a person or a corporation, you must be powerless, or falling—into what? An unemployable underclass remains the bourgeois bogeyman and cautionary tale, the demonized other for middle-class resentments and fears. Yet the competitive pluralism intrinsic to any large-scale market checks and challenges anyone's will to power, whereas marketing itself enforces a continuous reassessment of otherness and difference among potential buyers. Equally to the point, the corporate workplace encourages collaborative as well as competitive energies, often beyond the imagination of academic artisans and entrepreneurs. An edgy tolerance for diversity has been one of capitalism's more unacknowledged cultural achievements.

Ideologies die operatic deaths, and individualism's deflection of capitalism's various contradictions into manliness has led to an exceptionally long aria–165 years and counting. From the beginning, the myth of the Last Real Man in America fuses idealizations of high civility with increasingly brutalized representations of lower-class violence. From the beginning, too, the myth has subsumed an elegiac simplification of history, grieving for the passing of frontier self-reliance and patriarchal dominance. In the cosmopolitan perspectives of another 160 years or so, the myth may well be set beside the grandfather clock and the Model T Ford as another example of persistent yokelism.

On the other hand, the myth's tenacity signals the vitality of capitalist paradoxes. Perhaps on a multinational stage, Real Man myths will even expand their market: the Last Real Man in Czechoslovakia, the Last Real Man in Argentina. Eventually there may well be more gender-neutral stories to tell. Yet myths of self-empowering will still mix elegance with violence to tease people away from thinking about what makes them feel unreal.

Notes

1. The *Celebrity Plus* cover presents Harrison Ford as, in smaller print, a "Crusader" who "Shoots from the hip in This Candid Talk." The story simply depicts him as a man at ease with himself, living in

Wyoming with his family, remembering his hard knocks, and fishing instead of playing Hollywood games. The *Gentleman's Quarterly* essay, by Diane K. Shah, entitled "All Together Now: Sean Connery Is an Icon," bears a similarly tangential relation to the "Last Real Man" packaging on the cover.

2. Barbara Gamarekian, "The Cartoonists' Art: Nothing Is Too Sacred," *New York Times*, Tuesday, 19 March 1991, B2.

3. Mark C. Carnes, *Secret Ritual and Manhood in Victorian America* (New Haven, CT: Yale University Press, 1989). See also Susan Jeffords, *The Remasculinization of America: Gender and the Vietnam War* (Bloomington, IN: Indiana University Press, 1989). As Walter Benn Michaels has pointed out for D. H. Lawrence's forays into New Mexico and classic American literature, such remasculinization through wildness depends on the previous extinction of the Indians to transform them from a social threat into an assimilable culture resource. See "The Vanishing American," *American Literary History* 2 (Summer 1990): 220–41. T. J. Jackson Lears, in *No Place of Grace: Antimodernism and the Transformation of American Culture 1880–1920* (New York: Pantheon Books, 1981), and many others emphasize connections between turn-of-the century feelings of powerlessness and fantasies of hypermasculinity.

4. Amy Kaplan, "Romancing the Empire: The Embodiment of American Masculinity in the Popular Historical Novel of the 1890s," *American Literary History* 2 (Winter 1990): 659–90. Kaplan applies this argument to turn-of-the-century chivalric romances of imperialism. See also Lora Romero, "Vanishing Americans: Gender, Empire, and New Historicism," *American Literature* 63 (September 1991): 385–404. My discussion of manliness on the frontier also builds on well-known studies by Leslie Fiedler and Richard Slotkin. Page references to Cooper's *The Last of the Mohicans: A Narrative of 1757* (1826; reprint, New York: Signet, 1980), are incorporated in the text.

5. In "No Apologies for the Iroquois," chap. 4 of *Sensational Designs: The Cultural Work of American Fiction 1790–1860* (New York: Oxford University Press, 1985), Jane Tompkins emphasizes the crossover liminalities throughout Cooper's narrative.

6. Donald J. Trump, with Tony Schwartz, *Trump: The Art of the Deal* (New York: Warner Books, 1987), 71–72. Trump goes on to talk with pride about stealing his younger brother's blocks and going to military school, where he found teachers he could admire, particularly a former marine drill sergeant who was "the kind of guy who could slam into a goalpost wearing a football helmet and break the post rather than his head." This Real Man would "go for the jugular if he smelled weakness," but he would treat you "like a man" if you "finessed" him with respect (72–74). Trump's autobiography shares

several characteristics with Cellini's: both seem to have been dic-
tated, both celebrate competitive prowess, and both show considerable relish for outstripping their fathers, though each pays ostenta-
tious respect to his father as well.

7. David G. Gilmore, *Manhood in the Making: Cultural Concepts of Masculinity* (New Haven, CT: Yale University Press, 1989), takes a cross-
cultural approach to the social construction of masculinities, arguing
that traditional manly codes of stoicism, physical strength, sexual
prowess, and bravery function to protect the social unit. Gilmore's
useful and unpretentious survey concludes that the "Ubiquitous
Male" criteria of "Man-the-Impregnator-Protector-Provider" function
in "either dangerous or highly competitive" social situations to force
men beyond their longing to retreat to "childish narcissism"
(222–24), a state repeatedly linked to Melville's Bartleby (109,
174–75). My own book, *Manhood and the American Renaissance* (Ithaca, NY: Cornell University Press, 1989), chap. 3, argues that all
ideologies of manhood draw on male fears of being humiliated, and
more diffusely of being seen by other men as weak and vulnerable
(72–73). Pericles' Funeral Oration to the Athenians is the most eloquent summation of precapitalist manliness I have run across; he
explicitly links honor in battle to a man's fear of humiliation and the
desire to have the respect of one's fellow men.

8. See Stephen Greenblatt, *Shakespearean Negotiations: The Circulation
of Social Energy in Renaissance England* (Berkeley: University of California Press, 1988), 75–76, on individual identity as a "way station
on the road to a firm and decisive identification with normative
structures," structures that he elsewhere discusses as masks and mobile improvisations whose instabilities themselves are part of power's
circulations. Compare also a fine review-essay by Thomas K.
McGraw, "In Retrospect: Berle and Means," *Reviews in American
History* 18 (December 1990): 578–96, which reassesses the Berle-
Means thesis about American capitalism's tendency toward industrial concentration and the separation of ownership from control.
McGraw speaks of the sociology of executives: their "submergence in
a corporate culture obsessed with competitive market performance,
their keen identification of self with company" (586). Alfred Chandler's recent book, *Scale and Scope: The Dynamics of Industrial Capitalism* (Cambridge: Harvard University Press, 1990), contrasts
American competitive corporate capitalism with England's more
family-based capitalism and Germany's more collaborative capitalism.

9. Kenneth Cmiel, *Democratic Eloquence: The Fight over Popular Speech
in Nineteenth-Century America* (New York: William Morrow, 1990),
92, also 58; Stuart M. Blumin, *The Emergence of the Middle Class:*

Social Experience in the American City, 1760–1900 (Cambridge: Cambridge University Press, 1989), esp. 269–92. As Blumin notes, the middle class' "individualistic, competitive values . . . were those most at odds with sustained, explicitly class-based organization" (257), despite "the increasingly distinctive three-class structure of daily social life" (288), especially in the cities, where "class segregation" increased (284) and an accelerating suburbanization of the middle class exacerbated class divisions. Blumin also suggests that middle-class values gained such ideological hegemony because the preindustrial upper class gave way to "more specialized celebrities" at the top (296), whereas manual workers had enough money to define themselves as middle-class consumers. Mary P. Ryan, *Cradle of the Middle Class: The Family in Oneida County, New York, 1790–1865* (Cambridge: Cambridge University Press, 1981) recurrently discusses the new middle class' fear of falling into the new working class—a more fundamental motive for upward mobility, in her view, than the drive for competitive success (184, 210, 238). See my notes to chap. 3 of *Manhood and the American Renaissance*; also Cmiel, *Democratic Eloquence,* on the "polysemic" diversity of language and self that accompanied the triumph of "middling" oratory over elite traditions of refined language and character. Cmiel notes the paradox that, after the Civil War, class divisions hardened while elite symbols diffused into mass culture (145–47).

10. Carroll Smith-Rosenberg, *Disorderly Conduct: Visions of Gender in Victorian America* (New York: Oxford University Press, 1985), 90, also 100–107. *Meanings for Manhood: Constructions of Masculinity in Victorian America* (Chicago: University of Chicago Press, 1990), a recent anthology of essays edited by Mark C. Carnes and Clyde Griffen, historicizes masculine gender constructions more complexly than I can do here. See esp. Anthony Rotundo's essay, "Boy Culture" (15–36) and Griffen's speculative overview (183–204). Filene's *Him/Her/Self: Sex Roles in Modern America,* 2nd ed. (Baltimore: Johns Hopkins University Press, 1986), 69–93, surveys late nineteenth-century American male anxieties, esp. in relation to women and domestic roles.

11. Page references to *The Deerslayer or the First War-Path* (1841; reprint, Garden City: Dolphin-Doubleday, n.d.), are incorporated in the text.

12. Compare Richard Slotkin, *Regeneration Through Violence: The Mythology of the American Frontier, 1600–1860* (Middletown, CT: Wesleyan University Press, 1973); my emphasis on the inversions of upward/downward mobility differs here from Slotkin's quasi-Jungian sense of the frontier beast-man myth as a mythic initiation into soul-archetypes, where manhood becomes a sacred marriage through violence with the anima and natural fertility goddesses (156, 539, 543).

In *The Fatal Environment: The Myth of the Frontier in the Age of Industrialization 1800–1890* (New York: Atheneum, 1985), esp. discussing General Custer, Slotkin's more sociological focus for myths of manhood could complement Cmiel's and my own sense of entrepreneurial role-playing. Slotkin argues (377) that the masculine imperatives of self-assertion and stern command, with their feminine inversions, lead to a double bind: self-reliant, yet subordinate to authority, a subordination that Custer split as masculine and feminine. Slotkin also emphasizes Custer's resolution of this split through role-playing and self-dramatization (378, 383).

13. Walter Benn Michaels, *The Gold Standard and the Logic of Naturalism: American Literature at the Turn of the Century* (Berkeley: University of California Press, 1987), situates McTeague's desire in relation to American anxiety about money circulation (148–54) and more profound insatiabilities of desire generated by capitalism. June Howard, in *Form and History in American Literary Naturalism* (Chapel Hill: University of North Carolina Press, 1985), comes closer to my view in framing Norris's contradictions about masculinity as part of "inconsistent fears" ranging from genteel class nervousness about proletarianization to petty-bourgeois feelings of entrapment "between the working class and the corporation" (95–96). The issues resolve into a sense of powerlessness diffusely projected on a monstrously empowered Other, which Howard links to manly brutality in both Norris and Jack London (51–63, 117–25, 140).

14. Jack London, *The Call of the Wild and White Fang* (Toronto: Bantam Books, 1981), 85–86: "Thornton fell on his knees beside Buck. Head was against head, and he was shaking him back and forth. Those who hurried up heard him cursing Buck, and he cursed him long and fervently, and softly and lovingly. . . . Buck seized Thornton's hand in his teeth. Thornton shook him back and forth. As though animated by a common impulse, the onlookers drew back to a respectful distance, nor were they again indiscreet enough to interrupt." Quotations from *The Call of the Wild* are incorporated in the text.

15. Christopher P. Wilson, *The Labor of Words: Literary Professionalism in the Progressive Era* (Athens, GA: University of Georgia Press, 1985), 155–56. Wilson notes the subtle undertone of "satire" created by adopting Buck's limited point of view concerning human desires (102–4). Wilson is also astute on the links between professionalism and narcissistic masculinity emerging at the turn of the century (xiv, 197–99). Like D. H. Lawrence's, London's emphasis on virility enables both a half-veiled homoeroticism and what Wilson calls a "rediscovery of threatened craft ideals" (104). Mark Seltzer's "the Love Masters" uses London's *Sea-Wolf* to culminate his complex argument about the machinelike disciplining of men's bodies as represented

50   David Leverenz

in various texts—"an erotics of discipline" yet a promiscuous transgression of boundaries, including the natural and the unnatural.
See Seltzer, *Bodies and Machines* (New York: Routledge, 1992),
149–72.

16. Victoria Kahn, "*Virtù* and the Example of Agathocles in Machiavelli's
The Prince," *Representations* 13 (Winter 1986): 63–83. I am indebted
here to discussions with Brandy Kershner. Kahn's essay brilliantly
teases out the differences between princelike and subjectlike readings
of the Agathocles-Borgia contrast—if we're taken in by humanistic
morality, we're unreflective subjects—before exposing "the essential
emptiness of the concept of *virtù*" (77).

17. Turner's "The Significance of the Frontier in American History"
(1893) is reprinted in *Frontier and Section: Selected Essays of Frederick
Jackson Turner*, ed. Ray Allen Billington (Englewood Cliffs, NJ: Pren-
tice-Hall, 1961), 37–62. An expanded version, "The Frontier in American History" (1920), is reprinted in *The Historians' History of the
United States*, vol. 1, ed. Andrew S. Berky and James P. Shenton (New
York: Capricorn, 1966), 462–73, quotations incorporated in text.

18. A great many studies in the last fifteen years have emphasized the
rise of the professions after the Civil War. Robert H. Wiebe, *The
Search for Order 1877–1920* (New York: Hill and Wang, 1967), esp.
chap. 5 on "A New Middle Class" (111–32), deftly sketches the complex tensions empowering an emphasis on class and a resolution
through the professions. In "Revisiting the Vanishing Frontier: The
Legacy of Frederick Jackson Turner," *Western Historical Quarterly* 18
(April 1987): 157–76, William Cronon notes Turner's fear that without the frontier, immigrants could not escape class conflicts (167).
Cronon argues that "almost in spite of himself," Turner "gave American history its central and most persistent story" (176), initially man
on the frontier but finally humans interacting with landscape, or
environmental history that began as western history (171). This sympathetic approach minimizes or misses Turner's insistence on man-
making as the goal of environmental interaction.

19. Compare Wiebe, *Search for Order*, 132; also Nick Salvatore, *Eugene V.
Debs: Citizen and Socialist* (Urbana: University of Illinois Press, 1982),
on Debs's appeal to native artisan traditions of American manliness
rather than to European traditions of socialism.

20. David McCullough's biography of Roosevelt's childhood, *Mornings
on Horseback* (New York: Simon and Schuster, 1981), esp. 90–108,
speculates that Roosevelt unconsciously used his asthma attacks to
gain days alone with his father: "father and the out of doors meant
salvation" (108). Roosevelt's National Progressive party, formed in
June 1912 after he had been humiliated at the Republican convention, was given its nickname by the newspapers because he told

reporters he felt as fit as a bull moose. The manly response to wounding caught the nation's fancy.

21. Theodore Roosevelt, *Ranch Life and the Hunting-Trail* (1888; reprint, Ann Arbor, MI: University Microfilms, 1966), quotations incorporated in text.

22. Grant C. Knight, *The Strenuous Age in American Literature* (Chapel Hill: University of North Carolina Press, 1954), 55, also 72 on Roosevelt the literary critic (as President!), esp. a 1907 essay criticizing London's *White Fang* for depicting a fight between dog and wolf that is "the very sublimity of absurdity." Knight situates Roosevelt's image and impact in the context of American imperialism (50–59, also 6–12). I am indebted here and elsewhere to Gordon Hutner.

23. Owen Wister, *The Virginian* (1902; reprint, New York: Grosset and Dunlap, 1929), quotations incorporated in text. On rhetorical play in *The Virginian* and its uses for dominating the independent, equality-minded heroine, see Lee Clark Mitchell, " 'When You Call Me That . . .' : Tall Talk and Male Hegemony in *The Virginian*," *PMLA* 102 (January 1987): 66–77. On the sometimes vexed Wister-Remington friendship, see Ben Merchant Vorpahl, *My dear Wister—: The Frederic Remington–Owen Wister Letters* (Palo Alto, TX: American West Publishing, 1972), which also thoughtfully sketches their lives and works. Wister had three serious breakdowns, a second in 1895 (171) and the last in 1909 (323), which he cured with another trip to Wyoming. On Wister's music background, see 9–10. Remington was a Yale football player whose drawings for Roosevelt's *Ranch Life* helped to establish his journalistic career (26), while his famous painting of Roosevelt's Rough Riders charging up San Juan Hill (a fiction) helped to launch his friend into national politics. Remington's letters to Wister about the Cuban invasion are flagrantly racist in their indiscriminate contempt for "a lot of d— niggers" (221), "the Dagoes or the Yaps" (225, also 233). Remington's burly macho postures contrast with Wister's more guarded gentility throughout, for example in asking about Wister's recent marriage, fresh from the success of the Spanish-American war: "How do you get on with your wife—who is boss? or haven't you had time to settle that yet. I believe that sometimes takes several campaigns. Annexation is attended with difficulties" (279). I am indebted for this reference to Carl Bredahl.

24. Edgar Rice Burroughs published *Tarzan of the Apes* as a magazine serial in 1912, then as a book in 1914. Quotations from the reprinted novel (New York: Ballantine, 1983) incorporated in text.

25. Marianna Torgovnick, *Gone Primitive: Savage Intellect, Modern Lives* (Chicago: University of Chicago Press, 1990), 52. Torgovnick's chapter, "Taking Tarzan Seriously" (42–72), teases out the tensions in various Tarzan books between the doubt-filled Tarzan, who can fleet-

ingly imitate maternal modes and learn from blacks, and the macho Tarzan required by the nearly all-male audience, gradually suppressing the character who dares ask, "What does a man do?" (70, also 68–71). See Gail Bederman's " 'The Women Have Had Charge of the Church Work Long Enough': The Men and Religion Forward Movement of 1911–1912 and the Masculinization of Middle-Class Protestantism," *American Quarterly* 41 (September 1989); 432–65, on the gender struggle in churches at this time.

26. Speaking French and (haltingly) English, Tarzan drives Jane away from a forest fire in Wisconsin, before he relinquishes her to her fiancé, the presumed Lord Greystoke.

27. Eric Cheyfitz, in *"Tarzan of the Apes:* U.S. Foreign Policy in the Twentieth Century," *American Literary History* 1 (Summer 1989): 339–60.

28. Alan Moore, *Batman: The Killing Joke* (New York: DC Comics, 1988), n.p. See also Frank Miller, with Klaus Janson and Lynn Varley, *Batman: The Dark Knight Returns* (New York: DC Comics, 1986).

29. Tom Wolfe, *The Bonfire of the Vanities* (New York: Farrar, Strauss & Giroux, 1987); quotations incorporated in text. Torgovnick, in *Gone Primitive*, 259, also links *Bonfire* with Tarzan's jungle.

30. Richard Slotkin, *Regeneration Through Violence*; cf. also Martin Green, *The Great American Adventure: Action Stories from Cooper to Mailer and What They Reveal About American Manhood* (Boston: Beacon Press, 1984), which argues rather simply that the American tradition of manly adventures is imperialist, while also claiming that it constitutes the finest aspect of American literature.

31. See Frederic Wertham, *The Seduction of the Innocent* (New York: Rhinehart, 1954), for a 1950s psychoanalytic (and homophobic) assault on Robin. Frank Miller's *Batman: The Dark Knight Returns* plays with Robin as a crossover gender figure.

32. Gilmore, *Manhood in the Making*, 221.

33. On traditional societies, see Gilmore, *Manhood in the Making*, though he implies the codes and ideologies have not changed much. On capitalism, see Chandler, *Scale and Scope*; Cmiel, *Democratic Eloquence*. Lears's *No Place of Grace* voices a hesitant admiration for religious and masculinist stances in opposition to inchoate modernization, for example, 138, on the "eloquent" and "admirable" manly stoicism of combat, regretfully assimilable to modern nihilism, or 258–59, on the "softened" quality of "'male'" and "'female'" ideals through therapeutic secularism rather than transcendent religion, yet the potential "heroism" of religious-based protest and dissent (181, 260). Lears's conscious ambivalence about the loss of manly strength and religious transcendence gives his book its own complex eloquence. An earlier essay by David Brion Davis, "Stress-seeking and the Self-Made Man in American Literature, 1894–1914," in *From*

Homicide to Slavery: Studies in American Culture (New York: Oxford University Press, 1986), 52–72, links the turn-of-the-century fascination with the "strenuous life" to the breakdown of traditional Protestant bonds between material success and spiritual salvation; stress-seeking man "became an embodiment of sheer vitality in a limitless void" (72).

34. Seltzer, *Bodies and Machines*, 166–72.
35. Eve Kosofsky Sedgwick, *Epistemology of the Closet* (Berkeley: University of California Press, 1990), 145. Sedgwick's extensive analysis of homosexual panic and gender incoherences in Melville's *Billy Budd* and James's "The Beast in the Jungle" locates the 1890s as a crucial moment for the binary construction of sexualities to opposed categories of homosexual and heterosexual.
36. Frank Norris, *McTeague: A Story of San Francisco* ed. Donald Pizer (1899; reprint, New York: Norton Critical Edition, 1977). See Norris, "A Plea for Romantic Fiction" (1901): "Realism is minute, it is the drama of a broken teacup, . . . the adventure of an invitation to dinner" (in *McTeague*, 314). Next quotation from Norris incorporated in text.
37. I am indebted here to discussions of *Tarzan* with a freshman honors class at the University of Florida, as I am indebted to Barry Qualls and Wendy Wall for discussions about *Batman.* See Carnes, *Secret Ritual and Manhood*, esp. 139–50, and Torgovnick, *Gone Primitive* 69, on maternal imitation, also 64–69 on ambivalence about matriarchy in other Tarzan books.

II

Crossing Cultures

2

Barthelme, Freud, and the Killing of Kafka's Father

Peter Schwenger

In 1919, when he was thirty-six, Kafka wrote a letter to his father—forty-five typewritten pages long, with three additional handwritten pages—which is a prime example of Derrida's wry observation that a letter can always not arrive at its destination (Derrida 1987, 444). In the case of Kafka's letter this assertion is true on a number of levels, and first of all the literal. Kafka's mother was given the hefty document to deliver to his father; she never did so. After keeping it for a while she gave it back, perhaps feeling that the estrangement between father and son was so great that attempts to explain it could never repair the damage, and might possibly make it worse. If we read the letter today, feeling rather like eavesdroppers, we ask ourselves about its destination in a figurative sense: Where is this letter going? What is the end point of its argument? The answer is again "the father." But we may now read, beyond Kafka's father, that which he may be said to represent: a certain element of writing—indeed of culture itself—which a number of theorists have called by the father's name. The problem posed by this element moves through the letter and beyond it to raise the question of how we can write to free ourselves from the patriarchal elements of writing. In this chapter I will use Kafka and Freud to explicate the problem. Then I will turn to Donald Barthelme and, briefly, the architect Philip

Johnson to suggest a process for resolving the problem—a process, I should stress, which is not to be taken as a destination, the destination of Kafka's letter. Yet all of these men, in their own ways, are addressing Kafka's father.

At one point in the letter Kafka (1966) confesses to his father that "my writing was all about you." He gives only one example, quoting the last line of *The Trial*—"He is afraid the shame will outlive him, even"—and connecting it to the sense of boundless guilt that Kafka had developed in relation to his father (73). The pressure of Hermann Kafka's domineering personality had invaded the child's very thoughts: "All these thoughts, seemingly independent of you, were from the beginning burdened with your belittling judgments; it was almost impossible to endure this and still work out a thought with any measure of completeness and permanence" (23). Still, completeness and permanence of some sort might have been available if the father's own behavior had these characteristics—but it was riddled with contradictions of which the father himself was unaware and that consequently did not diminish his confidence and authority in the slightest. Kafka draws his examples from the dinner hour, the obligatory family communion that often becomes the family battleground. Eating in the Kafka family was governed by innumerable edicts issued by the father and blithely disregarded by him, the one constant exception to the rule. For instance: "At table one wasn't allowed to do anything but eat, but you cleaned and cut your fingernails, sharpened pencils, cleaned your ears with a toothpick" (27). Kafka admits that these lapses were in themselves unimportant:

They only became depressing for me because you, so tremendously the authoritative man, did not keep the commandments you imposed upon me. Hence the world was for me divided into three parts: one in which I, the slave, lived under laws that had been invented only for me and which I could, I did not know why, never completely comply with; then a second world, which was infinitely remote from mine, in which you lived, concerned with government, with the issuing of orders and with the annoyance about their not being obeyed; and finally a third world where everybody else lived happily and free from orders and from having to obey. (27, 29)

We may as well disregard this last world, which we—the "everybody else" of whom he speaks—know to be a wistful illusion. We then have two worlds whose tension makes up much of Kafka's fiction: the remote, inaccessible world of authority, and the world of the bewildered paranoiac. Kafka's situation resembles that of many of his protagonists, and can be summed up in these words from the letter: "Nothing was in my very own, undoubted, sole possession, determined unequivocally only by me—in sober truth a disinherited son" (89, 91).

Yet Kafka, while bemoaning these problems, is in a sense attached to them. He pictures the resolution of his problems that would ensue if he were to marry and thus escape the old patterns, shifting the relationship with his father. "Then," Kafka says, "I could be a free, grateful, guiltless, upright son, and you could be an untroubled, untyrannical, sympathetic, contented father. But," he goes on, "to this end everything that ever happened would have to be undone, that is, we ourselves should have to be cancelled out" (115). Here Kafka verges on admitting that his father is necessary to his sense of self, a self, however unsatisfactory, to which he cannot help but be attached. At the very end of his letter he goes past that verge and allows his father to make essentially the same accusation in an imagined rebuttal of the whole letter. Here, in part, is what his father says to him:

You are unfit for life; to make life comfortable for yourself, without worries and self-reproaches, you prove that I have taken your fitness away from you and put it in my own pocket. Why should it bother you that you are unfit for life, since I have the responsibility for it, while you calmly stretch out and let yourself be hauled through life, physically and mentally, by me. . . . You have only proved to me that all my reproaches were justified, and that one especially justified charge was still missing: namely the charge of insincerity, obsequiousness, and parasitism. If I am not very much mistaken, you are preying on me even with this letter itself. (123, 125)

So Kafka, assuming the voice of his father, argues against himself; and there is powerful evidence to support that argument in Kafka's reluctance to marry and thus achieve the adulthood and freedom described before. Among Kafka's many explanations for that reluctance, the most significant one has to do with his writing—the writing that, we recall, is always about Kafka's father. He asserts quite simply that marriage will endanger his writing.

He does not specify *how* his writing will be endangered. He has indicated clearly enough, though, that tying the nuptial knot would immediately *untie* the Gordian knot of Kafka's relations with his father. And this he cannot afford to do, even if he were psychologically capable of it. For this relationship with his father is the ultimate source of his writing, of his art. The moment it is resolved, his writing must cease. In this sense, the father's imagined accusation of parasitism is fully justified.

Up to this point in the letter, the logic of Kafka's psychoanalysis has been crystalline, if complex; and he has been rigorously fair, even to the point of adopting his father's voice and arguing compellingly against himself. If it is possible at all for people to be clear and fair about such things, Kafka has been so. But at this point he is cutting down to the bone. And the scrupulous logic to which he has aspired throughout the letter is now completely overthrown. Continuing to speak of marriage and what it could offer him, Kafka has this to say:

The simile of the bird in the hand and the two in the bush has only a very remote application here. In my hand I have nothing, in the bush is everything, and yet—so it is decided by the conditions of battle and the necessity of life—I must choose the nothing. (117, 119)

The choice is an astonishing one, but it is by no means the most astonishing aspect of this passage. The *reason* for the choice intrigues me: "so it is decided by the conditions of battle and the necessity of life." Really, Kafka gives no reason. He neatly sidesteps responsibility for what is after all *his* choice, *his* decision. He does so first through a passive construction: "it is decided." And to answer the natural question of who or what decides, Kafka brings in only a couple of dimly perceived abstractions straight out of bourgeois parlor art: "the conditions of battle"—and we see, perhaps, a helmeted, heroic figure fighting "the battle of life"—and *lebensnot*, the necessity of life—the Greek *ananka* or fate, perhaps, complete with classical drapery. This moment is a flicker of bad faith, a retreat into foggy cliches at the very moment when Kafka owes an explanation (at least to himself) of the reasons for his choice.

That explanation can be found in Kafka's letter, but it must be assembled and extrapolated from scattered hints. Near the beginning of the letter, for instance, he speaks of the nothing that he is to choose at the letter's end. "This sense of nothingness that often dominates me (a feeling that is in another respect, admittedly, also a noble and fruitful one) comes largely from your influence," he tells his father (17). He does not pursue the parenthetical aside, despite its significant admission that the father's influence is in some way a fruitful one. Its fruits must be those previously mentioned products of the father's influence, Kafka's writings. We begin to realize that if his father had not actually existed, it would have been necessary for Kafka to have invented him.

In these circuitous ways we have arrived once more at that destination in Kafka's letter that is also an origin, the idea of the father. But really it is the origin only of another stage in the process: we may now move through the fissures of Kafka's letter and into Derrida's *Dissemination* (1981). In that work Derrida asserts bluntly that "writing is parricidal" (164). This assertion is justified in the context of Derrida's distinction between writing and the spoken word:

One could say . . . that the "speaking subject" is the *father* of the speech. . . . *Logos* is a son, then, a son that would be destroyed in his very *presence* without the present *attendance* of his father. His father who answers. His father who speaks for him and answers for him. Without his father, he would be nothing but, in fact, writing. At least that is what is said by the one who says; it is the father's thesis. The specificity of writing would thus be intimately bound to the absence of the father. (79)

Moving from the father's thesis to the situation of the son, Derrida gives this description:

Writing is the miserable son. *Le misérable* . . . . His impotence is truly that of an orphan as much as that of a justly or unjustly persecuted patricide . . . . Writing can thus be attacked, bombarded with unjust reproaches . . . that only the father could dissipate—thus assisting his son—if the son had not, precisely, killed him. (145)

These are figures of speech, of course, not real figures; nevertheless the two may sometimes be interchanged. So it is with Kafka's father. In all his blocky bourgeois solidity he is made to evaporate:

he becomes not so much a presence in Kafka's work as a pervasive absence, a nonexistent authority like that of *The Trial* and *The Castle*. Thus the son ensures that "the dead father, first victim and ultimate resource, not be there" (145).

These words of Derrida echo the terms of yet another text on the father, one that has plainly influenced him and may have influenced Kafka: Freud's *Totem and Taboo* (1961). The theory it advances can be applied to Kafka's fiction, to all fiction, and perhaps to all culture. In this book, Freud uses psychology in an attempt to resolve a problem in anthropology, that of the totem. Every member of a primitive tribe belongs to one or another totem, usually an animal. The people of the totem have a special relationship to the totem animal: it is sacred and may not be killed. Moreover, people may not marry within their own totem. Freud first notes some clinical cases showing that children often displace feelings for their father onto an animal. Then he points out that the two prohibitions of totemism—against killing the totem and against marrying within it—coincide with the two crimes of Oedipus. Finally, he lingers on certain ritualized exceptions to the rule, in which the tribe kills the totem animal and devours it. The animal is duly mourned in a clear attempt to disclaim responsibility for the killing; a festivity follows at which every sort of license is permitted. Freud now substitutes the real father for the symbolical animal, and suggests that all these tribal institutions are ways of coming to terms with one crucial event in the tribe's evolution. The earliest form of the tribe was probably, like that of many animal hordes, one in which a powerful male drives out all rivals, including his own sons, in order to keep all the females for himself. Freud suggests a scenario where the exiled sons learn to cooperate, with results that he bluntly puts in a single sentence: "One day the brothers who had been driven out came together, killed and devoured their father and so made an end of the patriarchal horde" (141). He then argues that the guilt for this act is handed down through the generations, in a kind of collective unconscious. The prohibitions of totemism appease that guilt; the debt to the dead father is paid and made fruitful through cultural forms—legal, religious, artistic.

This "fruitful moment of debt," as Freud has called it, is echoed in Kafka's words. A "fruitful" feeling of nothingness, he says to his father, "comes largely from your influence." And elsewhere he says "on every side I was to blame, I was in your debt"—*Von alle seiten her kam ich in deine Schuld*, where *Schuld* has the force of both "guilt" and "debt" (47). Kafka owed a debt not only to his father, but to Freud. He had broken through into his true voice with "The Judgement," a story he said had "come out of me like a birth" in one night's sitting in 1912; and he had thought of Freud while writing it. The Oedipal content of that story, as well as its relation to dream, could have been derived from Freud's writings before 1912. But it is significant that the first part of *Totem and Taboo* was published in that year.

Freud's theory may be applied to itself, because his problematic relations with his own father provided the impetus for explaining human failings, as well as the shape of that explanation. As much as Kafka, Freud could have confessed to his father "my writing was all about you." Marie Balmary and Marianne Krull have both published studies of Freud's relationship with his father. The more fully articulated of the two is Balmary's *Psychoanalyzing Psychoanalysis: Freud and the Hidden Fault of the Father* (1982). She begins with a couple of facts about Freud's father that have only recently come to light: His supposedly second marriage was preceded by another one completely covered over in the family history; and Sigmund was born not nine months after his parents' marriage but seven months. The possible Don Juanism of his father is the "hidden fault" that returns, like any repressed, in a multitude of unconscious betrayals throughout Freud's life, and may have played its part in Freud's renunciation of the seduction theory. In *Freud and His Father* (1986), on the other hand, Marianne Krull argues that Freud's renunciation of the seduction theory was a result of compromising evidence arising from his own self-analysis. Recognizing in himself the classic symptoms of the hysteric, Freud could not pursue the possibility that his father could, in any form, be guilty of originating those symptoms. Removing the Oedipal to the realm of fantasy allowed him to take all the guilt upon himself, as the son does in "The Judgement."

But guilt is also debt, and moreover fruitful debt, engendering perhaps the whole body of Freud's work, the payment of the parricide.

The cases of Freud and Kafka seem to validate the view that the father underlies all culture. Culture, in this view, is fundamentally patriarchal, and we are bound to it irrevocably by guilt even while we attempt to free ourselves from its bonds. Can we disentangle those bonds only by disentangling the fabric of culture itself? In Freud there is no disentangling; we must accommodate ourselves to the patriarchal pattern. But that problematic pattern, whose guilt-laden dynamics are said to have originated art, may be resolved by art and perhaps fundamentally altered by it. The suggestion comes from Freud (1961) himself:

In only a single field of our civilization has the omnipotence of thoughts been retained, and that is in the field of art. Only in art does it still happen that a man who is consumed by desires performs something resembling the accomplishment of those desires and that what he does in play produces emotional effects—thanks to aesthetic illusion—just as though it were something real. (90)

The "real" effect of art is probably due less to aesthetic illusion (a vague term in any case) than to the fact that the unconscious recognizes no illusion. The unconscious, Freud argued in renouncing his seduction theory, does not distinguish between real events and those of fantasy. To the degree that art partakes of fantasy, then, it becomes part of the unconscious and can work its changes there.

But, to get more particular, what *kind* of art can work best, that is, work its changes on the patriarchal inheritance of our unconscious? What artistic strategies are adequate to this deep-seated complexity? One answer is provided by a work that owes a considerable debt to both Kafka and Freud, and moreover deals explicitly with the patriarchal problem: Donald Barthelme's *The Dead Father* (1975).

Barthelme's book opens with this description, worth quoting in full for the tone it sets:

The Dead Father's head. The main thing is, his eyes are open. Staring up into the sky. The eyes a two-valued blue, the blues of the Gitanes cigarette pack. The head never moves. Decades of staring. The brow is noble, good Christ, what else? Broad and noble. And serene, of course, he's dead, what else if not serene? From the tip of his finely shaped delicately nostriled nose to the ground, fall of five and one half meters, figure obtained by triangulation. The hair is gray but a young gray. Full, almost to the shoulder, it is possible to admire the hair for a long time, many do, on a Sunday or other holiday or in those sandwich hours neatly placed between fattish slices of work. Jawline compares favorably to a rock formation. Imposing, rugged, all that. The great jaw contains thirty-two teeth, twenty-eight of the whiteness of standard bathroom fixtures and four stained, the latter a consequence of addiction to tobacco, according to legend, this beige quartet to be found in the center of the lower jaw. He is not perfect, thank God for that. The full red lips drawn back in a slight rictus, slight but not unpleasant rictus, disclosing a bit of mackerel salad lodged between two of the stained four. We think it is mackerel salad. It appears to be mackerel salad. In the sagas, it is mackerel salad.

Dead, but still with us, still with us, but dead. (3)

In what follows there are echoes at first of Gulliver among the Lilliputians: the gigantic figure is chained down, tiny arrows are sometimes found in its right leg. Its left leg, however, is artificial, and contains facilities for confession. "The confessions are taped, scrambled, dramatized, and then appear in the city's theatres, a new feature-length film every Friday" (4). This strikes the Freudian note: It is a clear though comical example of guilt giving rise to culture. Further flickers of Freud occur throughout the novel. "What is your totem?" a character asks (150); there is a briefly entertained proposal to eat the father (74); reference is made to "this little band of brothers." The band in question is made up of nineteen by and large faceless men, led by Thomas, the son figure. There are also Julie, his mistress, and the buxom Emma, who joins the party for no discernable reason. And of course there is the Dead Father.

Barthelme's novel is the story of a journey, a quest. Straining at a cable, the group drags the great figure of the Dead Father down the road, a transported colossus. At lunch break the Dead Father joins the group, makes passes at Julie, demands his rights and privileges, has tantrums, slays assorted fauna in the vicinity. Though "we *want* the Dead Father to be dead," as stated near the novel's beginning (5), he is not, exactly. This too is in keeping with Freud's theories in *Totem and Taboo*. The whole totem system,

according to Freud, is a form of deferred obedience to the Dead
Father, undertaken out of guilt. The prohibitions so rigidly enforced by the culture are a version of those enforced by the father
to ensure his power, especially his sexual power, within the tribe.
Thus the father whose death is celebrated in certain ritual killings
of the totemic animal is in another sense not dead at all, but lives
in the culture that continues to dominate his offspring. As "A
Manual for Sons" interpolated in Barthelme's book has it:

Fatherless now, you must deal with the memory of a father. Often that
memory is more potent than the living presence of a father, is an inner
voice commanding, haranguing, yes-ing and no-ing—a binary code, yes
no yes no yes no yes no, governing your every, your slightest movement,
mental or physical. At what point do you become yourself? Never,
wholly, you are always partly him. That privileged position in your inner
ear is his last "perk" and no father has ever passed it by. (144)

The goal of the journey is definitively to bury the Dead Father,
who is far too alive. That is to say, the son Thomas, like the son
Franz, is trying to purge himself of guilt and the patriarchal con-
trol that is its consequence. For instance, a story Thomas tells the
Dead Father opens with the bewildering paranoia of so many of
Kafka's tales:

One day in a wild place far from the city four men in dark suits with
shirts and ties and attaché cases containing Uzi submachine guns seized
me, saying that I was wrong and would always be wrong and that they
were not going to hurt me. Then they hurt me. (40)

And later Thomas tells the Father "when I explain myself I tend
to stutter" (56)—a problem he shares with Kafka, who explains it
as the product of his father's influence. But explaining this, and
everything else, in his letter has ultimately failed to serve Kafka's
purpose. Likewise, Thomas does not achieve his purpose by explanation, and does not even attempt to do so. Nor does he achieve
that purpose through the symbolic act of the journey, or of the
burial that concludes it. Thomas, or rather Barthelme, or rather
the reader, achieves the work's purpose through its *tone*.

The concept of tone fascinates Derrida, perhaps because it is
the most elusive element in literature, and yet often the one that
conveys the most. In *The Post Card* (1987), he calls tone "the final

index, the identity of some addressee who, lacking anything else, still dictates dictating" (145). But because identity, in Derrida's view, does not exist, neither does a stable tone; it "confuses itself and explodes all by itself, nothing to be done, unity of tone does not exist." He speculates, without quite believing himself, on possible techniques for underscoring this: "By mixing genres? By exploding the tone from tone to tone? By passing very quickly from one tone to another?" These are precisely the techniques that Barthelme adopts.

Barthelme's *The Dead Father* (1975) uses dozens, perhaps hundreds, of literary tones, genres, modes: snippets of larger systems that then play off one another. If culture, as Freud suggests, is a form of deferred obedience to a patriarchal law, it would seem to be impossible for any cultural artifact to break free of that law. For the law is not any *particular* order, but the very concept of ordering itself; and there is no such thing as a cultural artifact without an ordering principle, a law harking back to aspirations for control that are rooted in patriarchy, in the father. But Barthelme sees that the ordering principles differ, if only by a tone, in different artifacts. "Culture" is not a monolithic entity but an enormous heap of variegated systems of order. Culture is a scrapheap, like that described by the Dead Father in the novel as the product of his liaison with an attractive young lady:

We spent many nights together all roaratorious and filled with furious joy. I fathered upon her in those nights the poker chip, the cash register, the juice extractor, the kazoo, the rubber pretzel, the cuckoo clock, the key chain, the dime bank, the pantograph, the bubble pipe, the punching bag both light and heavy, the inkblot, the nose drop, the midget Bible, the slot-machine slug, and many other useful and humane artifacts, as well as some thousands of children of the ordinary sort. I fathered as well upon her various institutions useful and humane such as the credit union, the dog pound, and parapsychology . . . . I overdid it but I was madly, madly in love, that is all I can say in my own defense. (36)

The venerable myth of the male god who begets culture, such as Prometheus or Thoth, provides a major structuring principle behind this passage. But a counterprinciple arises from the broadening of the idea of culture to take in pop culture, including inventions of considerably less mythic dignity than fire or the alphabet.

There is a satiric edge to this passage, but it is difficult to decide which way it cuts. The mythic world and the modern world are rendered equally absurd. One's allegiance is to neither system of order: the reader is poised in the space between.

Juxtaposition creates this effect, and creates a similar effect in the catalog of objects. In admittedly minor ways, each of these objects represents a principle of order. But when all these principles are juxtaposed and jumbled, the effect becomes ludicrous. There is nothing innately amusing about credit unions, or about dog pounds, or about parapsychology. Through listing them all in one breath in this context, however, the disparate nature of their systems of order becomes apparent; and the chuckle, when it comes, is at the expense not of any one of these systems but at the expense of the idea of order itself. Lewis Carroll uses a similar technique for a similar subversive purpose when he speaks of "shoes and ships and sealing wax, / Of cabbages and kings."

The nonsensical disparities in Carroll's catalog are played against the linkages of its smoothly alliterative sound. In Barthelme's novel, too, sound is a major element. For not only does the ordering principle of culture wax and multiply; it becomes diluted to a mere sound, a tone, or rather a series of tones: the mythic, the pop, the epic, the lyric—but above all in Barthelme the innumerable versions of contemporary banality.

Of this last, the most extreme and the most intriguing versions are the conversations between Emma and Julie. In the following example, one or the other of them speaks each sentence or fragment; it is unclear *which* one, and it probably doesn't matter. Perhaps it begins with some jealousy between the two women over Thomas:

> Wake up one dark night with a puckle in your eye.
> We chat.
> About what?
> That's my business.
> Then perhaps he regards you kindly.
> Series of failed experiments.
> You have performed well under difficult conditions.
> Animals in which the brain strangles the esophagus.
> Years not unmarked by hideous strains.

Willfully avoided gathering to myself the knowledge
aforementioned.
And when not surly, pert.
The letter a failure but I mailed it nevertheless.
It's wonderful and reduces the prison population too.
I was surprised to see him in this particular bar.
Very young he's.
Parts of hero all over.
Many of them connected by legal or emotional ties.
Stares calmly at something a great distance away.

(153–54)

This is a good deal more far out than the first passage I quoted, a good deal further removed from an underlying sense of order. Though the conversation baffles our attempts to trace a coherent sequence in the whole, it also teases us with the feeling that each of its elements is a fragment from some perfectly familiar, even banal context. To restore one of these to its probable context: " 'You have performed well under difficult conditions,' he said to the slim young lieutenant standing at attention before him." This might be from one of those old-fashioned Henty novels for boys, which is pretty banal stuff. It's tempting to think, then, that the whole passage comments on the banality of communication be- tween people—an idea that is itself banal. Something else is going on here, and it has to do with the fact that these are two women in conversation. Feminist linguists like Robin Lakoff have deter- mined that women, far more than men, are capable of holding a conversation that is made up of indirections, obliquities, and unspoken understandings. Whereas men feel that they have com- municated only when they have fully articulated their points, pinned them down to logic and fact, women know they are com- municating even when the words themselves don't seem to be saying much. Such is the case here. The sense that each fragment is drawn from a familiar context only intensifies the opposing sense of soft ruptures and ricochets in the sequence. The conversa- tion proceeds in a series of tangents rather than in a straightfor- ward ("manly") way. All this suggests that these conversations between the two women represent the furthest remove from the principles of order that still govern other parts of Barthelme's patriarchal text. Exaggerating the technique that Barthelme uses—the juxtaposition of tones in order to undermine the principles of order they represent—these conversations are the strongest challenge to the presence and principle of the dead father in the text. A while ago I spoke of Emma being introduced into the story for no apparent reason. Perhaps Barthelme introduces her only so that these conversations between women can take place.

In extreme or less extreme versions, Barthelme is always writing about texts and contexts, and arranging delicately surreal battles between them. The effect is to undermine the authority of all texts, including his own. That authority is of course the authority of the father. The Dead Father, Julie says, is obnoxious, but "still he has something" (67). What he has, she decides, is "authority." Kafka describes his father as quintessentially "the authoritative man," and for Freud "the father is the oldest, first, and for children the only authority." In her book *Thinking about Women* (1968), Mary Ellman speculates about what might be the underlying characteristic of a "masculine" writing style: "authority," she concludes. If she is right, Barthelme's novel represents an interesting paradox: a male author authoritatively undermining male authority, both explicitly through his subject matter and implicitly through the strategies of his writing. And beyond the figure of the Dead Father, Barthelme's story undermines the Freudian authority that canonized this larger-than-life-size figure in the first place by telling a story.

Barthelme represents only one version of this kind of strategy, which I would argue is a basic strategy of postmodernism. By now, of course, any talk of a "basic strategy" of postmodernism is a kind of dancing through the minefield. This will be a short dance. In the sense in which I am choosing to see it (and choice is an important element of interpretation as it is of politics), postmodernism is characterized by a playing of "the Law" against itself in structures of irony. Often this is done by combining elements from various laws, and systems of order, in surreal juxtaposition. The clearest and most vigorous demonstrations of this postmodern aesthetic are found in contemporary architecture. As an example, take the building that has been said to have started it all, the AT & T building in New York, designed by Philip Johnson. A huge skyscraper is incongruously crowned with a classical pediment. The architect's model is especially surreal (fig. 1), charged with a curious power that is dreamlike, indeed Kafkan— this might be the castle keep to which Joseph K aspires. An "official" architecture, which usually represses a culture's unconscious, here expresses it. It's as if the commercial world of Kafka's big business father had been assimilated to the vision of the son. Yet this is not a simple case of Oedipal overthrow of the father, where the patterns of the unconscious are obeyed without even being recognized as such. Work like that of Philip Johnson brings that unconscious to the surface, conceivably helping to prevent a blind repetition of the Oedipal pattern.

The anxieties of the individual, then, and perhaps of the culture, are literally brought into the daylight in a building like this. But in stressing the anxiety related to this architecture I wouldn't want to overlook its wit and its playfulness. For these too are elements in the postmodern, as they are in Barthelme—and indeed in Kafka, who when first reading aloud *The Trial* to his friends repeatedly broke into laughter. Such playfulness is a form of release from both unconscious tensions and constricting patterns of authority. It provides a subversion of patriarchal authority that is not a rebellious challenge: that would only repeat the Oedipal cycle, as it is repeated in the dreary cycles of Greek mythology. Rather, authorities are turned against themselves, working to subvert the idea of authority. This allows one the freedom not to meet the force of the father but to *sidestep.*

I do not want to argue that the postmodern aesthetic, in architecture or literature, will instantly unravel knots in which the psyche has been tied for centuries. But I would argue that culture, far from being the passive child of an originary father, may be the means by which we come to a consciousness of the father's stature as something we have conferred on him, and that we can demystify. Rather than again burying the father in our unconscious and that of our culture, we must unearth him from the fictions created by our psyche. When we do so, the gigantic figure of the father dwindles down to the size of us. Daughters and sons alike, we have the promise of finally coming of age.

Figure 1. Architect's model of the AT&T Building. Photograph reprinted by permission of John Burgee, Architects.

Works Cited

Balmary, Marie. *Psychoanalyzing Psychoanalysis: Freud and the Hidden Fault of the Father*. Baltimore: Johns Hopkins University Press, 1982.

Barthelme, Donald. *The Dead Father*. New York: Farrar, Straus & Giroux, 1975.

Derrida, Jacques. *Dissemination*. Trans. Barbara Johnson. Chicago: University of Chicago Press, 1981.

———. *The Post Card: From Socrates to Freud and Beyond*. Trans. Alan Bass. Chicago: University of Chicago Press, 1987.

Ellman, Mary. *Thinking about Women*. New York: Harcourt Brace Jovanovich, 1968.

Freud, Sigmund. *Totem and Taboo*. Trans. James Strachey. London: Routledge, Kegan & Paul, 1961.

Kafka, Franz. *Letter to His Father/Brief an Den Vater*. Trans. Ernst Kaiser and Eithne Wilkins. New York: Schocken, 1966.

Krull, Marianne. *Freud and His Father*. Trans. Arnold J. Pomerans. New York: Norton, 1986.

3

Günter Grass's *Cat and Mouse* and the Phenomenology of Masculinity

Leonard Duroche

Homines, mihi crede, non nascuntur, sed finguntur.
—Erasmus

This chapter addresses what has been a puzzling lack in Grass scholarship to date. Although a great deal of attention has been given to Grass's social criticism, no critic has examined his critique specifically as one of the male system and no one has considered the significance of gender position in the construction and reception of Grass's narrative figures and narrative situations. When *Cat and Mouse* (*Katz und Maus* 1963) was written, gender consciousness, certainly *male* gender consciousness, had not been raised to a level where it was problematized by critics.[1] To my knowledge no one has yet explicitly thematized a number of pertinent questions: (1) To what extent does *Cat and Mouse* examine the masculinity models available in the specific historical context of National Socialism? (2) How do gender position and specifically the psychological and physical factors of male pubescence within the patriarchal system, particularly under the confused social psychological conditions of Nazism, determine the multiple narratives of the novella? After the appearance of *The Flounder* (1978; *Der Butt* 1977), which mythologized the battle between the sexes and created a minor uproar among feminist critics (see Erickson 1988, vol. 1, chap. 1), it is particularly puzzling that anyone could ignore the issues of gender in the earlier works, especially in *Cat and Mouse*. Among all Grass's narratives, *Cat and Mouse* focuses almost exclusively on the male lifeworld.[2] (3) Does it make sense to view Mahlke, like his predecessor Oskar in the previous volume of the Danzig trilogy, *The Tin Drum*, as singular in his deformity and abnormal, which is how the majority of critics has seen him? Or is it more likely that he is representative of male experience precisely because of his dysfunctionalism?[3]

In an attempt to address these concerns, I focus very much on the surface of the narrative rather than try to gather the narrative under larger overarching categories. Nor do I hunt for master metaphors or structural features to provide the key for unlocking the meaning *behind* the text. *Cat and Mouse* is an initiation story that, very much like *The Adventures of Huckleberry Finn*, deals with a boy growing up in troubled times, a dystopic German version of the theme. Like Huck, Mahlke, the protagonist, is a half-orphan. Unlike Pap, Mahlke's father is a positive father figure, a train engineer, who died heroically in a train accident while trying to save lives. Local geography, Danzig's position on the Baltic Sea, provides the physical setting, and Grass invests the sea with a complex symbolic significance that equals Twain's treatment of the Mississippi. The action in the first part of the novella takes place largely on the deck of a partially submerged Polish minesweeper. Like Huck's raft, the minesweeper is an adolescent male refuge from the adult world and the site of adolescent male rituals, including what Grass calls at one point the "masturbation olympics."

Narrated time in *Cat and Mouse* covers but a portion of Mahlke's life, from the onset of puberty to shortly before the end of World War II, and coincides with the rise and fall of the Third Reich. Two events mark puberty for Mahlke. The first is an achievement: learning to swim, becoming an expert diver. Grass calls it *freischwimmen*, which means earning a swimming proficiency certificate, but within the context of the novel takes on broader connotations of liberation (literally, freeing oneself through swimming). Only Mahlke can reach the furthest recesses of the submerged Polish minesweeper. The second event is biological, with challenging psychological consequences: Mahlke develops a very large Adam's apple which embarrasses him as it bobs up and down conspicuously, and that he tries to cover up with all manner of things.

When a former graduate of his school, decorated with the Knight's Cross, Germany's highest military honor, visits to give patriotic speeches about his experiences, Mahlke discovers what one critic has called "an appropriate fig leaf to cover his physical—and psychological—nakedness" (Thomas 1982, 98f.). When a second "hero" visits the school, Mahlke steals the medal. He later confesses, is expelled from school, finishes at an inferior school, and eventually winds up as a gunner in the tank corps. Mahlke finally gains the Knight's Cross legitimately by knocking out an impressive number of enemy tanks. Aided by the Virgin, his aim is unerring: Before a hit the Virgin appears marking the critical site—with her belly. She holds there not the Christ child, but a paternal icon, the picture of Mahlke's father. When he returns to his original school to give his long-planned hero's speech, he is turned down because he had earlier disgraced the school. He goes AWOL, takes flight finally to the minesweeper—at the suggestion of Pilenz, supposedly his only friend. The weather is cold and Mahlke has eaten himself sick on wild gooseberries. Pilenz, who goes with him, hides the can opener Mahlke needs in order to use his supplies. Then, Pilenz does not return at the time he had promised and when he finally does, there is no sign of Mahlke, who has apparently drowned. Pilenz writes the history of "the Great Mahlke" partly out of guilt, partly out of his own misguided hero worship.

Grass's narrative functions as a phenomenology of male adolescent experience, a rich description of the struggles and pain involved in the transition from childhood to youth and young adulthood.[4] That this struggle takes place in almost the very worst of circumstances, within a morally corrupt and finally collapsing social structure, does not restrict the significance of the novella to its own time frame. Much of what the novella explores has to do with the accumulated inheritance and consequences of the historical development of patriarchal culture within bourgeois capitalism. That is what justifies calling Mahlke's story a "male narrative." It typifies one possible path of an adolescent struggling to grow up. Largely unaware, Mahlke acts out specific narratives that history, time, and place have fabricated for him. Yet he believes his choices are his own. As Max Horkheimer reputedly said, "You can't talk about fascism without talking about capitalism."[5] National Socialism was only one, though a particularly horrible, result of the inheritance of patriarchy under bourgeois capitalism. Only partly and ineffectively dismantled following World War II in Germany and Japan and, despite the emergence of the women's and later the men's movements, left more or less intact elsewhere, modern hegemonic masculinity is still perpetuating social narratives that control men's lives, fabricating or reconfirming notions of the hero and constructing in young men malleable subjects to play the parts.

What are the issues or the questions that one asks of a male narrative? They are not unlike the kinds of questions that more traditional scholarship has already asked of texts, but they are framed from a conscious gender perspective and place at the center of investigating male experience, understood not as ungendered, "universal," human experience but as a construct of sociohistorical conditions. For the time period of Grass's novella and its current reception these are questions about father-son relations, including the problem of "die vaterlose Generation" (the generation without fathers) or, as Michael Schneider has more recently labelled it (1981, 9; 1984a, 4), "die vatergeschädigte Generation" (the generation damaged by its fathers). Since the 1980s, American men, and more recently European men, have intensified a search for the father, sometimes expressed more intensely as "father hunger," sometimes more mythically as the "Telemachos theme." That search has carried over into literature and intellectual life. It includes the theme of the dead (or the undead) father (see Rickels 1988).

A related theme is male expressiveness and particularly the inability of men to mourn for fathers or for brothers. Inexpressiveness suggests the machinelike nature of males as they have been socialized, particularly in wartime, thus the theme of the male body and men and machines. Also inevitable are the issues of male intimacy and friendship, and their flipside, male isolation and loneliness. More generally, a scholarship informed by a gender perspective asks what kinds of masculinity models exist or existed? Does a society provide meaningful rites of passage for male children through puberty and adolescence toward the production of positive adult males? Three of these issues touch on most of the others and are dealt with here. They are the themes of male intimacy and friendship, male writing/being written as male, and the relation of father and son.

Perhaps the best place to begin is with male friendship, because to address this issue is to take a stand on one of the "problems" to which earlier scholarship has devoted a good deal of attention: Is Mahlke "the" main figure or is Pilenz, his biographer and the first-person narrator of the story, equally important? What is the nature of their "friendship?" Croft (1987, 119) argues that "Pilenz as narrator proves to be as significant in the novel as its hero Joachim Mahlke"; Hollington (1980, 53) agrees. Keele (1988, 66) contends that Pilenz is the real subject of the book, whereas Cunfliffe (1969, 87) argues he is "not himself an important figure." Hayman (1985, 51) claims that "Grass has never since filtered so much of his message through a personal relationship." Reddick (1988, 109) asserts that "all this ambivalence and private psychology . . . are certainly not of central importance." And so on and so forth. I shall argue that *Cat and Mouse* is specifically an exploration of male relation.

If we focus on the gender issue, the appropriate questions are not whether Pilenz is a real friend or a traitor, but what are male relationships like, in general? How is gender scripted? How can narration, the act of writing or telling, examine varieties of male experience? One must consider *both* Pilenz and Mahlke. They are representative adolescent males caught *in* and, to a greater or lesser degree, compromising *with* the hegemonic male system. That is an overarching system offering to men as well as to women prefabricated scripts and limited choices that they may elect or reject. To look at both young men as situated within the context of the patriarchal system broadens the focus to encompass *all* social relations, self-self, self-other, self and society.

It is useful, I believe, to consider what feminist theorists have written concerning the impact of patriarchy on friendship among women and to consider why it should affect men differently. Dale M. Bauer opens her recent book, *Feminist Dialogics: A Theory of Failed Community* (1988), with a discussion of the threats to female friendship. The argument of the book, she says, has to do with "women's misreadings of the patriarchal ground of all of their relations: with each other, with their daughters, with their husbands and lovers, with their own histories." Using a short story by Edith Wharton as an example, Bauer argues "that the patriarchy, far from being the natural or originary foundation of human culture, in fact, functions to reduce experience . . . to some manageable minimum, to erase heterogeneity and Otherness" (ixf.). The effect of this is to make women "essentially ignorant of each other as women." What she says of women applies to men as well. To rephrase Bauer, *all* human beings caught up within the male system are "essentially ignorant of each other [as human beings], thereby allowing the displaced anger they feel to be vented on the other rather than on the cultural system by which they have been defined" (x).

One may draw two conclusions from Bauer's argument. The first helps explain Grass's title. The novella opens with teenage boredom and aggression. It is summer vacation. Boys wait for a ball field to be freed up so they may play. One of them, most likely Pilenz, sees Mahlke lying on the ground, his huge Adam's apple bobbing, and sets a cat loose on the "mouse." The first conclusion is that the game of cat and mouse is already inherent in the system, the role of the outsider and the persecution impulse are already parts of an inherited script. Kaiser makes this point when he reminds us that neither Pilenz nor Mahlke can remember who set the cat on Mahlke: "That indicates the degree to which in this moment Pilenz acts out of an impulse of the entire group, which forms Mahlke's environment, the extent to which the act is embedded in the situation, and actually flows from it" (Kaiser 1971, 13; see also Croft 1987, 119). *Cat and Mouse* is about the tension between conformity and heterogeneity in males' relation to one another and to the group. The novella revolves around the desire to establish one's own identity and the impulse to erase Otherness, as if erasure—of Self or of the Other—were the only path to identity. Pilenz's seemingly self-contradictory identification with and aggressivity toward Mahlke may make somewhat more sense if we remember the features of the Lacanian Imaginary before it relates to the Symbolic Order. Fredric Jameson (1977) writes that

> this is the type of relationship . . . which we have seen to result from that indistinct rivalry between self and other in a period that precedes the very elaboration of a self or the construct of an ego. As with the axis of Imaginary space, we must again try to imagine something deeply sedimented in our own experience, but buried under the adult rationality of everyday life (and under the exercise of the Symbolic): a kind of situational experience of otherness as pure relationship, as struggle, violence, and antagonism, in which the child can occupy either term indifferently, or indeed, as in transitivism, both at one [sic]. (356)

A second conclusion, if one applies Bauer's position to men, is that the isolation of and alienation between men is of a particular kind. The human gaze, so Sartre taught us, can be a loving gaze establishing connection between Self and Other. But it can also objectify and hold the Other from a distance, thus reinforcing the separation between Self and Other. The latter stance, as contemporary film criticism so frequently reminds us, characterizes male behavior. In *Cat and Mouse* the male gaze dominates. A strong visual quality characterizes the writing. Exteriors are lovingly and enviously depicted, suggesting at times a voyeurist narrator. Yet there is an almost total lack of access to the Other. Grass reminds the reader often enough of Mahlke's taciturnity and inability to open himself. As Hollington has said: "The emphasis . . . is on external and visible behavior" (Hollington 1980, 53). Pilenz almost never has access to the interiors, physical or psychological, where Mahlke dwells. His ignorance of his friend's inner life, for which critics often excoriate him, reflects a sad but true aspect of male friendship:

> And as for his soul, it was never introduced to me. I never heard what he thought. In the end, all I really have to go by are his neck and its numerous counterweights. (40)
> (Und seine Seele wurde mir nie vorgestellt. Nie hörte ich, was er dachte. Am Ende bleiben sein Hals und dessen Gegengewichte. [545])

Pilenz's very act of writing, besides being a penance and an act of mourning, is also a futile attempt to write the Self by writing the Other. The exploration of narration as a cognitive tool in men's attempts to understand who they are is by now a fixed feature in male consciousness-raising and in male gender studies. Grass's attempt to show both the power and the pitfalls of narration—uncovering fictions, inventing fictions—anticipates and parallels other literary descriptions of male rites of passage. The way in which the structure and events of *Cat and Mouse* resonate with other texts suggests that Grass has seized upon deep truths about the pain and struggle of adolescent male behavior. Thematic similarities are striking, for example, in Stephen King's (1983) novella "The Body," the text on which the film *Stand By Me* is based, which incidentally also thematizes male writing. King depicts the loss of intimacy and growing alienation from other males that begins with puberty: As boys approach that threshold, the acceptance and intimacy of childhood become mixed with aggression, separateness, and finally indifference. The narrator, very much like Pilenz, is writing the history of one particular summer's experiences with his then-teenage friends, most of whom are now dead. At one point he says something about language that also sheds light on Grass's text: "The word is the harm. Love isn't what these asshole poets like McKuen want you to think it is. Love has teeth; they bite; the wounds never close" (423). Pilenz may be treacherous and ultimately on the side of the cat, but he has also been bitten. He loves and he hurts; that is, he wounds and he is wounded. He writes about the great Mahlke to separate from Mahlke, but he is perpetually drawn back to him. He writes to discover who he is, but cannot separate from the Other. The complexity of male friendship in *Cat and Mouse* demands that one say something more about "love's bite." Grass portrays the strong homosocial desire that is possible between men. As in Twain's *Huckleberry Finn* or more recently in King's short story, there is in Grass's novella a deep sense of male intimacy. Though it is this very intimacy that may finally make treachery possible, there are undeniably strong homoerotic overtones in the narrative. It is disturbing—though in a homophobic culture not surprising—that so many critics have confused male intimacy with homosexuality. Croft (1987, 119) implies it and Thomas (1982, 109) takes it more or less for granted, to name just two examples. Croft, in fact, applies the terms "sterility and therefore deadness" to Mahlke's supposed homosexuality, reflecting an implicit (hetero)sexist and probably bourgeois capitalist attitude toward sexual economy, which is unable to see any relation as productive, that is, nonsterile, unless it is reproductive (119f.).

My point here is not to pick on fellow critics, but simply to suggest that our biases, when "reading" men's lives and relationships, are very deeply ingrained. Whereas men are socialized in ways that lead them (us) to confuse intimacy and sex, Grass seems to know the difference between the two. In *Cat and Mouse* he portrays young men discovering sexuality, still not fully aware whether they are male or female (548/47). Girls may begin to appear on the horizon, but boys are still also interested in, or have not yet been frightened away from, developing male relations to other males. Grass has Pilenz make the point that if Mahlke was more interested in men than in women, it was certainly not because he was *verkehrt* ("queer").

As for Pilenz's own homoerotic relation to Mahlke, there are other explanations. A good deal of it is envious admiration, identification with the human sublime, with *der große Mahlke* ("the great Mahlke"). Keele calls Pilenz's *fictional* attendance and search for Mahlke at the 1959 Regensburg reunion of former Knight's Cross recipients, an event that actually happened (supported by the West German army), "a bitter indictment by Grass of postwar militarism, a powerful statement that there are those in the Bundeswehr [other 'survivors' like Pilenz] seeking a resurrection of the old, messianic glory of the Nazi era. These sexual duds, Grass implies, seek in the mysticism of phallic gun barrels the fulfillment they cannot attain in normal life" (Keele 1988, 73). Rickels, in an altogether different context, speaking of what he calls "mourning sickness," says that "what is threatened with extinction during mourning is heterosexual libido itself: he who cannot stop mourning becomes the widow of his heterosexuality" (1988, 5).

Grass's graphic descriptions of emergent male sexuality are further ways in which he satirizes dysfunctional male narratives. Earlier criticism has made much of Mahlke's sexual exploits while tending to overlook what motivates him. That is not so much a sense of competition with other men, but with his own father. The male relation that ultimately is most important for him is that between father and son. As for the supposed grotesqueness of his Adam's apple and its sexual symbolism, the novella makes it clear that it is not objective size, but the self-perception and the self-conscious perception of one's peers—in this case young men uncomfortable in their own bodies—that is important. Mahlke's uncontrollable Adam's apple, like Pinocchio's suddenly elongating nose, stands for the awkward male teenage body, which seemingly has a life of its own. Mahlke ultimately comes to terms with his body changes and body image and even admits that perhaps his "mouse" was not all that much bigger after all. Though one of his friends gives his "article" the qualities of a disease, a goiter (555/ 59), the real disease is his masculinity, or hypermasculinity. In the figure of Mahlke and through the legends his admiring buddies tell about him, Grass satirizes a genitally organized sexuality and the fantasy that bigger is better. The point is not whether Mahlke's potential is productive or sterile (Croft 1987, 119), but rather that it is *over*productive. Overproductivity and overcompensation have their own liabilities, whatever the nature of the economy, and represent imbalances. Leonard reminds us that Mahlke's "deformation" is not only involuntary, in fact, something nearly every currently living male has inherited; she also points up the double edge of male strength: "What starts off as a promising act of emancipation, turns into an act of self-annihilation" (Leonard 1974, 29f.). Though Pilenz attempts to describe through his narrative what the "hero" should be, it is interesting that at the same time he doubts the very concept of "hero." There is something simultaneously attractive and grotesque about the ideal. Thus he is simultaneously awed and repelled. He admires and envies the status of the hero and offers his narrative as a memorial. But he also kills the hero, and his own nonbelief foils all resurrection scenarios. For these reasons, it is worth paying more attention to the act of writing—and of being written, both of which Grass thematizes through the novella.

Gerhard Kaiser's (1971) compact little book on Grass offers essentially a phenomenology of narrative consciousness in its first few pages. As his point of departure, he compares the function of narrative in Grass's tale with that of a nineteenth-century author, C. F. Meyer. Meyer's *Die Hochzeit des Mönchs (The Monk's Wedding)* is a story within a story in which the interior story, the defrocking of a monk, is not so much the theme as is its telling. Kaiser contrasts this kind of reflection on the narrative process with that of *Cat and Mouse*, which is yet a degree higher: Pilenz is not only a narrated narrator, he knows he is being narrated, or as he says, invented (*erfunden*; 527/8).

Kaiser contends the awareness of being the product of another consciousness is part of a modern development of narrative that shifts from thematizing consciousness to thematizing language, in which consciousness is already constructed. I contend that this development is not strictly "literary," but is reflected in male experience in the "real world" as well, in what Husserl called the Lebenswelt ("lifeworld"), that complex structure of consciousness that emerging from our "being-in-the-world." Being gendered is one part of "being-in-the-world." The male lifeworld originates in the gendered encounter with a world already structured before our own advent, from our unique perceptual relation to that world, and from the attempt to construct our own meanings against the background of the preexisting meanings of the world into which we are born.

Narration does not construct a fictional world of social relations with the aid of language; rather those relationships already exist in language itself. Grass seems unusually aware of that. *Cat and Mouse* exemplifies how that plays out in male experience. Pilenz, or more accurately, the fictional consciousness speaking, recognizes itself as linguistically constructed and is aware that the only possibility of elevating itself to the status of linguistic subject is by recognizing and negating its object character. That, Kaiser contends, can no longer be done by attempting to break out of the constraints of language, by creating a new language, but only by seeing through language. To the extent that the concept of the individual as an entelechy within society has been placed in question, *historia (die Geschichte)* has become a dubious category, whether understood as the history of collectives or the story of individual persons. Thus in the place of a world *mediated* through history and stories there is now only consciousness, a consciousness that understands—or misunderstands—itself and the world only as histories and stories. It takes the "world" as "tellable," without coming to any positive conclusions about the nature of "tellability." Which "stories" are liberating? Which stories are imprisoning, confirming the status quo? As Kaiser points out, even Pilenz, the invented narrator of *Cat and Mouse*, who knows he is invented, at first passes himself off as a sovereign master of the tale, who plans it in ad lib fashion.[6] Kaiser draws one set of conclusions from these observations, dealing with the problematization of narration in a narrow sense. I would like to draw attention to a second set of implications, namely the way in which both the contents of the text and the reflection on the writing of the text are suggestive for an understanding of narrative in a broader nonliterary sense and thematize the notion of male as invention.

Pilenz, far less innocent than Mahlke, seems very much aware that he as male is "invented." He is not terribly bothered by that. Several times he repeats the notion, expressed in the first chapter: "Over and over again the fellow who invented us because it's his business to invent people obliges me to take your Adam's apple in my hand and carry it to every spot that saw it win or lose" (8; "Der uns erfand, von berufswegen, zwingt mich, wieder und wieder deinen Adamsapfel in die Hand zu nehmen, ihn an jeden Ort zu führen, der ihn siegen oder verlieren sah" [527]). At one point he asks: "If only I knew who made the story up, he or I, or the one who is writing this in the first place!" (131; "wenn ich nur wüβte, wer die Mär erfunden hat, er oder ich oder wer schreibt hier?" [593]). And at another point: "Who will supply me with a good ending?" (188; "Wer schreibt mir einen guten Schluβ?" [623]).

Mahlke's naivete contrasts almost grotesquely with Pilenz's self-knowledge. Leonard (1974) writes that no other character in Grass is as completely a victim as Mahlke: "Not only does the system exploit his physical courage and extraordinary will-power, but in the end it refuses to grant him the recognition for which he has fought so tenaciously. Mahlke is unaware of this exploitation"

(32f.). His unawareness is sad but, again, representative. With his unraised consciousness Mahlke believes he has played by the rules and has done what "real men" are supposed to do.

Kaiser (1971, 8) postulates a difference betwccn the narrated narrator and the narrator's narrator, arguing that the author as ultimate narrator, in a final ironic continuation of the topos of *deus artifex*, manifests a freedom that is absolute and unconditional. I wish to argue that all the narrators, *including* the author as *apparent* last narrator, are caught in a wilderness of mirrors behind which there is always another force "inventing" the narration and the narrator. Such a view posits the fictionality of the subject both in art *and* in reality. That is not to argue, however, for a *mise en abîme*, a Romantic infinite regress. There is an original inventor: the "wilderness of mirrors" has its ultimate source in the real relations of production in bourgeois capitalist patriarchy.[7] Given the sociohistorical setting of *Cat and Mouse*, the theme of male as fiction, the fictionality of our masculinity, is particularly apt. One entire generation of males and much of the following, although in one sense "invented" by their society, were also forced to attempt to invent themselves in the absence of fathers. And that leads me to the significance of the father in the fatherless generation.

Without wanting to be as Freudian, or post-Freudian, as Laurence Rickels, I am going to attempt to approach the problem of the father in *Cat and Mouse* via ideas and implications found in Rickels's recent book, *Aberrations of Mourning* (1988). It, like *The Fictional Father* of Robert Con Davis (1981), is another attempt to deal with the power of the dead father, that figure who, be it in our critical practice, the tales we tell, or the lives we lead, is said to haunt us all. Rickels explores "a phantasmatic *Geistesgeschichte* not addressed within the traditional framework of theories and histories that emphasize only Oedipal structures." I find the search for other than Oedipal models of father-son relationships particularly appealing. Rickels tries to provide "a reading of both reading and writing that would go beyond notions of patricidal writing," beyond killing the father (1988, 1).

To apply Rickels' ideas to *Cat and Mouse* is to read the novella as an attempt to bury the dead, or—as Rickels would argue—the undead father. That attempt connects with the inability to deal with the dead, with the important themes of "the homeless dead," "the missing grave," "the imitation corpse" (8), and with the enormous difficulty or impossibility of the survivors to mourn and thus "detach [their] memories and hopes from the dead" (7). These are themes that have not only prevailed in West German literature, including Grass, but that have taken on new urgency with the attempts of those students who came to intellectual maturity during the Student Revolution of 1968 to come to terms with their own fathers, many of whom had been Nazis. Michael Schneider, perhaps the most widely read commentator on the student generation's preoccupation with the father, speaks of a "Hamlet complex" (Schneider 1984a), of an entire generation haunted by the father, and entitles one of his essays "Not all those who are buried are dead" (Schneider 1984b). *Cat and Mouse* clearly has its Oedipal aspects, but embedded in it, too, are scenes that, following Rickels, we might call "Oresteian," scenes manifesting drives within the son that center "on the urge to retrieve a lost father" (Rickels 1988, 174). In the introduction to his daring psychohistory, which the dust jacket calls "a Nietzschean challenge to and within the Freudian system," Rickels speaks of a primal identification with the father and alludes to Freud's rendering of "the death-wish bond with the father [as] the model of all mourning sickness," a task that can be done "only by keeping the mother in the shadow—as the shadow—of the moving target" (12). Here it is perhaps appropriate to remind readers that Pilenz names three motives driving Mahlke's ambition: (1) the Virgin Mary, the only woman in his life; (2) the urge to distract attention from his Adam's apple; (3) the wish to be recognized by an all-male institution, symbolized by *"unser Gymnasium"* (our high school). I identify this third motive force as the desire for male, particularly adult male—that is, symbolically—paternal approval. As Miles (1975) has said, "It is the applause of the school which he covets above almost any other" (90). While the tendency has been to focus on the first two motives, I shall argue for the greater importance of the third.

Much of what Mahlke does seems aimed at a "return or reanimation of the missing father" (Rickels 1988, 177). In his long-planned hero's speech he wants to speak not so much of himself, but of his father. A shot in the wrong direction, his attempt to become a hero on a par with the father fails. Those who dwell on the Christian imagery and ironic parallels between the life of Mahlke and the life of Christ can borrow an alternative reading from Rickels, in his etymological play with *Versöhnung:* "Reconciliation—*Versöhnung*—remains the implicit aim of both sign and son: to become son (*Ver-söhnung* [a play on the words *Sohn* = son and the German for reconciliation]) means to become the acknowledged second person, sign, likeness—and ultimately, the original image—of the father" (Rickels 1988, 181). Mahlke not only literally walks in his father's footsteps (he wears his father's shoes and many of his clothes), he assumes the role of the adult male in his house and his mother and aunt defer to him as if he were the father. Rickels speaks of a "substitutive economy of symbolic positions organized around the father, who . . . is already his own shadow when alive and then, once dead, is broadcast live" (3). Such a description applies quite literally to Mahlke's father. Mahlke's postpubescent life seems dedicated to finding a position from which he can relate to and vie with his hero father, the only positive male model in the entire narrative. He at first seems to find that place when he discovers the radio room, which, though it is above water, can be reached only from below. One must dive deep into the belly of the boat and swim a long way underwater. Only Mahlke can do so. He constructs there a shrine suggestive of ancestor worship, complete with sacred relics. His descent into the belly of the sunken minesweeper represents an "Orphean journey," dedicated to penetrating "the underworld only to excavate and commemorate the father, and never to the point of bringing back a lost object—an object which, since capable of being lost, would not be paternal" (3).

When Mahlke forsakes the boat in his *Flucht nach vorne* ("retreat forward," his attempt to overcome the system by joining it), he leaves the realm of positive sacrificial heroes to attempt the passage into manhood on his own. As Reddick (1988) and others have argued, it is "precisely his phenomenal 'Flucht nach vorne' that first exposes his 'mouse' to the gaze of 'one cat and all cats,' and that makes him even more exposed and vulnerable in direct proportion as his seeming successes become ever more brilliant" (115f.). But that does not establish Mahlke's singularity, rather just the opposite. If we transfer Mahlke's *Flucht nach vorne* from Nazi Germany to the offices and washrooms of the corporate world, the mouse as a symbol of a distorted, aggressive, achievement-oriented supermasculinity remains just as meaningful, and the implication that this is a masculinity that necessarily self-destructs strikes us not at all as odd but as quite familiar.

The turning point for the novella comes when Mahlke returns to his school to receive his reward, his recognition in giving his hero's speech, and is rejected by the false father, Klohse, the school director and Nazi party leader. At this point *Cat and Mouse* becomes a story of failed initiation. Mahlke's *Untergang*, his descent into the underworld at the end of the novella, is a retreat from awareness won on the threshold of manhood, an awareness that Reddick (1988, 115) calls "disastrously partial," or—in the words of a colleague—"disastrously insightful." Mahlke discovers an obscene and duplicitous world. His retreat is not unlike the retreat of other male protagonists unable to cope with their first confrontation with the complexity of the world and with death, as for example, in Hemingway's "Indian Camp." The difference, adding to the profound pathos of Grass's initiation story, is rooted in the historical context, in the inevitable absence of a wise adult male to bring the boy safely through the initiation experience. There is neither an adult male, a loving father, in whose arms he may nestle, safe as though a little boy again, nor a trusting peer to support and stand by him. There is only an age-old male isolation. At the very end Mahlke attempts to join the father, but his entry into the father's realm is prevented by the envious and abandoned son/brother who hides the key, the *Büchsenöffner* (can opener).[8]

But *Cat and Mouse* is not only about burying the dead father. It is also about burying the dead brother, whether one reads that as applying to either Pilenz's biological brother or to Mahlke or to both. Pilenz must deal with dead fathers and sons in different ways. He too has a "dead" dad who is nightly "killed" by the replacements in his mother's bed, who wear the slippers of the usurped husband without realizing the significance of that in the eyes of the son. (Once again this is the "Hamlet motif.") The death of Pilenz's biological brother also elevates the latter to a revered status, one that Pilenz envies and hates him for. His blood brother is beyond his reach, but not Mahlke. Ultimately the choices offered to the men in Grass's dystopic world seem to be between choosing or "refusing to survive the [death of the heroic] father"[9] or attempting to placate the haunting ghost of the murdered, but unburied brother.

One of the conundrums of Grass criticism has been the inability to reconcile the social optimism of his political writings with the apparent pessimism of his literary texts. A possible solution lies perhaps in recognizing—and then liberating oneself from—the essentialist tendencies implicit in much current scholarship, not just on Grass. Many critics have invested Grass's literary phenomenology with normative character and positive ontological status, that is, they seem to have understood his narratives not as descriptions of the way things (including men and women) have been and are sociohistorically, but the way they necessarily are and have to be. Though one should not always trust authorial commentary, we can take at face value, I believe, the statement Grass made in his *Text und Kritik* interview: "In my Novelle *Cat and Mouse* . . . I have undertaken the attempt at portraying the fabrication of a military hero by society" (cited by Hollington 1980, 64; his translation).

Gerhard Kaiser's (1971) distinction between the unfreedom of the invented narrator and the freedom of the author figured earlier in discussing masculinity models as fictions. That distinction can also help resolve the seeming contradiction between Grass's literary and political writings. Kaiser argues very convincingly for the logical necessity of differentiating between the inevitability of events in Grass's (or any other author's) narratives and the possibility of change in the real world. He reminds us that the rules governing scientific experimentation also apply to narrative "possible worlds" (my term, not Kaiser's). Though verisimilitude may hold sway so that fictional events "appear under the guise of the real," the represented world "is defined once and for all as invention, play, intellectual experiment, and its proximity to reality thus has the simulation character of experiment."[10] Even if the fictional world, as a phenomenological-psychological reduction of modes of lived experience, necessarily looks very much like the "real world" as we perceive it in the natural attitude, there is nothing that guarantees the ontological necessity of the fictional world. This is a point well worth remembering when reading male fictional narratives, particularly when we can discern more than a single voice (see Duroche 1987). As Kaiser (1971) says:

Even experiments simulating natural conditions do not in fact take themselves to be nature nor wish to be confused with it. They differentiate themselves from the latter by the fact that no matter how the experiment is set up, the inevitability in the running of the experiment is always subordinated to the premise of the free choice of experimental conditions [the narrative premises of the narrator]. Thus this tale [*Cat and Mouse*] operates inevitably and inexorably under the conditions postulated. It does not produce however an inevitable and unchangeable world, does not inflate artistic consequences into metaphysical necessity, but rather presupposes that with conditions set differently different consequences would necessarily ensue. The unchangeability within the story manifesting its own inventedness implicitly points to the changeability of the world. Its changeability does not enter into the narrative's formation because it precedes it. (9f.)

Following from the previous position, Kaiser then presents his argument that both the story and its narrator thematize their production *by* and groundedness *in* another consciousness. Kaiser points to the radicalization of social problematics that began with classicism and reaches into our own time. One result of that development has been to narrow the arena in which subjects can act, as subjects. He speaks of a narrowing of the stage of human self-realization "with the reality of action and consciousness [of the subject] shrinking to simply the reality of consciousness alone." In this process "the figures of the linguistically constructed fictional world of literature have increasingly been allowed to [compelled to] change from subjects into the objects of their life circumstances." To understand this state of affairs is to understand how we are "written," as men and as women. The awareness that we do not think, feel, and act as subjects but as objects calls forth in us a loud "No!", a refusal to accept that state of affairs. The consequence is to produce a critical consciousness-raising by seeing through language. To understand our inventedness is to understand the possibility of other possible worlds. In Grass, so

Kaiser contends, "the possibility of action is still present in the narrative, though relativized as the consciousness of the narrator's narrator." Consciousness becomes the new "place of action." It is ultimately the consciousness of the reader, that is the dynamics between the reader and the text, between enunciation and the enounced, that grounds the political potential of narration and brings forth the impetus to change.

To read Grass in the way I have suggested is to discover the political potential of narration as a possible cognitive tool for the examination and reconstruction of masculinity. There is more than one story to tell. It is difficult to think of a single contribution to recent Grass commentary that excels Helen Croft's 1973 study. But as in so many critical encounters with Grass's text, she becomes victimized by her methodology, by Jungian essentialism and the freezing of the future by the patterns of the past. It is logical that she should reach the conclusion that Grass's "ultimate vision is that of a *humanity* unable to cope, and without any real hope of rejuvenation" (Croft 1987, 121; my emphasis). That would certainly seem to be the case for the conception of masculinity that Grass describes in *Cat and Mouse*. But is that the one readers are stuck with? New possibilities open up if the reader understands that conception as a social construct and Grass's narrative as satirical critique of that construct. A social construct has a history and an ability to change, even if *very* slowly. If critiquing the inherited male past is a first step toward change, then Grass has made in *Cat and Mouse* a major contribution to the process of reconstructing masculinity.

Does Grass ever offer more than a critique and a horror story? Not in *Cat and Mouse*. At the level of story it offers essentially aversion therapy. Only at the level of discourse, in thematizing narration, does it suggest to the attentive reader the possibility of alternative masculinities. Are there any glimmers of hope elsewhere in Grass's work? The answer is a cautious "yes." *Very* faint glimmers are seen not only in *The Flounder*, but even as early as *The Tin Drum*. The last lines of *The Flounder* offer a note of hope in describing the male narrator's determination to catch up with Ilsebill, mythic representation of woman, so that perhaps the seesaw domination of one sex over the other can finally end (see

Erickson 1988, vol. 1, chap. 4). In the final scene of *The Tin Drum*, Oskar, another damaged male who is misshapen but finally growing, ascends the escalator, slowly resolving to confront *die schwarze Köchin* (the Black Cook: "Black Witch" in the English translation), what one might call Oskar's "shadow self." But as Pilenz is fond of saying, that is another "dismal complicated story, which deserves to be written, but somewhere else, not by me and certainly not in connection with Mahlke" (551/53).

Notes

1. I have tried to provide English translations for all German quotes. I have quoted the German only in the case of Grass's own texts and have used the standard Manheim translations with the first number referring to the German, the second to the English text. Unless otherwise noted, all other translations are my own.
2. For the brevity of her discussion Irène Leonard offers some of the most incisive commentary and comes closest to seeing Mahlke as *male* victim of a *male* system. (See Leonard 1974, 32f). Miles (1975) is one of the few to recognize explicitly that the novella deals with what it meant to be a young male under Nazism. Thomas (1982) focuses somewhat more than many others, though only implicitly, on exclusively male issues. Behrendt (1976, 132) is typical in speaking of Mahlke's oversize Adam's apple as "the symbol of *human* striving."
3. I have also explored this thesis, male pathology as norm, elsewhere. See Duroche (1986–87).
4. Kaiser (1971), to my knowledge, is the first and only other writer to suggest this way of looking at the novella:

   The point of this narrative stance [Pilenz's repetitive, unending, unendable, self-correcting narration, which forces him not only to speak *about* but also *to* Mahlke] consists in preventing the reader from reading Mahlke's story as that of an exceptional pathological case which is being presented here objectively, as a clinical example, so to speak. The reader is forced to read the story as something else: not the pathology of an individual, but the pathology of a society, the history of a social relation, of which the presentation is part of that relation." (19)

   I shall return to the idea of the last sentence when discussing the implications of writing as a male.
5. A statement attributed by Michael Schneider to Max Horkheimer (Schneider 1981, 12f; Schneider 1984a, 7). The most brilliant, though chilling, exposition of the connections between patriarchy and fascist

mentality is Klaus Theweleit's *Männerphantasien* (1980; *Male Fantasies*, 1987, 1989), which provides part of the theoretical background for this chapter. Theweleit presents a very comprehensive study of the psychosocial circumstances out of which the Freikorps, and from them, fascist mentality arose, and of the connections between bourgeois patriarchy and fascism. The book is indispensable for any study of twentieth-century Western patriarchy, images of the body, connections between man, machine, technology, and male-dominated culture.

6. This paragraph paraphrases the argument of Kaiser (1971, 10–12 passim).
7. I am indebted to my colleague Russell Christensen for this and several other formulations within this chapter.
8. Interpreting Gottfried Keller's death bed dream, Rickels (1988, 184) speaks of the appearance of the knightly, armored dead father as "death's delegate in a conserving can."
9. Rickels (1988, 259) in reference to Kafka.
10. Much of what follows in this and the next paragraph is either direct translation (quoted material), or close paraphrase of Kaiser (1971, 9ff.).

References

Bauer, Dale M. *Feminist Dialogics: A Theory of Failed Community*. Albany, NY: State University of New York Press, 1988.

Behrendt, Johanna. "Die Ausweglosigkeit der menschlichen Natur: Eine Interpretation von Günter Grass' *Katz und Maus*." In *Günter Grass: Ein Materialenbuch*, edited by Rolf Geißler. Darmstadt: Luchterhand, 1976, 115–35.

Croft, Helen. "Günter Grass's *Katz und Maus*." *Seminar* 9 (1973): 253–64. Reprinted in *Critical Essays on Günter Grass*, edited by Patrick O'Neill. Boston: G. K. Hall and Co., 1987.

Cunliffe, William Gordon. *Günter Grass*. New York: Twayne, 1969.

Davis, Robert Con. *The Fictional Father: Lacanian Readings of the Text*. Amherst, MA: University of Massachusetts Press, 1981.

Duroche, Leonard L. "Alternative Senses of Male Narratives: Other Voices/Other Choices." *Men's Studies Review* 4, no. 4 (1987): 6–7.

———. "On Reading Kafka's 'Metamorphosis' as a Masculine Narrative." *The University of Dayton Review* 18, no. 2 (Winter–Spring 1986–87): 35–40.

Erickson, Nancy. "A Contextual Analysis of Cooking Vocabulary in Günter Grass's *Der Butt* with Concordance." (2 vols. Ph. D. diss. University of Minnesota, 1988).

Grass, Günter. *Cat and Mouse*. 1963. Reprint. New York: Harcourt, Brace and World, 1987.

———. *Danziger Trilogie: Die Blechtrommel. Katz und Maus. Hundejahre.* Darmstadt: Luchterhand, 1980.

———. *Der Butt.* Darmstadt: Luchterhand, 1977.

———. *The Flounder.* New York: Harcourt Brace Jovanovich, 1978.

Hayman, Ronald. *Günter Grass.* London: Methuen, 1985.

Hollington, Michael. *Günter Grass: The Writer in a Pluralist Society.* London: Marion Boyars, 1980.

Jameson, Fredric. "Imaginary and Symbolic in Lacan: Marxism, Psychoanalytic Criticism, and the Problem of the Subject." *Yale French Studies* 55/56 (1977): 338–95.

Kaiser, Gerhard. *Günter Grass: Katz und Maus.* Munich: Wilhelm Fink, 1971.

Keele, Alan Frank. *Understanding Günter Grass.* Columbia, SC: University of South Carolina Press, 1988.

King, Stephen. "The Body." In *Different Seasons*, 289–433. New York: Signet, 1983.

Leonard, Irène. *Günter Grass.* New York: Barnes and Noble Books, 1974.

Meyer, Conrad Ferdinand. *Sämtliche Werke: Historisch-kritische Ausgabe.* Edited by Hans Zeller and Alfred Zach. Vol. 12, 7–98. 1883. Bern: Benteli, 1958–1991.

Miles, Keith. *Günter Grass.* New York: Barnes and Noble Books, 1975.

O'Neill, Patrick, ed. *Critical Essays on Günter Grass.* Boston: G. K. Hall and Co., 1987.

Reddick, John. *The "Danzig Trilogy" of Günter Grass. A Study of the Tin Drum, Cat and Mouse and Dog Years.* New York: Harcourt Brace Jovanovich, 1988.

Rickels, Laurence A. *Aberrations of Mourning: Writing on German Crypts.* Detroit: Wayne State University Press, 1988.

Schneider, Michael. "Fathers and Sons, Retrospectively: The Damaged Relationship between Two Generations." *New German Critique* 31 (1984a): 3–51.

———. "Nicht alle sind tot, die begraben sind." In *Nur tote Fische schwimmen mit dem Strom* . Cologne: Kiepenheuer and Witsch, 1984.

———. "Väter und Söhne, posthum. Das beschädigte Verhältnis zweier Generationen." *Den Kopf verkehrt aufgesetzt.* Darmstadt: Luchterhand, 1981.

Theweleit, Klaus. *Male Fantasies.* 2 vols. Minneapolis: University of Minnesota Press, 1987, 1989.

———. *Männerphantasien.* 2 vols. Frankfurt: Verlag Roter Stern, 1979. Reprint. Hamburg: Rowohlt, 1980.

Thomas, Noel. *The Narrative Works of Günter Grass: A Critical Interpretation.* Amsterdam: John Benjamin, 1982.

4

Naguib Mahfouz, Men, and the Egyptian Underworld

Miriam Cooke

If you would like to know what men are, then you should be a woman. If you would like to know what women are, then you should ask God.

—Jacob Lorenz

Any discourse which fails to take account of the problem of sexual difference in its own enunciation and address will be, within a patriarchal order, precisely indifferent, a reflection of male dominance.

—Steven Heath
"Difference," *Screen* 19, no. 4 (1978–79): 53.

At any given moment, gender will reflect the material interests of those who have power and those who do not. Masculinity, therefore, does not exist in isolation from femininity—it will always be an expression of the current image that men have of themselves in relation to women. . . . Those people who speak of masculinity as an essence, as an inborn characteristic, are confusing masculinity with masculinism, the masculine ideology. Masculinism is the ideology that justifies and naturalizes male domination. As such, it is the ideology of patriarchy. . . . It gives primacy to the belief that gender is not negotiable—it does not accept evidence from feminist and other sources that the relationships between men and women are political and constructed.

—Arthur Brittan
Masculinity and Power (London: Basil Blackwell, 1989), 3–4.

In this chapter I shall be examining some of the early novels of Naguib Mahfouz in an attempt to uncover the dynamics of gender construction. As Brittan writes, masculinity and femininity are never givens but power-based constructions that are in a state of perpetual negotiation in everyday life as well as in literature.

At a time when metanarratives are coming under scrutiny and criticism, it is appropriate to examine those of modern Arabic literature as well, neopatriarchy for example. In his innovative theorization of modern Arab (read, any neocolonial) society, Hisham Sharabi[1] has described the dichotomization of emergent classes as neopatriarchy. At the top is the newly empowered, traditionally patriarchal, yet spiritually bankrupt bourgeois man schooled in the ways of the European ex-potentate; at the bottom is the ever poorer and weaker subaltern. Naguib Mahfouz's novels and short stories may be considered to be multiple, Egyptian elaborations of such a totalizing discourse[2]: His men are either obsessed by the empty striving for advancement within a circumscribed, deified[3] bureaucracy, or, they are alienated, disillusioned revolutionary intellectuals who search—often aided by drugs and drink—for the meaning of existence in a modernizing, amoral, and Godless world. A subplot of this master narrative is the psychological and sexual victimization of women by selfish, greedy men. In her full-length study of Mahfouz's women, Fawzia al Ashmawi-Abouzeid describes Mahfouz's oeuvre as yet another kind of metanarrative: "the struggle between tradition and modernity as well as the evolution of customs and relations between men and women in contemporary Egyptian society."[4]

To read Mahfouz's fiction as metanarrative is to approach his work from only one of many possible directions. Perhaps part of the problem, for a Western reader at least, is that literature from the Arab world as well as literature from all parts of Asia and Africa, those dark continents of which we know little, is read as allegory. Allegory is one of a text's subtexts for which the protagonists are vehicles. For the literary detective, these novels wear their plots as coats. Once this coat has been peeled off, all are relieved to find the reassuring meaning; whatever does not fit the broad strokes of the allegory is artifice that should not interfere with the social or political message. The sleuth work has been accomplished and the reader can proclaim the coat to have been well tailored or cut with an axe.

In this chapter, I shall try to read Mahfouz without expectations of allegory derived from mandates for sociopolitical commitment. Liberating the text from its immediate subtext opens up semiological depths that would otherwise remain masked by that seemingly impermeable level. The text is now susceptible to different readings that uncover new facts and foci. Protagonists can be read as not merely carrying messages, but as being textual constructions that construct the text. If they are not credible, nothing else will be.

Mahfouz has pluralized the actors on his urban Egyptian stage to portray men and women from the rich, the petit bourgeois and the destitute classes. Heterosexual relations are paradigmatic of relationships of power pertaining throughout Egyptian society. Male characters are constructed out of their relationships with others according to the binary model of master/slave. Men who cannot control their own lives, or those of insubordinate men, turn to women as objects over which they can have dominion. The relationships of Mahfouz's men with women are always explicitly grounded in asymmetric power. Women's insubordination, in other words any hint of autonomy, threatens these men's fragile identities and represents the final stage in their alienation. They cannot confront and therefore they escape women's challenge, thereby stunting any possibility of growth. Their conception of masculinity is too rigid to accommodate interaction with women on the basis of equality. The women, however, enter into relationships for a variety of reasons. Because they are less programmed in their needs and desires, they are more difficult to fathom. Women's lack of clear definition, despite apparently self-evident categorization, emblematizes the incomprehensibility of forces confronting Mahfouz's men.

Yet, Mahfouz seems to be saying something else. He told Salwa el-Naimi: "Our world is 'masculine' and one cannot imagine it otherwise. . . . Women continue to struggle to become part of social life. But I could not describe a world in which women play the same roles as men."[5] But is this the point? For a world in

which women play the same roles as men does not yet exist, nor is
it perhaps desirable that it should. Sameness implies mimicry and
therefore a replication of a system of asymmetric power. Therefore, because domination is inherent to these same roles, a world
in which women played the same roles as men would look the
same and would be as unjust and patriarchal as one in which men
were the sole players. What matters is equal access to power,
defined as audibility and effectiveness of voice. Reading with the
protocols of the text, even though apparently against the author's
intention, I argue that Mahfouz's fiction echoes with women's
voices as they act out their lives in society, whether it be in the
home or with the men in the "public sphere." Yet, I am not
claiming that he has concentrated on them at the expense of
delineating male protagonists. His fiction often betrays the delicate balance of power maintained in real life relations among
men, among women,[6] and between the genders.

Mahfouz's women are not images, flat symbols of good or evil
in Egyptian society. Yet this is precisely what most critics have
asserted. Fawzia al Ashmawi-Abouzeid concludes her study of
Mahfouz's women with a taxonomy of what female protagonists
represent: (1) social situations; (2) a whole class; (3) a type of daily
life; (4) the evolution of customs over three generations. She adds,
"The role of the female character consists in making this social
evolution more concrete and to clarify the nature of male/female
relations in contemporary society" (161). Her study focuses on
three protagonists: Nafisa of *The Beginning and the End (Bidaya
wa nihaya)* is the "[incarnation of the] middle class Egyptian
woman of the between-wars period who is living through a harsh
economic crisis and of a struggle between tradition and modernity." Her quest is "passive" (161). Nur of *The Thief and the Dogs
(Al-liss wa al-kilab)* is another incarnation, this time of the "proletarian woman *[fatat al-tabaqa al-sha'biyya]* whom misery and social ill-fortune have turned into a prostitute" (162). Finally, Zahra
of *Miramar* is the "[incarnation of] the Egyptian fallaha [peasant]
after the 1952 Revolution. . . . [she] is a symbol of the myth of
Woman/Egypt" (163–65).

In *Ramziyat al-mar'a fi al-riwaya al-'arabiya wa dirasat ukhra*
(Symbolism of women in the Arabic Novel and other studies,

Beirut, 1981), Jurj Tarabishi has analyzed the portrayal of women in *Respected Sir* and *Miramar*. He is more interested in Uthman Bayyumi's mystical quest as well as in the development of the four male characters in *Miramar*[7] than he is in Mahfouz's women, the avowed subject of his inquiry. He calls Uthman's struggle with women "not so much a struggle between the sacred and the profane as between depravity and life, between selfishness and life. . . . Uthman escapes women because they are the mirror in which he sees reflected the barrenness of his soul. . . . His relationship with Qadriyya is not with her but with himself" (91–92). This is also true for the four men in *Miramar* who use Zahra as a reflection of themselves (120). It seems that Zahra is a symbol, but a "living symbol" who is skillfully drawn despite her symbolic role. Tarabishi concludes that Zahra's future is in her hands (124), but he does not consider that fact significant enough to warrant revision of the mirror/symbol role.

In the interests of uncovering political allegory, Menahem Milson has reduced characters to symbols to further his detective work:

Naima in *Fear (Al-Khawf)* and Saniyya in *Hanzal and the Policeman (Hanzal wa al-askari)* represent the idea of Egypt, the motherland and the people. This is a most important icon which appears in quite a number of allegorical stories of Mahfouz: Zahra in *Miramar*, the young women in *The Lord Giveth Death and Life (Yumit wa yuhyi)*, the woman in labor in *The Child of Pain (Walid al-ana)*, Qaranfula in *al-Karnak*, Saniyya al-Mahdi in *Only One Hour Left (al-Baqi min al-zaman saa)*, Randa in *The Day the Leader was Killed (Yawm qutila al-za'im)*. . . . The outstanding qualities of . . . secondary female characters are charm, endurance, fortitude in adversity and hope.[8]

For Mona Mikhail, Mahfouz's women are symbols who "tend to embody ideas and ideals. . . . Mahfouz's classical 'putain respectueuse' of *The Beginning and the End (Bidaya wa nihaya)* or that of *Miramar* represents an always illusory truth."[9]

It may be that the persistent symbolization of Mahfouz's women is due to the fact that until recently the study of women's roles in men's literature has been confined to the discussion of images in isolation from their impact on the evolution of the male characters. If a woman made only brief appearances, critics did not feel she warranted much of their discursive space. I shall argue that Mahfouz's women are much more than symbols. They are as critical to the development of plot as are male protagonists. What is more, they are often critical to the development of male characters. While Mahfouz's men need women, his women would like to—and quite often do—escape their need for men. Female protagonists are much more than Luce Irigaray's masquerading woman whose desire exists only as a mirror to masculine desire. On the contrary, Mahfouz's women have ambitions and desires that propel the narrative in ways that masquerade would not allow.

To understand the significance of Mahfouz's women, we must strip away the sexist bias that has informed canonical readings and view his works through a feminist optic. Such a reading will resemble the first visit of a Western tourist to the Arab world. This tourist, filled with prejudices and stereotypes, ventures into the streets of Casablanca, Tunis, Cairo, and Baghdad and suddenly realizes that the women are not all veiled. When we read Mahfouz's novels we are like that tourist, conditioned by the oft-repeated and apparently axiomatic commentary that his female protagonists are flat symbols of this and that. When we come across a woman with a complex personality who is motivated by individual goals that have nothing to do with men except as instruments of her advancement, we label her amoral. We gloss over the intricacies of her evolution in the plot, all the while commending Mahfouz for having drawn a credible woman among the panoply of paper dolls.

Because of the profusion of characters in a majority of Mahfouz's novels and short stories, it is not always possible, or indeed desirable, for each character to be rounded. Mahfouz himself has said that "from a minor real detail, I manage to create a whole life."[10] The reader should then be sensitive to the fact that this is just as true for the men as it is for the women. Yet, when critics have described sketchiness, or flatness, in Mahfouz's character portrayal, it has often been the women who have been singled out for attention.

Mahfouz has provided us with a wide tapestry in which women's experience is elaborated and valorized. Mahfouz does not allow the reader to get away with any one image, because for him no group, however apparently homogeneous, behaves in uniform fashion. It is important to read Mahfouz's oeuvre as a whole so that the resonance from one novel to the next can be felt and echoes of a simply delineated woman in one story can be read in the thoughts and actions of a woman in another story. Fully aware of the sexist preoccupations and prejudices of his fellow men, Mahfouz has depicted among the vast caste of women strong moral individuals who have been able to survive despite male opprobrium at trespassing on their turf. But he has also given us the weaker women who have not been able to overcome the obstacles. He has satirized men who respond in stereotypical fashion to women's new and unexpected roles. He has painted the canvas of Egyptian society, always striving to get the whole picture, either by proliferating characters or by embedding a single character in a vivid social context. Mahfouz's women do not live in a world apart where they suffer independently; his men and women are part of the same universe, they are locked into mutually dependent relationships so that what one does influences the other.

In fact, Mahfouz's men are often flatter than his women. The women cannot be reduced to a few types. What draws many of the women characters together is terminology: beautiful or ugly daughters, piously self-sacrificing or assertive mothers, virtuous or adulterous wives, fading or alluring spinsters, and above all prostitutes. The simplicity of these designations is deceptive, for Mahfouz creates memorable women whom readers grow to love or hate as though they knew them personally. Some are educated, some illiterate, some kind and some mean, some chaste and some loose. Vivacity is achieved by the introduction of the unexpected into a mundane character. For example, in *The Beginning and the End*, the reader learns that the tender-hearted, recently bereaved widow has never kissed her children (203). This piece of information explains previous and later behavior not only of the widow but of all who come into contact with her. And then, as though he were wont to stereotype, Mahfouz writes of this same woman that "unlike many of her sex, Samira was not a chatterbox" (231). Samira has been eased out of any possible pigeonhole, and although she is only a secondary character, we feel that we know her as an individual distinct from the others we have and will meet in Mahfouz's literature.

However, the most interesting and creative women are the "prostitutes," those literary figures whom Simone de Beauvoir has described as projections of male fantasy.[11] What does this word prostitute mean to Mahfouz? In his 1946 novel *Khan al-Khalili*, he wrote that "the real woman is the prostitute who has rejected the mask of hypocrisy and who does not have to pretend to love and to be modest and loyal" (39–40). Twenty seven years later, he takes this definition further. In *Love in the Rain (Al-hubb taht al-matar)*, Mahfouz has Husni Hijazi say: "But 'prostitute' no longer means anything" (87). Does this mean that throughout this considerable oeuvre, Mahfouz is using a signifier whose signified is other than expected? I would suggest that this is indeed the case, and that this is why so many have misread Mahfouz's women: They have viewed them from a single vantage point that, like the assessment of plot in relation to allegory noted earlier, allows only for praise or regret of in-depth characterization.

The *Concise Oxford Dictionary* defines a prostitute as one "who offers her body to promiscuous sexual intercourse esp. for payment or as religious rite." Does this exchange adequately express the motivations and actions of Hamida of *Midaqq Alley (Zuqaq al-Midaqq*, 1947), Nafisa of *The Beginning and the End* (1949), Yasmin of *Children of Gebelawi (Awlad haratina*, 1959), Nur of *The Thief and the Dogs* (1961), Riri of *Autumn Quail (Al-summan wa al-kharif*, 1962), Basima in *The Search (Al-tariq*, 1964), Warda of *The Beggar (Al-shahhadh*, 1965), and Qadriya of *Respected Sir* (1975)? If we deconstruct this word in the context of all of Mahfouz's works that contain prostitutes as main or subsidiary characters, we will see that what they have in common is not so much a commodification of body for survival, but rather an urge for independence.

This subsuming of Mahfouz's prostitutes under a single rubric of revolt is not meant to essentialize but rather to open new possibilities of analysis. Through the lens of revolt the behavior of Mahfouz's prostitutes acquires a level of activism absent from the creation of prostitutes in conventional male writing.[12] Reading the behavior of Mahfouz's prostitutes as acts of revolt allows us to understand their literary roles also.

Mahfouz's depiction of prostitutes makes explicit what remains implicit in his other women: men reify all women so as to avoid dealing with the reality of their lives and experiences. This objectification protects men against their own weakness and allows them to weave fragile delusions of power and control. One of the best known examples can be found in the first volume of the Trilogy, *Palace Walk* (*Bayn al-Qasrayn*, 1956). Sayyid Ahmad Abd al-Jawwad is the stern patriarch who rules his household with unrelenting rigidity. During one of his very rare absences, his secluded wife Amina is urged by her children to visit the Husayn Mosque. While she is out, a car knocks her over and injures her slightly. The affair comes out into the open. To her surprise, the stern patriarch does not punish her at once: he waits until she has recovered from her accident and then throws her out. This moment of independence that she stole forces him briefly to view her as an individual and one whom he loves. His love frightens him because it makes him vulnerable, and so he has to close her out. Mahfouz's men are safe only as long as the women with whom they consort are subsumed in their roles. A measure of Mahfouz's control in characterization is that it remains allusive.[13] Amina is not unrealistically transformed by her experience, she is merely shown to have become wiser. The Amina of *Sukkariyya*, the third volume of the *Trilogy*, is a gloomy, inflexible woman, a far cry from the bright innocent of *Bayn al-Qasrayn*. Abd al-Jawwad's Achilles heel has been glimpsed. Time takes care of the rest.

Mahfouz's prostitutes are self-willed, strong individuals who for the space of the novel, or part of the novel, find themselves linked to a man—as client, lover, wife, or mother—whose need for her is greater than is hers for him. In *Children of Gebelawi* (1959), Rifaa tries to save Yasmin from her pimp, the alley strongman. He marries her. Yasmin is disappointed that Rifaa is more interested in her soul than in her body, more interested in what she represents than in who she is. She rejects this spiritual commodification and returns to her pimp. Her indignation is such that she becomes instrumental in Rifaa's execution. In contrast with this Judaslike figure, Mahfouz two years later in *The Thief and the Dogs* (1961) creates a completely different prostitute. Nur, meaning "light," is the only enlightenment that the alienated protagonist can find. She is more honest, more patriotic, and closer to God than is the God-fearing shaikh.[14] Yet, like many other women in Mahfouz's fiction, Nur is a resource Said Mahran is unable to tap because all he wants is to control her.

Prostitutes are often portrayed as stronger and more intelligent than the generality of womankind. Basima in *The Search* tells her son: "Your mother is far more honorable than their mothers. I mean it. They don't know it, but if it weren't for their mothers my business would have floundered" (5). Sabriyya al-Hishma, whose name means the Patience of Modesty,[15] uses her profession to achieve the kind of respectability and security of which she had always dreamed: she collects enough money to be able to leave her brothel, and at the age of fifty she marries a young man and lives happily ever after. These women are aware of the social opprobrium attached to their label, but it does not stand in the way of the accomplishment of their goals. For them it is not a problem; it is for the men who choose to interact with them.

Here is the crux of the matter. The men who choose to interact with these prostitutes do so with the understanding that they are quite simply prostitutes, women who sell their bodies and who in that transaction temporarily lose possession of those same bodies. Mahfouz demonstrates again and again that this is not the case. The woman who sells her body not only retains control of that body, but also of its surplus value. She is doubly empowered: she is in control of the illusion that she is surrendering just as she is in control of the man's desire and burgeoning need for her body and not that of any other woman.

Mahfouz uses prostitutes to demonstrate men's inability to deal with women except as masks and symbols. In *Respected Sir*, Uthman Bayyumi is the son of a cart driver who is promoted up and up until he becomes director-general. Throughout his journey to the top, Uthman feels he might be aided by marriages to daughters of influential superiors, yet the time never seems quite right. This is particularly the case because the eligible woman he fancies when he is at a particular civil service grade is no longer a social superior and therefore helpful when he has moved up.

While he waits, this respected civil servant virtually lives with Qadriyya, the somewhat unattractive "half black" prostitute he has frequented since youth. From time to time, he resorts to the local matchmaker, only to be disgusted with her suggestions. One candidate is an aging, though attractive, never-married headmistress whom he finally manages to seduce and in whom he then promptly loses interest. At another time, he courts one of his office personnel. But, as always, when the woman seems to want marriage, Uthman escapes. He is afraid that marriage, at least with someone of her station, will hinder his plans (85). Marriage must bring advantages, not responsibilities. He can think of only one escape from this fear that connection with women who need him engender: marry a prostitute, the emblem of passivity and of masculine power. Surely Qadriyya will not threaten his control of his own life and affairs.

However, marriage is not for the autistic; it compels recognition of another as a human being. Uthman comes to realize that Qadriyya the prostitute is above all a woman with a will and a way of life of her own that she is not willing to sacrifice because of a change in her institutional status. When she had earlier spoken to him of her political concerns and commitments, he had dismissed them as irrelevant (42). He had never felt the need to keep himself politically informed, much less to sympathize with the political activities of a prostitute. Anything she had done that did not relate directly to the pleasure he gained from her body was of no interest, and it presented no threat. But then he marries her, this unattractive woman with her political passions and her drink and drug addictions. Marriage makes them both miserable: Qadriyya because she has to contend with a man who has never taken women seriously as individuals; Uthman because he has never taken women seriously as individuals lest they threaten his smug sense of self.[16]

Respected Sir exemplifies the problematic relations all Mahfouz's men have with women. Middle- and upper-class women represent their class and nothing more. They are prizes to be coveted because of what association with them promises. Prostitutes are symbols of pleasure. Men cannot imagine that the function masks an individual, and that once they have stripped away the function, by marriage for example, what is left is the individual. As long as Uthman keeps Qadriyya on the side and does not have to deal with her on a level of equality, he does not have to try to understand who she is. He continues to preoccupy himself with other women, but as always at the level of function: Who are their parents? Will they help him fulfil his grandiose ambitions? Would they make attractive wives? These are flat questions, and because our viewpoint is Uthman's we get flat answers going little beyond yes or no. Whenever these women start to encroach on his life, start to make demands however undemanding, he immediately backs away, afraid of losing part of himself in a relationship where he will not always be in charge. Losing his life's companion, the "half black" fat prostitute, to his wife deprives him of the only kind of relationship it was possible for him to have with anyone— that of taker. The novel ends with Uthman ruminating the only satisfaction he can wrest out of life: a splendid tomb.

Many of Mahfouz's male protagonists are torn between attraction to and fear of women. Umar in *The Beggar* and Isa in *Autumn Quail* hope to reconcile desire and disgust through association with a prostitute. Umar cannot keep away from women, yet rejects all who need him; the greater the need, the more violent the rejection. First, he abandons his pregnant wife who had cut all ties with her Christian family by marrying a Muslim. He turns to the prostitute Warda assuming that she will demand nothing beyond financial recompense. But Warda has feelings and Umar turns from her at the moment that she begins to love and, he fears, need him. He grows to hate women, which is exemplified by his relentless chasing after anonymous women. Warda perspicaciously observes: "Men don't believe in love unless we disbelieve in it" (85). Isa, a high ranking civil servant in the pre-1952 government, loses his position as well as his hope for an advantageous marriage after the Revolution. Like others of Mahfouz's men who have despaired of life, Isa takes up with a prostitute called Riri. His relationship with her is not human but symbolic; it concretizes for him his own degradation. She was "a symbol of the utter humiliation into which he had sunk" (80). Yet even at his most abject, Isa clutches at the shabby remains of his masculinity in an attempt to protect himself against any weakness. When Riri announces that she is pregnant—in other words that she is establishing herself in a relationship of wife and therefore of possible demand—he rejects her summarily. He even ignores her when they run into each other in a cafe. Years later, he sees her in her husband's cafe with "his" daughter. By that time he has come to need her and the stability she offers in the new role she has assumed. She, on the other hand, no longer needs him. This is one of the topoi of Mahfouz's writings: incongruence of needs in time and kind.

But what is the motivation for these women into whose minds we are not allowed to enter? How did Qadriyya, Warda, and Riri become prostitutes? Were they victims of terrible circumstances? That is the usual literary explanation proffered for the fall to prostitution, often with the added flourish that this victim's virtue exceeds that of those whose business is virtue. Yet, if we turn to two earlier novels we will read of prostitutes—Hamida in *Midaqq Alley* and Nafisa of *The Beginning and the End*—whose destinies elaborate another story. These are not so much stories of a fall, but of a rebellion couched in terms of a fall.

It is in *Midaqq Alley,* his best known novel in the West because of its early translation into English, that Mahfouz creates one of his most convincing women. Hamida, the beautiful orphan adopted by the alley matchmaker, is the evil product of socialization by vicious women. In fact, she is so strong and determined that Mahfouz can ironically describe her as "most unfeminine" (21). Here he sets up the norm of femininity: weakness, passivity, and vacillation. Hamida knows this, and she eschews the feminine condition. She has to break out of a world that expects her to be other than she wants to be, a world that condones older women's oppression of young women. She will only break that particular cycle if she can escape the constrictions of her space. We get to know Hamida through her conversations with the alley inhabitants. We sympathize with her claustrophobia, and are ultimately relieved to escape its stranglehold even though the agent of this release is a pimp, ironically named Ibrahim Faraj, or Abraham the Liberator.

Hamida becomes one of the few women characters in Arab men's literature to make a real choice. She makes her decision as an individual with complex interests and goals. Although it is true that she may have chosen prostitution because her choices were limited, she did not choose it because she was forced. Mahfouz does not present society as uncomplicatedly oppressive. Hamida has rejected her destiny as a traditional Egyptian woman for whom marriage is the sine qua non for social acceptability. She is not condemned by her circumstances to sell her body—she is engaged to a respectable young man and has a secure, if poor and unexciting, future in the alley. She chooses to emulate the Jewish factory girls whose economic freedom gives them the means to dress well and to seem to be in control of their lives and their bodies. This is what Hamida craves, despite the pain she inflicts on all who care for her. Freedom from the alley means more, much more, than security in an oppressive world.

Hamida has thought carefully of her options and has chosen outside what was offered. Certainly, Hamida's fate can be explained as an allegory for the invasiveness and corruption of western values leading to the fragmentation of traditional society. And the use of a female protagonist as the vehicle for this allegory indicates how this form of imperialism is perpetrated through women, the vessels of honor and culture. Moreover, the fact that her decision mirrors and participates in a stage of Egyptian feminism does not mean that we should reduce Hamida to yet another kind of symbol.[17] This symbol would be of the morally reprehensible influence of Western notions of equality and women's rights at the expense of community. For Hamida emerges out of a milieu in which there is almost as little freedom for men as there is for women to act out a new pattern. Had she been upper class such a decision might have led to an exemplary path like that trod by Huda Sha'rawi, the pioneer of Arab feminist activism. Under such social and economic circumstances, her courage and anger at her limited horizons as a woman could have helped others, as did Sha'rawi's. But Hamida is not upper class. She is from the lowest echelons of society, and, what is worse, she is an orphan. She has no status and no resources other than her beauty and intelligence. She uses the one to exploit the other so that she can effect the break. Mahfouz does not indicate whether Hamida is happy. Here we have an example of his intuition of a twentieth-century Egyptian woman's dilemma: rejection of socially sanctioned norms of behavior had become for some women an imperative for which the cost could not be counted.

Why does Hamida not choose to work in the factory like the Jewish girls instead of opting for the most compromising of all women's occupations? Is it because the rewards are more immediate and less strenuous? Or is it that working in a factory or even only as a seamstress, as does Nafisa in *The Beginning and the End*, was no more valued, no less shameful than earning an honest wage as a prostitute? As always, the issue is the woman's independence. This independence is at the core of men's fear of women, disguised as indignation at the threat directed at family honor.

In *The Beginning and the End*, Mahfouz traces the "fall" of another woman. In this case, however, the woman is from the petite bourgeoisie and far from being beautiful, she is plagued by her ugliness. More than most of his women, Nafisa demonstrates Mahfouz's ability to create not only a woman but a prostitute from within. Nafisa is not universal woman but a unique individual. Nafisa and her three brothers are introduced just after their father has died suddenly without leaving provision for his family. There is general consternation because none of them has a skill or training. However, Nafisa has been sewing for friends and neighbors gratis, and the family realizes that her dressmaking skills are their only immediate resource. Although her three brothers—a drug addict and two schoolboys—are at first shocked that they have sunk so low as to have a seamstress in the family, their attitude does not outweigh their satisfaction with her earnings. Very soon none can imagine life without the fruits of Nafisa's labors.

Mahfouz allows the reader to enter Nafisa's confusion as the certainties of class and status are undermined. What was previously inconceivable is now possible. This is particularly true as far as her relations with people outside the family are concerned. She no longer has to play the game by the rules of the class into which she was born. No man of her class has ever expressed the slightest interest in her. The only one to have paid her attention is the grocer's ugly son. Whereas she is securely fixed in the ranks of the lower middle classes, Sulayman is beneath contempt, a worm whose lechery she shunned with horror. Yet, with the destabilizing of her social situation, she begins to humanize the worm. She sees in him the possibility to rebel against the limitations of her physical handicap. She can break out of the prison of her petit bourgeois upbringing and of her ugliness; she can initiate contact with a man. She seeks rather than tries to escape Sulayman's admiration.

Sulayman is delighted with this turn in events. Before her father's death, Nafisa had been a social superior and therefore his hope for improvement in status. He has dared to hope because she was so ugly that she repelled peer suitors. However, now that she has become one of the lower classes, she represents something else: satisfaction of lust. He is soon able to make this desperate woman do what she knows she should not do or what she would never have done before: walk hand in hand with him in a disreputable part of town. He finally lures her into his family apartment while everyone is out. This is not a scene of easy seduction presented from the male or the outsider's perspective. Mahfouz articulates Nafisa's experience as though seen through her eyes. Nafisa's monologues that combine admonitions to herself as well as desperate justifications lead the reader through each tiny decision that leads to her submission. When Sulayman has his way, the moment is evoked in her mood: "a mixture of anxiety, pleasure and despair" (104). She knows that she is losing control, but the hope of realizing her goal as a woman, which was to attract a man and to get married, makes her act in ways she would never have anticipated.

But Sulayman is a man like all the others; women will always be one-dimensional, reducible to icons and epithets such as respectable or shameful. He has had his pleasure and now despises this shameful creature. The courting pretense is over, he has proven his virility at no cost at all—he even asks her to lend him money she knows he will not return. Another monologue takes the reader into Nafisa's confusion: "How can I squander money like this . . . when our home needs every millieme I earn. . . . He is not a man. . . . But I love and want him. . . . I have no one else in the world" (116). He has not acted as he should have and therefore Nafisa declares him not to be a man. Yet, much to her dismay and confusion, she thinks she loves and needs him. For him, this is a victory. For her, this is a shock because she realizes that she has no one else to care for her. Moreover, she has now become a particular kind of woman, without the assurance that she is indeed such a woman, for the usual exchange has not happened, or at least it has happened in reverse.

Confirmation of her ignominy and doom comes soon with the announcement of Sulayman's engagement. Ironically, she is asked to sew the bridal gown. Betrayal gives Nafisa the courage to confront the scoundrel, to mock his unmanly subjugation to his father—the ultimate insult—and finally, in a farcical scene, to beat him in public. Sulayman begs her to stop, and when she will not he threatens to call the police. Although he acts like a woman, he can paradoxically invoke male prerogative, saying "You have no claims on me" (131). As a man he has socially sanctioned rights that allow him to escape what a woman could not escape: answerability for amoral behavior. Even at her bravest and most rebellious, Nafisa's actions serve only to consolidate an unmanly man's manliness.

Nafisa has encouraged the advances of a social inferior whom she despises but has come to need because he is her only hope for affection. Here Mahfouz indicts the family that uses Nafisa, in fact needs her, but whose members condemn her because of what they have driven her to do: earn her living and theirs as a seamstress. Her brothers, despite their radically different characters, are chips off the same block. Their equivalence is nominally marked: Hasan, Hasanayn, and Husayn. Each name is derived from the same root HSN, which means good. Hasan is good, Hasanayn is in the dual form and means doubly good, and Husayn is in the diminutive form and means quite good.

Husayn is the most virtuous in his manner and therefore the most sinister and hypocritical. Nafisa gives him the money that allows him to start his career as a teacher in Tanta. Piously mouthing concern at the need to take dirty money, he starts his new life full of good intentions toward his family. Now he is going to be the breadwinner and this bread will be clean. For the first few months he sends home a substantial share of his salary. With time, however, he is less happy to part with so much and one month he determines to tell them that he is sick. He keeps the money to buy himself a suit. His mother is worried and comes to Tanta to make sure her son can cope. He lies without flinching. His defense of this purchase out of the allowance he should have sent to his family is heinous: he has acted against the interests of his family, yet he has convinced himself that he has done no wrong. He continues to bemoan his misfortune at having the siblings he has and longs for the return of the soul to the family when it has been cured of its evil ways (200). Mahfouz's intertextual reference to Tawfiq al-Hakim's patriotic novel *Awdat al-ruh* (*Return of the Soul*, 1933), which extols the woman as a symbol of purity and Egypt, is ironic. Nafisa is a symbol of shame; all know that their honorable and successful futures depend on Nafisa's dishonorable employment. Without her dishonor there can be no honor for them.

Hasanayn represents lust: lust for his chaste fiancée prefigures his lust for power and social standing that allows him to betray his family. He sees in Bahiyya, the daughter of the esteemed Ahmad Bey Yusri, the hope for social advancement: "Mount her and you'll mount a whole class" (246; cf. 276, 287), as well as the satisfaction of carnal desire. Throughout his three-year engagement, he can only talk to Bahiyya of his desire, knowing that her honorability mandates modesty. Yet, as soon as Bahiyya is pronounced by his illustrious colleagues at the War College to be unsophisticated, he loses interest. His disinterest grows with her growing interest and reaches crisis when she offers herself to him (298, 315–16). In the meantime he is fashioning a respectable facade. He moves the family out of their neighborhood and tries to keep Nafisa at home and out of the sight of their new neighbors. Like Husayn, he hopes that papering over the past will assure another future. Yet, like Husayn he continues to use the money that Nafisa earns from her prostitution and that Hasan earns from pimping to establish his highly respectable career.[18]

Hasan does not have the pretensions of his brothers. He knows he has failed, and in some ways his marginality mirrors that of Nafisa. Yet he, too, despises and ignores Nafisa. Before establishing himself as a pimp and alley bully, he tries singing for a living. When he hears of Sulayman's wedding, he offers his services. No one is more surprised or gratified than Sulayman, who had expected the brother's visit to be one of revenge for his sister's disgrace. The offer to sing at his wedding implied condonement— even if only through ignorance—of his dishonorable behavior and of her betrayal. Subconsciously, patriarchal forces regroup to close out space for women, except in their routinized roles. As her world collapses, Nafisa turns against her mother (126). This turn is as powerful as it is unexpected. With the death of the father, her mother has become the primary authority figure. In some ways, she has assumed the male role and in the mimicry had become male. This female father figure incarnates Nafisa's shame.

Shame is incurred when Nafisa leaves the home to earn her family's living. The transition from seamstress to prostitute is easy and almost irrelevant. After rejecting the lewd advances of a mechanic, she gives in. She is hurt at his roughness after he has had his way, yet she eventually picks up the ten-piaster piece that he has thrown at her. She knows that the decision to take the money is part of a continuum that began with her family launching her into the outside world to sell her services on their behalf and will end with her determination to sell her body on her own behalf. In this connection, it is worthy of note that Mahfouz repeats throughout that Nafisa gained pleasure from her sexual encounters. This is not to say that Nafisa is happy, but that through this vocation she finds a level of satisfaction of which she would otherwise have been deprived. In a society that values women for their physical charms, an ugly woman has no place, no right to happiness, and certainly no right to physical pleasure. With the loss of Sulayman, Nafisa knows that she has no hope of marriage. By offering her body, she can attract the attention of men who would be repelled by her face.[19] Unlike the beautiful Hamida, who became Titi so as to gain autonomy and independence, the ugly Nafisa used her body to glean seconds of pleasure and tenderness even if they were then turned into the coldness of cash and cruelty.

For her two younger brothers her work as seamstress as well as her unmarriageability epitomize the family's degradation. The

irony underlying the novel is the anxiety that all feel about
Nafisa's job and status simultaneous with their ignorance not only
of her prostitution but above all of her independence of them and
of social convention. The family's blindness to the reality of their
sister's and daughter's life reflects Mahfouz's awareness of the
shallowness, selfishness, and insensitivity of men and their surro-
gates with respect to women.

It is Nafisa's suicide that reveals the chasm dividing the world
of men from that of women. When the ruthlessly ambitious young
officer is summoned to the police station to identify his sister, who
has been caught with a man, he is horrified. He does not, nor ever
will, know that this is not the first incident. His outrage is such
that he feels honor-bound to kill her to safeguard the family reputation. But he cannot do the deed. Nafisa senses his anguish and
offers to kill herself—the ideal solution. He has been instrumental,
yet he does not have to compromise his situation further by soiling
his hands with shameful blood and will not have to render an
account to the world of the reasons for this murder. When Nafisa
throws herself into the Nile, Hasanayn feels a slight twinge. Yet
when the body is dragged out on to the bank he is just one of the
curious onlookers. His decision in the last lines of the novel to
throw himself into the Nile from the same spot Nafisa had chosen
does not mitigate his crime, but only suggests at best that he has
been inspired by his sister's courage, and at worst that he cannot
face a life his family has so tarnished for him and that he can no
longer patch over. This depiction of blindness, terminal selfishness, and cowardice parodies patriarchal obsessions with honor
as vehicled through women who are perceived to be without subjectivity. There is no act that Nafisa can commit, however de-
praved or noble, that will make her real to the men with whom
she deals. To them, she is as flat as a mirror. Yet, as a mirror she
reflects and thereby creates their image.

This chapter has examined a few of Mahfouz's novels that revolve
around the relationships men have with prostitutes. I have sought
to demonstrate that Mahfouz's prostitutes are not fallen women
but rather modern women who have been exposed to new options
and values and who have rebelled against traditional social expec-

tations. They are forging a different future during a period of transition. Despite the gravity of this challenge, men continue to be preoccupied with themselves and with existential issues. They are blind to reality, particularly that of the women with whom they absentmindedly consort. When these women assert themselves, the men withdraw.[20] This inability to relate to women except as fantasy or stereotype replicates or perhaps constitutes their alienation.[21] Mahfouz mocks his men whose delusions of power and knowledge women expose.

From his first publication, a collection of short stories entitled *Whisper of Madness* (*Hams al-junun*, 1938), to the most recent classically intertextual novels like *The Nights of the Thousand Nights* (*Layali alf laila*, 1982) and *The Travels of Ibn Fattuma* (*Rihlat Ibn Fattuma*, 1985), Mahfouz has created a caste of men and women whose actions and beliefs affect each other. In the longer works, Mahfouz explores heterosexual relationships in depth. In the shorter fiction there is more allusion. It is the intensity of women's relationships with men rather than their symbolization of larger forces that makes Mahfouz's portrayal of women exceptional.

In considering his vast and varied oeuvre, can we argue that Mahfouz writes as a feminist? If the criterion is attention to the multiplicity and evolving nature of urban Egyptian women's experience, then perhaps. Mahfouz has opened up the deprived and angry lives of women in the poor and not so poor areas of Cairo. He has written of the first women students at the Egyptian university where he was matriculated only two years after women were first admitted. He has written of the changing reaction to women's education over half a century. He has focused on changing marriage customs; he proceeds from a time when neither men nor women could see their prospective partners to a time when they were introduced through the photograph,[22] to a still more recent time when women proposition men.[23] He has concentrated on the workplace and shown how time has changed men's attitudes.[24] He recognizes at the same time that this new economic freedom also entails emotional freedom: women have earned the right to choose whom to love and especially whom not to love.[25] He has written of powerful women who were part of what he calls the women's renaissance or who were members of the Women's Wafdist Committee,[26] and who did not have to bow to society's conventions. Above all, he has entered the Cairene and Alexandrian underworlds and has fully fleshed out the lives of prostitutes who are not merely symbols or projections of fantasy but often complex personalities who use their humiliation against their humiliators.

But is he a feminist? Mahfouz's depiction of women has changed over the past fifty years. In his sociorealist novels of the 1940s and 1950s, he displayed a sensitivity to women's issues and particularly to prostitution as a form of rebellion that may be dubbed feminist. However, in the existential novels of the 1960s that revolve around a single male, many of the women seem flat and transparent. Young women during this period represent the extremes of emotion latent in the men who are so self-absorbed they can only see and interact with these women as aspects of themselves. In the 1970s, his attitude changes once again. By constantly proffering the male perspective and reiterating the strangeness of women's new visibility, Mahfouz emphasizes the importance of caution. Like Camelia Zahran, these women had to "bear in mind the eastern complexes which their male colleagues inherited from their forefathers at home" (*Al-maraya*, 282). If women did not remain constantly on their guard men would be vindicated in their fearful preconceptions.

During the latter half of Mahfouz's career, we read of men's fear of phallic mothers, "the real killers" (*The Search*, 78). In *Wedding Song*, Sabir says, "She is my foremost enemy: father is insane, an addict, but mother is the engineer of all the evil in the world" (80). The man who is intoxicated with one woman will be like the son under the control of his mother; he will lose his reason because he will need the object of his obsession no matter how vicious and adulterous she may be. The only solution beyond numbers is to control this woman with an iron fist, to not allow her any freedom or to allow oneself feelings. The woman who is not controlled will surely control. Mahfouz attempts to overcome the negative attitude toward women prevalent in twentieth-century Egypt but he is increasingly trapped in a web of prevailing notions and fears.

When he wrote *Midaqq Alley*, *The Beginning and the End* and the Trilogy over thirty years ago, Mahfouz must have felt free to create specific, complex women who gradually attained a measure of autonomy. Subsequently, his women have become flatter, more sketchily delineated. We can only surmise about the reasons, but it could be that as women have attained greater acceptance in society they have become more threatening. It is not so easy to be a male feminist in a world full of women.

Notes

1. Hisham Sharabi, *Neopatriarchy* (London: Oxford University Press, 1989).
2. In his introduction to the English translation of Elias Khoury's *Little Mountain* (Minneapolis: University of Minnesota Press, 1989), Edward Said has written, "Mahfouz's precedence assures [later generations of Egyptian writers] a point of departure . . . discursive patterns of a narrative structure that was not merely a passive reflection of an evolving society, but an organic part of it. . . . Mahfouz's novels, his characters and concerns have been the privileged, if not always emulated, norm for most other Arab novelists" (xiii).
3. "The State is an exhalation of the spirit of God, incarnate on earth" (*Respected Sir*, Questet, 1986, 143–44; originally published as *Hadrat al-muhtaram*, 1975).
4. Fawzia al Ashmawi-Abouzeid, *La Femme et l'Egypte Moderne dans l'Oeuvre de Naguib Mahfuz 1939–1967* (Geneva: Labor et Fides, 1985), 160.
5. Interview with Salwa el-Naimi, "Notre Père Mahfouz," *Magazine Littéraire* 251 (March 1988): 28.
6. "The Visit" from the *Black Cat Tavern* collection (in Arabic, 1967) explores the terrors and anxieties of the faded beauty who never married and who has no support system. She is physically and psychologically dependent on her callous servant who is economically dependent on her.

   In *Wedding Song* (Cairo, 1984; originally published as *Afrah al-qubba*, 1981), we read of two prostitutes who confront the same circumstances with different outcomes: one is killed; the other becomes a brothel madam. Tahiyya, the murdered actress, is never given a voice. Her story is recounted by four protagonists, none of whom has ever seen her as a person. The reader glimpses a woman whose only function has been to fulfil men's dreams and desires. On the other hand, there is Halima al-Kabsh, the mother-in-law who, despite the resentment she feels toward her, understands Tahiyya as no man ever had or could. She is able to learn from a woman's experience.

7. In fact, he writes after eighteen pages on the men: "Is it not time for us to talk about Zahra herself?" (120) and he does so for just over four pages.

8. Menahem Milson, "Najib Mahfuz and Jamal Abd al-Nasir: The Writer as Political Critic," *Asian and African Studies* 23, no. 1 (March 1989): 10.

9. Mona Mikhail, *Images of Arab Women: Fact and Fiction* (Washington, D.C.: Three Continents Press, 1978), 92. In a more recent work entitled *Brides at the Feast: Studies on Arab Women* (*Ara'is fi al-mawlid dirasat hawla al-mar'a al-'arabiyya* [Cairo: Dar al-'Arabi, 1987]), Mikhail discusses Hamida as a fallen virtuous woman (saqita fadila) and as a victim (78). However, she does insist that Hamida is a strong woman who is rebelling against society.

10. Salwa el-Naimi, "Notre père Mahfouz," 28.

11. Simone de Beauvoir, *The Second Sex* (New York: Vintage, 1974), 157–223.

12. "Even among male writers who are sympathetic toward prostitutes, the tendency is to create the character from without, to rely on the role of 'prostitute' in defining the character, rather than to single out the individual in that role. . . . [Their men] see the women's actions in terms of themselves and are blind to their meaning for [the women]." Amy Katz Kaminsky, "Women Writing about Prostitutes," in Pierre L. Horn and Mary Beth Pringle, eds., *The Image of the Prostitute in Modern Literature* (New York: Frederick Ungar, 1984), 120, 125.

13. She is quite unlike the mother in the Moroccan novel by Driss Chraibi, *La Civilisation, Ma Mère!* (Rabat, 1972), whose exposure to the world after protracted seclusion leads to violent self-consciousness and political activism.

14. Compare also the shaykh and the prostitute in "The Mosque in the Alley" (*Dunya Allah*, Cairo, 1963).

15. *Al-maraya* (Cairo: Maktabat Misr, 1974), 174-77.

16. Men's fear of women is a topos in modern Arabic literature. Fiction writers have often described dangers imagined to be inherent in beautiful women, cf. Yusuf Idris, "Affair of Honor" (Hadithat al-sharaf), in which the merest suspicion of illicit relations was enough for the innocent woman to be punished; Yahya Haqqi, "The Empty Bed" (Al-firash al-shaghir), in which a young man is so disturbed by women's sexual responsiveness that he finally resorts to necrophilia.

17. "One can easily tell that Mahfuz gives great importance to his female characters and that he uses them as a mirror in which the evolution of customs is reflected. Through his paper characters, he elaborates

the stages in the emancipation of the flesh and blood contemporary woman" (al Ashmawi-Abouzeid, *La femme et l'Egypte*, 160).

18. Like Nafisa, Hasan has a perspective from his marginal position and he is amused by the irony. When Hasanayn highhandedly demands that Hasan return to the straight and narrow, Hasan retorts: "If you really want me to abandon my tainted life, then you, too, must abandon yours" (294).

19. "How delicious is flirtation even if it is a lie. She was in a shameful situation but this restored the self-esteem and dignity of a woman whose wings had been broken" (165). Note the use of the broken wings image so common in feminist literature.

20. In *Chatter on the Nile* (*Tharthara fauq al-Nil*, Cairo, 1966), the mostly male occupants of the houseboat reject Sammara Bahjat when she confronts them with the emptiness of their lives and their social irresponsibility.

21. In *The Beggar* (*Al-shehhadh*, Cairo, 1965), Umar's daughter Buthayna writes teleological poetry as had her father when he was young. Yet he cannot understand her spiritual yearnings, assuming that women write only about love. The woman who is his mirror hides behind his reflection whether she wants to or not.

22. See, for example, *Hikayat haratina* (Cairo, 1982), 30.

23. See, for example, *Al-maraya*, 27, 82, 320.

24. "We had become as accustomed to having girls in our midst as to the rumors flying around during the difficult period before marriage" (*Al-maraya*, 282).

25. See, for example, *Al-maraya*, 112.

26. See, for example, *Al-maraya*, 9, 55, 87.

III

Crossing Sexualities

5

Man among Men: David Mamet's Homosocial Order

David Radavich

Apart from C. W. E. Bigsby's booklength study (1985), curiously little scholarly attention has been paid to the insistent masculinity of David Mamet's plays. Published in editions frequently bedecked by the author's tauntingly phallic photo-portrait with cigar, the major plays either totally exclude or marginalize women, concentrating instead on myriad variations of homosocial male order. Mamet's dramatic world is both self-consciously and half-consciously male, with references to homosexuality, fear of violation by other men, insistent desire for male friendship, and pursuit of domination and acceptance operating at the core of the dramatic conflict. In one interview, Mamet admitted, "I don't know anything about women. . . . I'm more around men; I listen to more men being candid than women being candid" (Fraser 1976). Only two of his more successful plays, *Sexual Perversity in Chicago* (1978) and *Speed-the-Plow* (1987), include female characters at all, who, in both instances, are experienced by the male characters and by the audience as essential disturbers of the natural male order. The central body of Mamet's work concentrates on a single-minded quest for lasting, fulfilling male friendship protected from the threats of women and masculine vulnerability on the one hand and the destabilizing pursuit of power and domination on the other.

123

Mamet's concerns about masculinity take on a particularly intense resonance in the latter part of the twentieth century, as the traditional bastions of male companionship have increasingly been called into question. Eve Kosofsky Sedgwick (1985) has described homosocial desire in a "pattern of male friendship, mentorship, entitlement, rivalry, and hetero- and homosexuality . . . in an intimate and shifting relation to class" (1). This reference to class may be expanded to include age, rank, and other social factors creating a functional inequality. Chapter 1 of her pathbreaking *Between Men: English Literature and Male Homosocial Desire* details "male homosocial desire within the structural context of triangular, heterosexual desire" (16). Mamet's *Sexual Perversity* and *Speed-the-Plow* highlight this triangular configuration, whereas other of his plays deal with the struggle to form and define exclusively male bonds. A desire for dominance, usually between men of unequal rank or age, battles with an equally strong desire for loyalty and acceptance, resulting in a hard-won, intense, fundamentally unstable intimacy established in the absence of women.

From the outset, Mamet's plays have asserted the primacy of male friendship: "A man needs a friend in this life. . . . Without a friend, life is not. . . . It's lonely. . . . It's good to have a friend. . . . To help a friend in need is the most that any man can want to do" (97–98). This excerpt from the Seventh Variation of *The Duck Variations* (1978) represents a paean to such friendship, as two men in their sixties engage in "Spectator Sports" together, in this case observing ducks (not "chicks"), as a means of solidifying their bond. The men of Mamet's later plays bond through frequenting bars (*Sexual Perversity*, 1978), performing together (*A Life in the Theater*, 1977), or driving business deals (*Glengarry Glen Ross*, 1983; and *Speed-the-Plow*, 1987), but in each case the primacy of close male friendship is asserted in the face of intruders, either rival men or, more seriously, women.

Sexual Perversity presents the challenge in the form of Deborah, erstwhile lesbian, who becomes involved with Dan, the steady buddy of Bernie. In the course of the play, many sexual perversions are trotted out for verbal display, as the title suggests, but most involve the degradation of women: "The Way to Get Laid Is to Treat 'Em [Women] Like Shit" (22). In an early extended narrative, Bernie describes his encounter with a "chick" who dresses for sex in a Flak Suit, asks him to make war noises, then douses them both with gasoline and sets all on fire. A later narrative centers on King Farouk, who arranges to have "his men run a locomotive right through the broad's bedroom" and later "whacks her on the forehead with a ballpeen hammer" (34–35). Bernie acts as spokesman for most of these "perversities," though Deborah and Joan act out some of the vicissitudes of lesbian affections and jealousy. The one "perversion" omitted in the play—probably the most common variation from heterosexuality in our culture—is adult male homosexuality. Its absence appears all the more striking as Bernie successfully undermines and fights off the challenge Deborah presents to his relationship to Dan, so that at the end the two men reunite in a friendship that, although nominally situated in a heterosexual context of "casing chicks," nonetheless posits a male bond of superior endurance.

Although lacking some of the intellectual trappings of traditional comedy, Mamet's plays embody many of its major elements, including the disruptive intrusion by an outsider followed by chaos and the final reunion of the happy couple (in this case male). In *Sexual Perversity*, Dan's sexual interest in Deborah threatens to shatter the male bond, forcing Bernie to counterattack with measures that one usually associates with heterosexual dating: outings to the movie house, evenings in Bernie's apartment, and sojourns to the beach. After this concerted effort on Bernie's part, Dan succumbs to his eventual partner's way of thinking, explaining to another co-worker, "And *he* [Bernie], he puts his arm around my shoulder and he calms me down and he says, 'Dan, Dan . . . don't go looking for affection from inanimate objects'" (53). The subtextual reference to women as "inanimate objects" brings the supremacy of male bonding full circle by play's end.

In the absence of a clear cause for Dan's break-up with Deborah, the bonding activities with Bernie that negate or exclude women serve to reassert the primacy of their same-sex friendship. Both men find it difficult to appreciate the otherness of female experience, which they consider either frivolous or irrelevant.

While in bed with Deborah, Dan cannot imagine "having tits": "That is the stupidest question I ever heard. What man in his right mind would want tits?" (40). When Deborah confesses to having fantasized about other women the last time they made love, Danny responds, "The last time I masturbated I kept thinking about my left hand" (40). The solipsistic impulse, albeit in a comic context, serves to isolate both men from a deeper experience of the feminine. The fear of the female, and of female sexuality in particular, dominates Mamet's early plays, as males jostle for position and affection among themselves apart from women.

American Buffalo ([1975], 1981), one of Mamet's most successful plays, features an all-male cast in a Chicago pawnshop where homosocial desire finds its decadent arena. Unlike *Duck Variations*, with its placid contemplations, this play foregrounds homosocial pursuit and defense and introduces the cuckolding and rape imagery important to Mamet's portrayal of American capitalism. In an interview Mamet reiterates the important link: "Look at Delorean. He completely raped everybody in Northern Ireland with that scheme" (Roudané 1986, 74–75). Although in *Sexual Perversity* Bernie and Dan work together in a faceless contemporary office, the underworld of second-rate business functions in *American Buffalo* as a more symbolic setting for Mamet's portrait of capitalism gone awry.

At the outset of *Buffalo*, Dan chastises Bob for incompetence, exerting his dominance in a pattern that clearly establishes Mamet's concern with the man "above" and the man "below." In *Sexual Perversity*, Bernie functions as Dan's superior in experience, offering fatuous advice and controlling much of the subsequent action. Don maintains supremacy in *American Buffalo* more clearly through financial control of Bob, and through his rôle as teacher/mentor and status male. The allusion to education embodied in Joan is transferred here to both Teach and Don, who continually moralize, philosophize, and pontificate about the nature of life, people, and business. The "knowledge" actually taught, however, is both corrupt and clumsy, so that by the end, the traditional mentoring of males in the world of business has collapsed into mutual incompetence.

American Buffalo differs from other Mamet works in the intense triangular relationship among the men, where Teach clearly poses a threat to the central if unequal bond between Don and Bob. Their friendship is only haltingly acknowledged—at the end, after injuries and humiliation/threat bring them together—but Teach recognizes it and hopes to establish his own relationship with Don by replacing Bob and ousting Fletcher. The men jockey for one-on-one friendship within whose boundaries emotional loyalty can be assumed and women can be regarded with mutual distrust. Denigrations of women abound: "Only . . . from the mouth of a Southern bulldyke asshole ingrate of a vicious nowhere cunt can this trash come" (803–4). And whenever Teach seeks to vent frustration with himself or his fellows, he resorts to homosexual slander ("you fruit") or images of impotence/emasculation ("dick on the chopping block") (884, 893). Clearly, insults that homosexualize or womanize men negate their potency, thereby diminishing their status and value.

Anxiety about manhood pervades these plays, at least partly the result of "improperly construed [masculine] initiations" (Raphael 1989, 144). "Makeshift" males struggle with "the deep-seated fear that [they] might never become 'men'" (145, 190). In *American Buffalo*, Teach responds to Don in anger, "I am not your wife. . . . I am not your nigger," where, presumably, the secondary status of both doubles the rhetorical effect of his outburst (888). Later, feeling rejected, he laments, "There is no friendship," and "I look like a sissy" (895). The threat of being emasculated, either by women (Grace and Ruthie, a lesbian couple) or by men, is ever-present, only to be allayed through a strong male bond that empowers each male in it. Hence the "honor among thieves" element in *American Buffalo* maximizes potency through a supposed pooling of expertise (in this case, a shared incompetence) (Roudané 1986, 76). At the end of the play, Don, through a clever Mametesque pun, tacitly acknowledges the intimate connection between sex and business: "It's all fucked up. . . . You fucked my shop up" (894). The twisted initiation ritual embodied in their struggle results in closer male bonds but leaves in its wake both physical wounds and the destruction of the locus of their enterprise.

Supplementing the central, all-male triangle in *American Buf-*

falo is a recurring motif of cuckoldry, whereby coins function as
the battleground for sexual revenge on the successful man ("fucking fruit") as well as on the wife ("dyke cocksucker"): "Guys like
that, I like to fuck their wives" (847, 820). For the first time,
Mamet ties business practices to the sexual/power act of rape in a
singularly evocative metaphor of masculine revenge for perceived
inadequacy. Indeed, rape and prostitution, primarily of men by
men, becomes the central metaphor for American capitalism in
Mamet's later plays. The desire for an enduring male bond is
inextricably linked to a mutually conceived crime for the dual
purpose of perpetration and profit. Beneath the comic surface, the
dramatic structure reveals the swirling, conflicted emotions of
men for and against other men.

A *Life in the Theater* (1977) contains the most penetrating stage
metaphor of homosexual interconnection in all of Mamet's work.
The older actor, Robert, discovers that his zipper is broken and
reluctantly agrees to allow his younger colleague, John, to pin his
fly for him. As Robert stands up on the chair, he urges John in
the endeavor:

ROBERT: Come on, come on. *[JOHN puts his face up against ROBERT's
crotch.]* Put it in. . . . Come on, for God's sake. . . . Will you stick it in?
JOHN: Hold still. There. *[Pins fly awkwardly.]*
ROBERT: Thanks a lot. (144–45)

This arresting metaphor captures the latent homosexual desires
and fears implicit in the playwright's characterization of male
friendship. Robert, symbolically emasculated by a broken zipper,
stands physically above John on the chair and metaphorically
above him by age and experience, while the young man attempts
to "pin" him—a clever pun on sexual penetration and domination. At no point in the entire scene, clearly intended as a stage
ruse for the audience's titillation, do the two males acknowledge
either the humor or the sexual implications of their actions; subsequent interactions reflect no awareness of this sequence of events.
The symbolic failure of the pinning suggests a taunting almost-
consummation that results instead in collapse and lack of connection.

The sexual triangle implicit in several Mamet plays receives up-front treatment in *A Life in the Theater*, although the shared woman never appears. John accuses Robert of impregnating his wife, Gillian, but in a consummately comic scene, does not seem overwhelmingly shattered by the revelation: "What are we going to do about this?" (31). Elsewhere, the two men assert the primacy of their bond as Robert denigrates his female co-star, "When we're on stage she isn't there for me," and John responds by acknowledging his desire for substitution: "I wanted to be up there with you" (14–15). Later, John wipes the makeup off Robert's face, and they go out to dinner together, an occasion reported subsequently by John in a telephone conversation as "going out with . . . an Actor" (24). At the end of the play, Robert cries, complaining that John makes him "feel small" (49). The transaction becomes complete when the older man gives the younger one money, solidifying the reversal in power and the insistent connection between (unconsummated) sex and lucre.

In contrast to *A Life in the Theater*, *Glengarry Glen Ross* (1983) showcases the sexopolitical battle of the male "pack," with one-on-one friendships relegated to somewhat lesser status. In yet another all-male play of characters now middle-aged, the focus shifts to male rape ("fucking up the ass") and enslavement (18). And the "screwing" is not merely verbal. The audience watches Moss "screw" Aaronow by forcing him into a criminal plot, one of many attempts by the men to emasculate other men, either psychologically or financially. In a moment of frustration, Roma declares, "We're all queers," and Levene accuses Williamson of "not having balls," establishing a figurative equivalence between homosexuality and castration (27,49). As Leverenz (1989) has pointed out, such cut-throat sexual dueling among males "has to do with manhood: a way of empowering oneself through someone else's humiliation" (245).

The sexual images in this play therefore turn correspondingly negative. Moss insults the police investigator by referring to him as a "cop without a dick" (41). Roma turns later to Williamson: "You stupid fucking cunt. . . . I don't care . . . whose dick you're sucking on" (65). Here, the eunuch, the homosexual, and the female become equally debased versions of the male, as gender slurs are used to harass, insult, and blackmail other males. Such language of bravado, domination, and humiliation is immediately understood and never questioned by any of the characters. When Levene thinks he has made a legitimate blockbuster sale, he announces his triumph in genital terms: "And now . . . I got my balls back" (70). The phallus thus valuates the currency not only in business but also in society at large. In the ethos of Mamet's plays, a man symbolically deprived of his penis through personal insecurity or deprecation by other males becomes, by definition, a faggot or a cunt, debased both sexually and professionally.

What's curious about *Glengarry*, and about most of Mamet's better-known works, is the marginalizing of any real sex. Gould and Karen spend a night together (on a male wager) in *Speed-the-Plow* but say virtually nothing about the love-making itself afterward. In *Sexual Perversity*, Dan and Deborah lounge together in bed, discussing the apartment, Deborah's lesbian experiences, and the virtues of "come" and penises. The noticeably tentative affection disappears altogether later in the play, for reasons unknown. In *Glengarry Glen Ross*, Roma declares sex essentially meaningless: "The great fucks that you may have had. What do you remember about them?" (28). In the masculine world of Mamet's early plays, men primarily pursue not sex but position ("above" or "below"), power, and male loyalty.

Somewhat later, in *The Woods* and *Edmond* (1987), what Sedgwick (1985) calls "homosexual panic" emerges as a central theme (89). In the latter play, Edmond and Glenna discuss their hatred of "faggots":

EDMOND: Yes. I hate them, too. And you know why? . . . . They suck cock. (Pause.) And that's the truest thing you'll ever hear. (266)

The context here, decidedly tongue-in-cheek, provides a stark contrast with Nick's confessions to Ruth in *The Woods*. Having invited Ruth to share a vacation by the lake, Rick makes clear his disinterest in making love: "Why don't you leave me alone?" (86). Finally, Nick confesses to a homosexual past:

NICK: I have to tell you something. . . . I have to tell you we would come up here as children. *[Pause.]* Although some things would happen . . . . Although we were frightened. . . . And many times we'd come up with a friend. With friends. We'd ask them here. *[Pause.]* Because we wanted to be with them. *[Pause.]* Because .... *[Pause.]* Wait. Because we loved them.

RUTH: I know.

NICK: Oh, my God. *[Pause. He starts to cry.]* I love you, Ruth. (115–16)

Ruth's knowledge and acceptance in this passage provide the essential absolution, allowing Nick to break down and purge his anxieties. If the play ends inconclusively, Nick nonetheless moves tentatively beyond what Ruth calls "this manly stuff" he has "made up" (102).

Speed-the-Plow (1987) seems to move beyond the homophobia articulated in Mamet's earlier plays. Here, the homosexual imagery is noticeably positive and comic, accepted without reservation by the two main characters. Rather than hurling gay-bashing insults at each other, as in earlier plays, Fox and Gould refer to themselves as "two Old Whores" and the "*Fair*-haired boys" (23, 31–32). References to "*your* boy" and "*my* boy" turn males into commodities, and other gay references flow freely in the assumedly more tolerant atmosphere of the Hollywood movie set. Fox proposes filming a "*Buddy* picture" featuring black guys who "want to get him [the protagonist] . . . going to rape his ass" (12). The intimate link between rape and business is reiterated: "It's 'up the ass with gun and camera' " (27). As studiously as Mamet's earlier male characters refused to acknowledge homosexual elements in their behavior, Gould and Fox trade gay one-liners with a new-found freedom of expression: "They'll *french* that jolly jolly hem"; "Just let me turn one more trick" (33).

Like *Sexual Perversity* and *American Buffalo*, *Speed-the-Plow* again features a tight male bond threatened by an intruder and eventually reestablished after a threat of dissolution. Karen's rôle emerges more fully than in *Sexual Perversity*, partly because Joan and Deborah have become fused into one voice, offering a direct frontal attack on the bastion of male unity. Again, the relationship between Gould and Fox is noticeably unequal (Gould has been "bumped up" above Fox), and sexual references link directly to business:

GOULD: You put as much energy in your job as you put into kissing my ass . . .

Fox: My job is kissing your ass. (39)

Their relationship dates back some eleven years, with Gould, in his new position, functioning as Fox's protector. As archetypal woman, however, Karen represents a severe threat to this male harmony, advocating the "moral high ground" that both Gould and Fox have abdicated in their pursuit of success in the world of men.

Karen is a secretary, symbolically temporary both professionally and sexually, with no surname, rendering her several stages inferior to either man, so that Fox, with obvious impunity, can threaten to have her killed if she does not leave. Unlike Gould, Karen exhibits a complete awareness of the sexual implications of their appointment to discuss the merits of the radiation screenplay, offering to palliate their mutual loneliness in a night together. Gould, the same man Fox wagered could not bed Karen, seems caught off guard by the straightforwardness of her proposition. Karen's probing dialogue reduces Gould to monosyllabic questions: "You came to? . . . I asked you here to sleep with me? . . . *I'm* frightened. . . . Why did you say you would come here anyway . . ." (76–77; final ellipsis in original).

Fox counterattacks by calling Gould a "wimp," a "coward," a "whore," and a "ballerina" (92–94). In one of his most extreme insults, Fox claims, "You squat to pee" (92). The womanizing deprecations, noticeably lacking homosexual equivalents in this play, finally collapse as Fox utters his two quintessential claims on Gould's attention: "I love this guy, too" and, more poignantly, "Bob: I need you" (102, 104). In all of Mamet, this is the baldest statement of homosocial desire for intense male friendship, forceful enough to overrule any female objection. When Karen later admits that she probably would not have slept with Gould had he not favored the "radiation script," their night together crumbles into a sham of (self-)deception and strategy, with whatever affection they might have exchanged evaporating into silence. Gould decides in favor of the *"Buddy* play," and the work ends suitably with the male "couple" reunited, albeit without any overt sexual interaction.

In *Speed-the-Plow*, the perception of women as sexual "weakeners" or "corruptors" of men receives its most direct expression. Karen's influence on Gould diverts his attention and attitudes from what works in the male world (the "*Buddy* play") to what works in the world of higher, more humane values traditionally associated with women (the "radiation play"). More cogent than Deborah's in *Sexual Perversity*, her point of view nearly persuades Gould to take the "high road" he has abdicated in a long climb up the professional ladder. But Fox's claim proves the stronger, and Gould succumbs to the pressures of male bonding implicit in the world of business. Once again in Mamet, male friendship emerges as more powerful, more significant, and, ultimately, more enduring. As Roland Barthes (1978) described the potential threat of women in another context, "A man is not feminized because he is inverted but because he is in love" (14).

The male characters in Mamet's plays inhabit a homosocial milieu where male bonds offer the primary reality, where women threaten the tightly stretched, fragile if enduring fabric, and where sexuality is largely expressed in words and distorted transactions rather than in mutually satisfying love-making. The Mamet males, with the possible exception of Fox and Gould, fear the sexual intimacy their bond implies, turning that fear outward instead into a denigration of females and of other males as homosexuals and *castrati*. Sedgwick (1985) sees this "homosexual panic" as a central motivating force in the maintenance of the capitalist patriarchy (89). Not surprisingly, Mamet's plays wed male bonding to the often corrupt practices of business. The instability of the bonding, the fierce competitiveness with which his characters struggle to escape the dichotomy of their announced desires for women and their more enduring preference for the company of other men, suggests both the decay of the relatively comfortable old professional order and the panic of being forced to acknowledge the needs such relationships imply.

As Leslie Fiedler so provocatively pointed out in his *Love and Death in the American Novel* (1966), the masculine desire for an innocent, intimate bond transcending sex and operating outside the perceived strictures of female society has remained an enduring theme in American literature: "In our native mythology, the tie between male and male is not only considered innocent, it is taken for the very symbol of innocence itself; for it is imagined as the only institutional bond in a paradisal world in which there are no (heterosexual) marriages or giving in marriage (350)." Mamet's characterizations of male friendship establish him firmly within this tradition, evoking images of latter-day Huck and Jim attempting to negotiate the shoals of modern life on a raft. But the contemporary playwright's interpretation of this theme differs considerably from earlier manifestations by foregrounding the tensions inherent in such relationships and by deconstructing their self-willed innocence. The agitated "casing" of Dan and Bernie, the hard-won, unstable intimacy of Don and Bob or Gould and Fox, ranges far from the stylized boyhood innocence of Twain's Huck and Tom. More than any other American playwright, Mamet enacts a searching, multivalent drama of homosocial desire questioning and assessing itself.

As strategist, Mamet is essentially a comic satirist, with an underlying sense of anxiety and pain. On the one hand, his plays can be savagely funny in attacking the predatory instincts of Western enterprise capitalism. And his exploitation of sexual taboos for ridiculous effect places him squarely in the comic mainstream of verbal dexterity and social "tweaking." On the other hand, the central quest for satisfying male friendship underlies all his works, adding a more serious element that encourages audience sympathy for men seeking to find loyalty and acceptance in a world disturbingly competitive, hostile, and transitory. The duality of this conception results in a darkly comic artistic vision suited to a society in transition, moving from the comfortable economies of empire to the new, less stable realities of shared power and enterprise.

The structure of Mamet's major plays typically revolves around fortifying and defending besieged male friendships that nonetheless cannot be fully acknowledged or relied on. This sets up an inherently ironic perspective. Although most of Mamet's work results in a united male "couple," the dénouement cannot assure much equilibrium, given the professed heterosexual imperatives and inherent competitiveness of males as the playwright portrays them. Male friendships in Mamet are also destabilized by inequalities of age, rank, or experience, as well as by the men's inability to weave male friendships into their relations with women. The men in the later plays seem more comfortable with the terms of their bond, but without successful integration into the larger world of dual-gender interactions, such friendships must remain fragile, isolated, and defensive.

Yet the troubling, contradictory elements of Mamet's view of masculine reality provide much of the taut intensity of his dramatic view of decadent, wounded patriarchy. The old loyalties have broken down or become corrupt, and the formerly comfortable structures of male interactions have given way to confusion and dissatisfied longing (Robert Bly's, 1990, "grief for the absent father"). Pervading the major plays is a spirit of melancholy for something lost, a kind of lamentation for male friendship that seems ever-volatile and subject to unpredictable dissolution. Mamet's contribution has been to articulate the intimate connection between sexual and business practices and to underscore the homosocial desire driving relations among men. His characters seem caught in a shifting social pattern they do not comprehend, locked into what Rich (1984) calls "archaic sexual attitudes" (B4). Yet whatever faults they may have, whatever incompetence, stupidity, or dishonesty, they are driven by the extremity of their situations to admit a need and affection for each other that hitherto remained unvoiced. Mamet's searching, half-articulated stage vision of contemporary masculinity dramatizes the struggle of American males to accept and affirm one another in a shifting climate of gender expectations and identities.

Bibliography

Barthes, Roland. *A Lover's Discourse: Fragments*. Trans. Richard Howard. New York: Hill and Wang, 1978.

Bigsby, C. W. E. *David Mamet*. Contemporary Writers Series. New York: Methuen, 1985.

Bly, Robert. *A Gathering of Men with Bill Moyers*. PBS Interview. WILL-TV, Champaign-Urbana. January 8, 1990.

Fiedler, Leslie. *Love and Death in the American Novel*. New York: Stein and Day, 1966.

Fraser, C. Gerald. "Mamet Plays Shed Masculinity Myth." *New York Times*, 5 July 1976, A7.

Leverenz, David. *Manhood and the American Renaissance*. Ithaca, NY: Cornell University Press, 1989.

Mamet, David. *American Buffalo.* 1975. In *Nine Plays of the Modern Theater.* Ed. Harold Clurman. New York: Grove, 1981.

———. *The Duck Variations.* In *Sexual Perversity in Chicago and The Duck Variations.* New York: Grove, 1978.

———. *Glengarry Glen Ross.* New York: Grove, 1983.

———. *A Life in the Theater.* New York: Samuel French, 1977.

———. *Sexual Perversity in Chicago and The Duck Variations.* New York: Grove, 1978.

———. *Speed-the-Plow.* New York: Grove, 1987.

———. *The Woods; Lakeboat; and Edmond.* New York: Grove, 1987.

Raphael, Ray. *The Men from the Boys: Rites of Passage in Male America.* Lincoln: University of Nebraska Press, 1989.

Rich, Frank. "Theater's Gender Gap Is a Chasm." *New York Times,* 30 September 1984, B1,4.

Roudané, Matthew C. "An Interview with David Mamet." *Studies in American Drama, 1945–Present* 1 (1986): 72–81.

Sedgwick, Eve Kosofsky. *Between Men: English Literature and Male Homosocial Desire.* New York: Columbia University Press, 1985.

6

Male Heterosexuality in John Hawkes's
The Passion Artist

Peter F. Murphy

A critical sequence in John Hawkes's fiction: *The Blood Oranges* (1970) to *Virginie: Her Two Lives* (1981), presents a radical theory of male heterosexuality. During this ten-year span Hawkes also published *Death, Sleep and the Traveler* (1974), *Travesty* (1976), and *The Passion Artist* (1978).[1] The first three of these novels make up what Hawkes came to call "the sex triad."

As one of the few contemporary male authors affected directly by the feminist movement, Hawkes is at the forefront of the male response. His fiction examines such issues as: domination/submission, father-daughter incest, pornography, the "Lolita" complex, men's relationship with their mothers, jealousy, and power. With the recent conflict within feminism over erotica versus pornography, Hawkes gives an honest and vivid portrayal of one man's involvement; often his vision resembles that of many men.

The Blood Oranges introduces an important theme for a critical engagement with male heterosexuality. Cyril, the male antagonist, articulates an explicit theory of nonmonogamous marriage. His theory diverges quite dramatically, though, from the typical double standard of most male writers. In *Death, Sleep and the Traveler* and *Travesty* Cyril's theory unravels in the specific behavior of the male characters. Cyril's suggestion that husbands and wives should make love with whom they please and that each should help the other in accomplishing their seductions becomes problematic in *Death, Sleep and the Traveler*. Allert, the husband, is quite unhappy with the knowledge that his wife has a boyfriend. As if to retaliate, Allert falls in love with Ariane, whom, it seems, he murders. A lovely young woman who believes in free love, Ariane seduces Allert by playing her flute in the nude. She represents another recurrent male fantasy in Hawkes's novels: small, diminutive women. The Lolita complex informs this novel as it does many of his other works of fiction.

In *Travesty*, the theory of nonmonogamous marriage explodes and claims for its victims not only Papa, the male protagonist, but his daughter, Chantel, and his wife's lover, Henri. Both *Death, Sleep and the Traveler* and *Travesty* demonstrate the difficulty men, not women, have with open relationships. They provide the basis to begin rethinking the recurrent male obsession with nonmonogamy and free love. It is, after all, Papa who kills himself and two others, not his wife, who sleeps comfortably at home.

In *Virginie: Her Two Lives*, Hawkes relies on a female narrator for the first time in his fiction. Formalistically similar to Virginia Woolf's *Orlando* (1928), the story describes a young girl's life during two different historical periods: 1740 aristocratic France and 1945 post-World War II Paris. In 1740, Virginie helps Seigneur operate a school for women and in 1945 she and Bocage run a surrealist bordello. As a parody of de Sade, Seigneur represents the full spectrum of male heterosexuality. An ironic perversion of a Sadeian discourse, *Virginie* can be read as a feminist text.

The Passion Artist commands a central position for a critical appreciation of Hawkes's ideas about male heterosexuality. Exploring the sexual awakening of one man, Konrad Vost, the novel focuses on the relationship between masculinity and femininity. More than any other of Hawkes's novels, *The Passion Artist* "lays bare the horrors of the masculine mind" (O'Donnell 1983, 116). Vost's sexual development occurs in the surrealist context of a riot-torn women's prison and a stark and desolate marshland. His own life is desolate, as well. Claire, his wife, died several years earlier, but he cannot accept her death. His young daughter has become a prostitute. His mother, Eva, has been imprisoned for the murder of his father. In this novel, as in much of his fiction,

Hawkes combines "dislocation of cause and effect, distortion of rational processes, insistence on the psychic truth beneath the recognized surfaces" (Greiner 1985, 12). In an anti-real, Kafkaesque setting, Hawkes explores relentlessly the contradictions as well as the possibilities of male heterosexuality.

Vost's transformation begins when he volunteers to help put down a riot in La Violaine, the local women's prison in which his mother is incarcerated. His experience inside the prison battering the prisoners and eventually as the captive of his mother and her bestfriend, Hania, provide valuable insights into Vost's sexuality in particular and male heterosexuality in general. While hunting escaped prisoners, Vost fantasizes about some of the women escapees and learns firsthand the intimidating power of masculinity. These encounters force Vost to confront the ordeal of women's lives and become a better man. In this context, innocence and purity are illuminated against the setting of male violence against women, submission and domination, marriage, bestiality, and pornography.

The Passion Artist explores the fantasies, manifestations, doubts and transformations of male heterosexuality in the context of a world besieged by hatred, fear, and shame. The novel conveys Vost's sexual awakening from the artist of dead passion (as was Papa in *Travesty*) to "an artist . . . of the willed erotic union" (TPA, 181). Vost evolves from being a man who hates his body and denies his sexual longings to one who finally feels comfortable with his sexuality. This long and brutal voyage culminates in Vost's acceptance of his role as a man, due in no small part to his experience of what it is like to be a woman. As he endures the life of a woman, Vost learns about the potential for men's liberation.

His participation (along with many other men) in squelching a violent rebellion by the women inmates focuses many of the issues raised in this novel. What transpires between the men and the women, as well as among the men, explains much of what it means to be a man in contemporary society. Through the image of the riot, Hawkes examines male fantasies about and male bonding around violation in its various manifestations and the relationship between power and sexuality.

The volunteers represent the complete gamut of males in our society. They are "husbands, fathers, bachelors" (TPA, 46), "workers, shop owners, professional men" (TPA, 53). They come from all classes of society and represent every relationship men have with women, except friendship. If they were friends they wouldn't be in the prison trying to squelch the riot; they would empathize with the women and defend their right to rebel. The possibility that such men exist is given explicit consideration.

Initially, the men seem to feel ashamed about their participation in putting down the women's rebellion; even though Vost knows two of the men, they don't speak or even acknowledge each other's presence. Most of the men are relatively innocent of inflicting pain on anyone and prefer to stand far apart from each other. At the same time, however, they are "fully or partially aware of the fact that the blows [they were] about to strike would fall on the flesh and bones of a woman" (TPA, 47). They felt either guilty about their actions or eager to begin. These husbands, fathers, bachelors (brothers) want to beat their wives, daughters, mothers, sisters.

The extent to which Vost becomes involved with the suppression of the women and the extent to which he enjoys his brutality against them emerge as crucial points in the novel. He "prepared to drive the stick into the face of the disbelieving woman. . . . He swung his arm with all the strength he could manage and brought the stick crashing against the side of the woman's head. . . . And for a moment he wished that the rioting all around him would never cease" (TPA, 54–55). Vost's obsession provides a perceptive portrayal of a male fantasy and in this way enlists the reader directly into the novel's prose. The issues of power, sadomasochism, bondage, and pornography are engaged powerfully, allowing readers to confront their own complicity in such violence. At first, the reader might feel horrified. Almost immediately, though, he feels compelled to consider the accuracy of the fictional portrayal. If violation were sanctioned, especially against women, many men would find it difficult to control themselves. More than half of the men surveyed in a recent poll said that they would rape a woman if they were absolutely sure they would get away with it (Sidran 1981, 30). In light of this, Vost's behavior in the woman's prison is not incredible at all. In a society in which such violation is an everyday occurrence, Vost represents Everyman.

In the context of this "sanctioned violation" (TPA, 53) Vost "found himself wanting nothing more than to beat the woman first to surrender and then to unconsciousness. He was not given to physical exertion. . . . Yet he was determined that he himself would administer the blows that would fell this woman who had become victorious in a man's clothing" (TPA, 51). Vost's outrage is exacerbated by the women's attire; they transgress gender boundaries when they put on men's clothes. Vost's trial, later in the novel, reveals the possibility that women have a similar confused and antagonistic response to men attired in women's clothing. Here, as elsewhere in the novel, Hawkes seems to be suggesting a similarity between the sexes. Opposition to rebellion against gender boundaries may not be innate to the male condition but rather a socially learned, culturally reinforced stereotype that neither men nor women can transcend easily.

While the riot continues, the voice of a young woman, a "young invisible victim" (TPA, 55), can be heard in the background. The vividness with which Hawkes describes Vost's attack on his victim, combined with the description of the young woman sighing in the background, accentuates the issue of violence against women. Invisible victims remain a major problem in contemporary society: as long as they remain invisible no one has to act. If we are neither victims nor perpetrators, we are innocent. But, as Hawkes makes clear throughout this novel, no one is innocent; we are all culpable and share similar fantasies of domination and submission. For Hawkes, "if we don't know our destructive potential we can't very well assume genuine responsibility for the world around us. . . . I'm just writing about the things that are most deeply embedded in the human psyche" (Fielding 1976, 45). Expanding on these ideas, Hawkes explains that his "work is an effort to expose the worst in us all, to cause us to face up to the enormities of our terrible potential for betrayal, disgrace and criminal behavior" (LeClair 1979, 27).

Vost is stimulated erotically by the stark and unbridled violence against women. Later, he changes and evolves. For now though, through the medium of the unbreakable length of wood the young woman's pain leapt to his clenched hands; in his hands and arms he could feel the small perfect body losing its form. . . . And, as the childlike woman took random useless steps, cowering and dangling her arms, the dress fell and exposed one shoulder while on the oval face the lips began to glisten with a wetness rising from deep within that miniature anatomy. (TPA, 56)

Even while he is battering this woman to death, her exposed shoulder remains a point of interest, of sexual excitation. Vost becomes even more titillated as her lips begin to glisten. The small, childlike woman resounds throughout Hawkes's fiction and in *The Passion Artist* it reaches new significance. Eventually, and despite her large size, Vost learns to love Hania.

One scene in particular explores the issue of submission/domination and the relationship between power and the erotic. Following the riot, Vost dreams he has been taken captive by the women in the prison. He stands trial for the crimes he has committed against these women and against one woman in particular. His accuser, a young woman, is "as small as a child yet clothed in a tight gown of a sparkling mauve material which exposed the diminutive anatomy that could belong only to an adult woman" (TPA, 63). This small and childlike woman, attired in a sensually colored gown, has complete power over Vost. She charges him with not knowing anything about women explaining that all he ever did was comment on her size without ever touching her. Despite the fact that he is condemned and powerless, a victim of her every whim, Vost finds his accuser sexually arousing. Even in his discomfort and humiliation he feels a growing rapture. Though accused of sexual impotence and complete ignorance of women he realizes

that all the agreeableness of her mannerisms concealed a petulance even more desirable than the legs, the hips, the musical voice . . . [and that] now, against his will, in the darkness of a condition that could not have been more contrary to that of erotic excitation, now he was overcome with the knowledge that in his locked and inaccessible loins the army of mice was beginning to run through the forest that was filled with snow. (TPA, 65–66)

In contrast to the assumption that men must dominate to obtain sexual pleasure, Vost finds himself sexually aroused to the point of orgasm, an orgasm he prefers not to have. The suggestion that men may also obtain pleasure from being submissive counters the assertion that pornography manifests an inherently male need to be the dominator. Current feminist arguments against pornography (e.g., Brownmiller 1975; Dworkin 1981; and Griffin 1981)[2] are confronted throughout the novel; Vost's journey examines the question of sexual difference.

Vost awakens from his dream to find himself in the hospital. He arrived there after having fallen in the ranks of the victims of La Violaine. The women had managed to rout the voluntary male militia and now control the prison. Vost leaves the hospital, decides to join the hunt for the women prisoners, and goes into the marsh after them. Here, Vost encounters the young woman in his dream. The bruises he had inflicted upon her body during the riot contribute to Vost's erotic sensations and enhance his vision of her beauty. Vost begins to fall in love with this young woman whom he had beaten unconscious and now spies upon. She brings out feelings in Konrad Vost that had always been fleeting and uncomfortable.

Vost's ambivalence about his sexual passion compels him to leave the scene immediately. As he leaves, he is threatened by one of the armed guards hunting for the escaped women. Vost betrays the young woman in an effort to save his own life: "The brute maleness of the man and dog [and] the stench of their intimidation" (TPA, 97), remind Vost that, confronted by the savage power of masculinity, one cowers. This firsthand experience of the fear and intimidation that male sexuality presents to women every day of their lives furthers Vost's sexual awareness.

From this immediate encounter with the malignant potential of masculinity, Vost confronts yet one more component of the female sexual experience: their assumed role as the means to men's sexual satisfaction. Lost in the fog that has covered the marsh, Vost stumbles upon an old abandoned barn in which he decides to spend the night. Unknown to him, he shares it with two women who have escaped from the prison. When these women giggle, Vost assumes, as would many men, that their giggling was intended for him. He believes they are flirting with him. He couldn't be more wrong, for these escaped women convicts proceed to "rape" Vost. They force him to fondle their breasts and vaginas so that they can have an orgasm but every time he tries to get them to reciprocate they abuse him. They maintain complete control of this sexual encounter and force Vost to satisfy them without any concern at all for his pleasure. One of the women "began squeezing rapidly the front of his trousers as if to arouse and crush desire in a single gesture" (TPA, 107).

Vost's "rape" parodies the sexual experience many women have at the hands of impatient, selfish men socialized to believe that women were created to satisfy their sexual needs. At the same time, however, it explicates, vividly, the experience of rape. "Submission, revolt, attack, submission; so the darkness was consumed in revolt, attack, submission" (TPA, 109–10), describes much female experience of sex at the hands of husbands, lovers, rapists.

Later, Vost is relieved upon awakening to discover himself a captive in La Violaine. He "found himself exactly where he had always wanted to be without knowing it: in the world of women and in the world of the prison ... where he would receive the punishment he deserved and desired. [Here he would] suffer at will the presence of the women he had spent his life avoiding" (TPA, 120). This direct confrontation with women, and in particular the environment of the prison within which it will occur, contributes much to Vost's awakening. Here he will "be brought to [a] rudimentary knowledge of submission, domination, the question of woman" (TPA, 121). Within the walls of this woman's prison and at the hands of Hania, his mother's bestfriend, Vost will learn the experience of women and will become a more sexually liberated male.

One of the first and certainly most important lessons he learns derives from his original characterizations of the two women who play such a significant role in his liberation: his mother and Hania. These women, who replace his wife, Claire, "promised him not sentimentality but flesh and light" (TPA, 122). They will give him not tender feelings of loss or regret but sexuality and the knowledge that accompanies it. Vost becomes aware that the stereotypical view of women as virgin/whore does not work. As Eva becomes the "notorious woman revealed," she can no longer be characterized as a whore. And Hania is "identified ... no longer as the nun [virgin] she had once been" (TPA, 121). Vost begins to see beyond the socially accepted characterization of women as either evil and dangerous or pure and sensitive.

In his prison cell strewn with articles of women's clothing, in this "splendor of depravation," Vost recognizes for the first time "the trespasser inside himself" (TPA, 125). Here, in confinement and at the hands of his female captors, Vost begins to comprehend his identity as a man. In La Violaine, which derives from the French viol, violteur, violenter, or violer—meaning to rape, to violate, to transgress—Vost becomes aware of his sexually prescribed role as a man—a violator and a rapist. At the same time, though, he realizes his own vulnerability. When Eva and Hania enter his cell, Vost struggles to "retain some semblance of pride in the midst of submission" (TPA, 128). Simultaneously, he realizes that for Hania indignity does not exist. Through years of submission and brutality at the hands of the prison guards and men in general, "there could be no indignity, nothing repugnant" for Hania (TPA, 130).

At this point, Eva shares her ideas about marriage with Vost. She explains the difficulty a woman has being a wife because most women find themselves not only married to a child but bearing children. She concludes with some radical insights into motherhood and female identity, insights echoing Simone de Beauvoir (1974) and Shulamith Firestone (1970): "We who spend our lives in prison know three things: that the family is the first prison; that among prisons the actual is preferable to the metaphorical; and that the woman is not a mother until she leaves her child" (TPA, 129). With this knowledge Vost becomes educated, even politicized. He realizes that he no longer grieves for Claire and that his marriage is over. Finally, he severs his ties with his dead wife, Claire. This contributes significantly to Vost's awareness. The more exposure to the female social experience Vost encounters, the more he appreciates their plight at the hands of men and patriarchy.

Eva amplifies her ideas of motherhood and of being a good wife when she relates her own experience giving birth to Vost. The ultimate moment of his recognition provides insights about himself that he needed to know, but of which he believed he would never be made aware. Eva was informed by a village doctor, who resented her small size and beauty, that her baby was dead inside her. The doctor prescribed abhorrent things for her to do to expel the fetus.[3] After much excruciating pain and violence to herself, she almost succeeds in aborting the baby. It lives, however, albeit extremely premature. Eva maintains that her son, Konrad Vost, holds the responsibility for the destruction of an otherwise beautiful experience by making it into something extremely painful and grotesque. Stressing that she had been married for a while before becoming pregnant, Eva seems to suggest that childbirth destroys innocence; but motherhood, not sex, makes a woman into a victim.

Vost is astonished by the graffiti on the walls when he awakens at dawn of his first full day at La Violaine. He reads the slogans and aphorisms written by the women inmates and is surprised by "the humorous or violent jottings of women whose vulgar cravings were the equal of the vulgar cravings of any man" (TPA, 155). Two inscriptions in particular impress him more than the others:

"In memory of a Sunday in summer" [made him wonder whether it was possible] that a woman, especially in this place, had been capable of such generosity. After all, the nostalgia and resignation captured in the expression were as shockingly appropriate to the mind of a man as were the obscenities that made him flush with embarrassment. (TPA, 155)

The second inscription, " 'Love is not an honest feeling,' [made him ponder] who but a man could have written these words? . . . Yet the authors of these sayings had in fact been women" (TPA, 155). The novel reiterates the point that women have sexual fantasies and sexual cravings similar to those of men. Hawkes seems well aware that one man can be embarrassed by the sexual longings of a woman just as a woman can be disconcerted by the sexual cravings of a man. This revelation resists the radical feminist position maintaining that pornography describes only male fantasies. According to one feminist perspective, pornography, written by men and for men, is evil and oppressive. This notion oversimplifies sexuality in general and distorts male sexuality in particular. As Ellen Willis (1981) points out in her response to the feminist opposition to pornography:

the view of sex that most often emerges from talk about "erotica" is as sentimental and euphemistic as the word itself; lovemaking should be beautiful, romantic, soft, nice and devoid of messiness, vulgarity, impulses to power, or indeed aggression of any sort. Above all the emphasis should be on relationship not (yuck) organs. This goody-goody concept of eroticism is not feminist, it is feminine (224).

One aphorism in particular stands out for Vost: " 'Between my legs I do not have a bunch of violets.' " This statement "excluded him forever; it was the clue to the object of his desperate quest; it could not have been written by a man" (TPA, 156). Here, as elsewhere in the novel, Vost searches for the difference between men and women. For Vost, learning that the vagina is not a bunch of violets helps move him beyond his previous characterization of a vagina as "the nostril of a dead bird" (TPA, 67) or as "a small face beaten unrecognizable by the blows of a cruel fist" (TPA, 151). Soon, with Hania, Vost will come to realize the beauty and desirability of women's sexual anatomy.

First, however, Eva Laubenstein introduces the theories of Dr. Slovotkin, the prison doctor. Slovotkin's obsession with the difference, if any, between the man and the woman seems to echo the object of Vost's own desperate quest. Unlike Slovotkin, though, Vost is less a theorist than a simple man confused about his own sexuality as much as he is by women's. Slovotkin, on the other hand, parodies the contemporary "feminist" man. Obsessed with his theory of androgyny, Slovotkin tries to have sex with every woman in La Violaine. That "he never tired of taking his victims or stating his theories" (TPA, 157), sounds a little like the radical man at the cocktail party who mouths feminist theories for the sake of getting laid.

Slovotkin has a theory though, and an important one for the overall meaning of this novel. Eva explains it at length:

Slovotkin proposed, first, that the person is essentially a barren island and that for each of us life's only pleasure is the exploration of other barren islands: in this way being a man or woman merely enhances the interesting differences of people who are in fact the same. He proposed, secondly, that in the souls of their bones the man and woman are opposites: as extreme as that. Finally he proposed that the man and woman are both the same and opposite. (TPA, 157)

Slovotkin's opportunistic use of feminism confirms Eva's point that his "dedication to his single question was no more than a ruse to feed his insatiable craving for the bodies of women" (TPA, 159). Slovotkin insisted, even in the face of death, that his first and third theories were correct. He asserted that, setting aside reproduction, men and women have the same capabilities. Simultaneously, he claimed that men and women are both the same and opposite. He concluded by explaining the impossibility of being the one without knowing the experience of the other.

This substantiates Eva's assertion of the similarity between Slovotkin and Vost. Vost seems to have known Slovotkin's theory, though without the premeditated opportunism of Slovotkin's work. In the woman's prison, which is a metaphor for women's experience in contemporary society, Vost has encountered a woman's life: the fear of male sexuality and the tendency to cringe before it. Like many women today, he has been used as a vehicle for sexual satisfaction without having the partner concerned with his satisfaction. He has experienced the submissive role of the woman and has been dominated in the sexual encounters he has had since joining the men in their efforts to squelch the women's riot.

Slovotkin's theory remains only superficial, however, as it becomes obvious that only women are qualified to speak about androgyny or the relative equality of the sexes: they have experienced the servitude of the female at the hands of the male. In taking Slovotkin's theory one step further, Eva points to a crucial truth: "The woman is not naturally a martyr; the man is not naturally a beast" (TPA, 160). This important addition to Slovotkin's theory highlights Eva's disagreement with the radical feminists' belief that men represent the enemy: naturally evil, inherently aggressive, and prone to violence against women. Eva maintains that women are no more naturally passive and gentle then men are naturally brutal; Vost demonstrates this insight throughout his entire experience at the women's prison.

As if remembering an important addition to any theory of sexual politics, Eva reminds Hania that only the childless woman retains her youth. Echoing her previous assertion that for women "the family is the first prison . . . [and] that the woman is not a mother until she leaves her child" (TPA, 129), Eva stresses the importance for women not to become mothers, or at least not to remain mothers. Motherhood as a woman's sole occupation destroys women's individuality and self-worth.

The culmination of Vost's sexual awakening occurs with Hania while he is a prisoner at La Violaine. As Hania undresses, Vost finds himself confronted once again with the issue of the difference or similarity between men and women. He sees in Hania "the presence of the hidden thighs that were as large as a man's and yet of the soft line belonging only to a woman" (TPA, 178). Parts of Hania's body, like many women's, resemble a man's just as many men resemble women. Here, as elsewhere in the novel, Hawkes seems to be pointing out the problematics of biology as destiny, especially when that argument suggests women are not physically capable of doing the same things men do.

Vost continues en route to his liberation. He has not arrived there yet. Upon seeing Hania naked he ponders, "why was it that when a man of his age saw for the first time hair and light glistening between a woman's legs he felt both agitation and absurdity? And yet was he even now beginning to learn that what he had thought of as the lust of his middle age was in fact the clearest reflection of the generosity implicit in the nudity of the tall woman?" (TPA, 178). Vost's middle-age crisis, or his insecurity as a man, is eclipsed by Hania's appeal as a caring, giving woman; these qualities make her attractive to him. He falls in love with Hania and, though this love has very little hope for the future, he begins to feel comfortable with his feelings. A significant moment in Vost's awakening emerges when he realizes his ability to feel comfortable with himself, to trust his emotions, and to be able to love someone.

Vost is a man in the social, cultural, and political sense of that identity. Unlike the women surrounding him in the prison, he has never learned certain things about himself as a sexual being or, like so many men, he has not learned how to express his emotions. He does not know how to sing and in particular he does not know the language of song, the discourse of celebration. And, Vost does not know how to dance. He is appalled to realize that even though he had been both a husband and a father he had never learned to dance. His male armor has not allowed him to relax and feel comfortable with himself. Like many men, Vost's sexual repression makes him afraid of his body, his emotions, and his feelings. Hawkes seems to suggest that whereas society may very well be patriarchal, men too are excluded from the discourse that supposedly belongs to them alone. They have to struggle against all the armor society has foisted upon them in the process of making them men. In order to do that men need to scrutinize male discourse in the same way feminists today seek a new language.

Vost's experience with Hania moves him closer to his liberation. While making love to him, Hania tells Vost to watch her as she performs fellatio on him. She points out that "passionate sensation depends on sight" (TPA, 179). Hania confronts another stereotypical distinction between men and women: for men, sexual experience is thought to be a more visible encounter than it is for women. Hania maintains, however, that the visual experience enhances sexual pleasure for both men and women.

Vost is amazed that even while continuing to take his penis in her mouth, Hania does not change her facial expression in the slightest. His confusion is exacerbated by his feelings of arousal. Vost has not recovered completely from his distress over his body and his fear of being repulsive to a woman. He still harbors feelings of doubt and apprehension about his sexuality and his attractiveness. Though on his way to a quasi-liberation he still has not arrived. Overcoming the socialization of manhood in this society necessitates a long, difficult struggle. Hawkes does not pretend that it is easy. Eventually, though, Vost becomes more comfortable with himself and his passions. As Hania takes his penis in her mouth his penis has become "that part of his anatomy that he could no longer deny" (TPA, 180). Finally, Vost accepts his sexuality. An important moment for his awakening, this newly found ability to acknowledge his passion moves Vost much closer to at least a semblance of sexual liberation.

Hania provides Vost with additional knowledge about the difference between men and women as sexual beings. She tells him that " 'in no other way, . . . can a woman so reveal her eroticism as by an act of the will. . . . As for you,' she said, 'the force of amorous passion is respect. You are now aware of your own respect and mine' " (TPA, 180). This respect is crucial for Vost, for throughout his life self-respect has been something he lacked. His love for Hania and his appreciation of himself and his body have allowed him to respect someone else as well as himself. When Hania asks Vost to perform cunnilingus on her, he discovered that her dilation was such that

the exterior of her body could no longer be distinguished from its interior; when she encouraged him to discover that the discolorations of the blown rose are not confined to the hidden flesh of youth, it was then that in the midst of his gasping he realized that the distinction between the girl who is still a child and the woman who is more than mature lies only in the instinct of the one and the depth of consciousness of the other. (TPA, 180–81)

These important insights do not help him discover the "small face beaten unrecognizable" or the "nostril of a dead bird," but a woman's sexuality: not just one isolated part, one organ, but rather a component of a much larger form, a part of a whole all intricately and intimately connected. Vost realizes that the difference between the young schoolgirl he was seduced by earlier in his life and the woman he has in front of him has nothing to do with physiology or age but rather experience. Hania's "depth of consciousness" makes her a desirable and satisfying woman.

As the night draws to a close, Vost finds himself "in the arms of the tall handsome woman who had loved him and seduced him as well" (TPA, 183–84). The possibility that a woman, and in this case maybe a wife, would be able to love and seduce someone at the same time provides a telling conclusion to the relationship between Vost and Hania. None of Vost's previous experiences with women had demonstrated both of these possibilities simultaneously. Most of the women he had encountered were interested primarily in seducing him. There was certainly not much love exchanged. Claire, Vost's wife, seemed capable of love toward Vost but not seduction. Hania emerges as all these women and more as she becomes the woman capable of both seduction and love. For Hania, women have vital, aggressive sexual needs upon which they are quite capable of acting.

Male sexuality, on the other hand, remains confused and uncertain. Though Vost has made progress toward sexual liberation he can share this accomplishment with very few men. His continued existence is problematic in a sexually oppressive society. As he leaves the prison early the next morning his old friend, Gagnon, shoots him down. As he dies, Vost knows "that the hole torn in his abdomen by Gagnon's shot was precisely the same as would have been opened in his flesh by the dog in the marsh" (TPA, 184). Men's omnipotence, coupled with a fear of their sexuality and a hatred of "the woman within" (Hoch 1979, 68) manifests itself in domination and control.[4] Gagnon's response represents the pathetic desperation of threatened male power.

Vost dies because the liberated man in contemporary society is a contradiction in terms. In the first place, there cannot be a fully, completely liberated man (or woman, for that matter). In the second place, as one moves closer to becoming a liberated man, he moves further away from being socially acceptable as a man. The liberated man, like the gay man, both of whom have had the female experience of male power, cannot be countenanced in a homophobic and sexist society that fears and hates female sexuality, especially when embodied in a man.

Notes

1. All quotations from the novel in the text are cited parenthetically in the text as TPA.
2. Andrea Dworkin highlights this position when she maintains, for example, that "the major theme of pornography as a genre is male power, its nature, its magnitude, its use, its meaning" (1981, 24). Later in this same book, Dworkin states that "male sexual aggression is the unifying thematic and behavioral reality of male sexuality" (57). Susan Griffin (1981) points out that "the world of pornography is a world of male gesture and male language and a male ethos" (52). This kind of reductionism posits a male essence and a male nature that are as damaging and reductionist as many reactionary ideas about women; for example that biology is destiny.
3. Contemporary American feminism has spent much time examining the history of women as victims of the medical profession. For example, see Ehrenreich and English (1979), and Drefus (1977).
4. For a more extensive examination of "the feminine other within the male unconscious" and how it informs current literature on men and masculinity, see Murphy (1989).

Works Cited

Brownmiller, Susan. *Against Our Will: Men, Women and Rape*. New York: Bantam, 1975.

Beauvoir, Simone de. *The Second Sex*. New York: Vintage, 1974.

Drefus, Claudia. *Seizing Our Bodies: The Politics of Women's Health*. New York: Vintage, 1977.

Dworkin, Andrea. *Pornography: Men Possessing Women*. New York: G. P. Putnam's Sons, 1981.

Ehrenreich, Barbara, and Deirdre English. *For Her Own Good: 150 Years of the Experts' Advice to Women*. New York: Doubleday, 1979.

Fielding, Andrew. "John Hawkes Is a Very Nice Guy and a Novelist of Sex and Death." *Village Voice* 24 (May 1976): 45–47.

Firestone, Shulamith. *The Dialectic of Sex: The Case for Feminist Revolution*. New York: Bantam, 1970.

Greiner, Donald. *Understanding John Hawkes*. Columbia, SC: University of South Carolina Press, 1985.

Griffin, Susan. *Pornography and Silence: Culture's Revenge Against Nature*. New York: Harper and Row, 1981.

Hawkes, John. *The Blood Oranges*. New York: New Directions, 1970.

———. *Death, Sleep and the Traveler*. New York: New Directions, 1974.

———. *The Passion Artist*. New York: Harper and Row, 1978.

———. *Travesty*. New York: New Directions, 1976.

———. *Virginie: Her Two Lives*. New York: Harper and Row, 1981.

Hoch, Paul. *White Hero Black Beast: Racism, Sexism and the Mask of Masculinity*. London: Pluto Press, 1979.

LeClair, Thomas. "The Novelists: John Hawkes." *New Republic* 10 (November 1979): 26–29.

Murphy, Peter F. "Toward a Feminist Masculinity: A Review Essay." *Feminist Studies* (Summer 1989): 351–61.

O'Donnell, Patrick. "Life and Art: An Interview with John Hawkes." *Review of Contemporary Fiction* (Fall 1983): 107–26.

Sidran, Maxine. "The Hating Game: Men's Response to Women's Independence: Don't Get Even, Get Mad." *Quest* (October 1981): 16–23.

Willis, Ellen. "Feminism, Moralism, and Pornography." In *Beginning to See the Light: Pieces of a Decade*, 219–27. New York: Knopf, 1981.

Woolf, Virginia. *Orlando*. New York: Harcourt Brace and Jovanovich, 1928.

7

Living Degree Zero: Masculinity and the Threat of Desire in the *Roman Noir*

Christopher Metress

I.

In "The Simple Art of Murder," his seminal manifesto on the poetics of that most masculine and most American of literary creations, the hardboiled detective novel, Raymond Chandler praises his gender-specific hero with a hard and handsome rhetoric:

> In everything that can be called art there is a quality of redemption. It may be pure tragedy, if it is high tragedy, and it may be pity and irony, and it may be the raucous laughter of the strong man. But down these mean streets a man must go who is not himself mean, who is neither tarnished nor afraid. The detective in this kind of story must be such a man. He is the hero; he is everything. He must be a complete man and a common man and yet an unusual man. He must be, to use a rather weathered phrase, a man of honor.[1]

Chandler's chivalric musings have long encouraged us to see the hardboiled novel as a redemptive arena of honorable masculinity in which complete and untarnished men seek to fulfill their desire for justice in a world gone mean with sin and depravity. For instance, George Grella links the hardboiled detective to the earliest American prototypes of heroic masculinity: "His characteristic toughness and redeeming moral strength conflict with the values of his civilization and cause him, like Natty Bumppo or Huck Finn, to flee the society which menaces his personal integrity and spiritual freedom."[2] John G. Cawelti concurs, saluting the hardboiled hero as "an instinctive protector of the weak, a defender of the innocent, an avenger of the wronged, the one loyal, honest, truly moral man in a corrupt and ambiguous world."[3]

154

Hardboiled fiction, however, is a "corrupt" and "ambiguous" genre and, as such, it contains within it contentious images of masculinity. As David Madden notes, "Just as one must distinguish between the formal detective story invented by Poe and the private-eye thriller initiated by Hammett, one must also distinguish between the latter and the 'pure' tough-guy novel, though they developed concurrently and cross-fertilized each other."[4] Thus, although Geoffrey O'Brien is right to assert that the "hardboiled novel was born complete in [Hammett's] *Red Harvest* in 1929,"[5] we need to realize that since its inception the hardboiled novel has developed along two distinctly different paths. The first path is the one pursued by the likes of Hammett, Chandler, Ross Macdonald, and John D. MacDonald, and it is readily known to us as the hardboiled detective novel (or, in Madden's words, "the private-eye thriller"). The heroes of this line are just that—heroes. They may be, as O'Brien says of Chandler's Marlowe, "disillusioned and increasingly bitter," but they are, nonetheless, "unmistakably chivalrous."[6] According to Cawelti, the hardboiled detective novel encourages us to identify with "important characteristics of the detective, his masculinity and courage, his integrity and sense of honor." Ultimately, such a work will reflect "common fantasies," fantasies, we must note, which fulfill distinctly masculine appetites: "the desire to escape from the anxious tension between conformity and resentment; the desire to replace the sense of inner corruption and insecurity and to avenge oneself upon the successful by physical force; the desire to completely dominate women and thereby overcome their sexual and social challenge."[7] However, if we understand hardboiled fiction as containing nothing more than the hardboiled detective novel, then we overlook a distinctive path within the genre, one that offers us a chilling contrast to the sometimes unsteady but ultimately redemptive images of loyal, honest, and moral masculinity inscribed in the world of the hardboiled detective novel. Among the poets of this other, richly suggestive path are such neglected writers as James M. Cain, Horace McCoy, Cornell Woolrich, Jim Thompson, and David Goodis. Rather than giving us complete men untarnished by and unafraid of the physical, social, and sexual challenges to their masculinity, these writers offer us fragmented men stained by absurdly tragic pasts and tormented by emasculating landscapes of frustration and paranoia. This alternative route within the genre has acquired many different names, such as Madden's "tough-guy novel," but despite its distinctly American origins it is best known by its French designation—the *roman noir*.

As concurrent and cross-fertilizing fictions, the hardboiled detective novel and the *roman noir* do share many of the same preoccupations, and there is perhaps none more revealing and fundamental than their preoccupation with the relationship between masculinity and desire. In the hardboiled detective novel, the hero is a common man, and as a common man he is necessarily faced with that most common of choices—that is, what will he desire and how will he secure that desire? The potential objects of desire for the hero are many, but these desires usually fall within the scope of four categories: power, money, sex, and/or justice. The men and women encountered by the detective are more often than not corrupted by an uncontrollable obsession for some combination of these first three categories of desire. Only the detective seeks the fourth desire—justice. His quest for this justice, however, is repeatedly threatened by the temptations of power, money, and sex. The detective succeeds as the hardboiled and masculine hero of his narrative because he is able to control his passion for these first three temptations and keep them subordinate to his more noble desire for justice.

We need only turn to the ending of Hammett's *The Maltese Falcon* to see this kind of struggle and subordination at work. After his swift and violent search for the Maltese Falcon fails, Sam Spade faces Brigid O'Shaughnessey, the deceptive seductress who is both his lover and the murderer of his one-time partner, Miles Archer. Spade tells Brigid that, despite his affection for her, he is going to turn her over to the police. Shocked, Brigid cannot believe that Archer means as much to Spade as she does; Spade offers Brigid eight reasons for turning her in. The first three reasons, worth quoting in full, reveal Spade's hierarchy of values, a hierarchy in which his passion for Brigid is subordinate to his desire for justice:

When a man's partner is killed he's supposed to do something about it. It doesn't make a difference what you thought of him. He was your partner and you're supposed to do something about it. Then it happens we were in the detective business. Well, when one of your organization gets killed it's bad business to let the killer get away with it. It's bad all around— bad for that one organization, bad for every detective everywhere. Third, I'm a detective and expecting me to run criminals down and then let them go free is like asking a dog to catch a rabbit and let it go. It can be done, all right, and sometimes it is done, but it's not natural.[8]

Spade enumerates four more reasons for his decision, but his eighth and final reason is perhaps the most revealing: "If [these first seven reasons] mean nothing to you forget it and we'll make it this: I won't [let you escape] because all of me wants to—wants to say to hell with the consequences and do it" (439). Remember, Spade is not without his lesser desires for money, power, and sex. At different moments in *The Maltese Falcon*, he indulges each of these passions. At the conclusion of the novel, however, Spade turns his back on them—on all those things that "all of [him] wants"—and seeks instead to do the right thing, to pursue and serve justice. It is this ability to contain—and ultimately reject— his improper desires and act upon the proper ones that makes Sam Spade the hero of his narrative; it is an ability that makes him both a common man—because he possesses desires—*and* an unusual man—because he can govern them.

What Chandler says of Marlowe is also true of Spade, for Hammett's hero is indeed "the best man in his world and a good enough man for any world."[9] He is "the best man" not because he is without desire for money, power, and women, but because he possesses a sense of justice and honor that can master those desires. We must note, as Chandler does in "The Simple Art of Murder," that the detective is very much a creature of passions. According to Chandler, however, the detective must strike a heroic balance between an emasculating rejection of desire and an inhuman surrender to desire, and, not surprisingly, it is his honor that helps him strike that manly balance: "I do not care much about [the detective's] private life," Chandler says of Marlowe, "[for] he is *neither a eunuch nor a satyr;* I think he might seduce a duchess and I am quite sure he would not spoil a virgin; if he is a man of honor in one thing, he is that in all things. . . . If there were enough of him, the world would be a very safe place to live in" (emphasis added).[10]

Chandler's detective, via his honorable masculinity, makes the world safe, if not for democracy, then at least for virgins. We cannot say this of the *roman noir*, however, for a world filled with the heroes of Cain and McCoy, of Thompson and Goodis, would be a very unsafe place indeed for both duchesses and virgins. The detective's code of honor, which demands that he fashion the scope and direction of his desires, is absent from the *roman noir* because desire (any desire, whether it be for love, for money, for justice, or for revenge) is the foundation for self-annihilation in these narratives. Whereas in the hardboiled detective novel the hero must learn, and can learn, to gain control of his passions, to fashion an honorable hierarchy of desire, in the *roman noir* such appetites cannot be so readily controlled and manipulated. Instead, the *roman noir* questions and negates the mastery of desire that is so fundamental to the masculine heroics of the hardboiled detective novel. If, as Chandler suggests, the masculinity of the detective hero is defined by his response to desire, then, as the novels of Cain, Thompson, and Goodis suggest, the masculinity of the *roman noir* hero is threatened by—not defined by—his response to desire. In the *roman noir* then, the problem for the hero is not how to order desire, how to subordinate and pursue passions in a manly and honorable way (avoiding the "unmanly" fates of both the eunuch and the satyr), but whether or not he can desire at all without initiating a swift process of self-destruction.

In this chapter, I want to pay particular attention to three novelists of the *roman noir*—Cain, Thompson, and Goodis—and how each of them explores the process of self-destruction engendered by the presence of desire. In his first novel, *The Postman Always Rings Twice* (1934), Cain establishes desire as the central problem of the *roman noir*, a problem that is also at the heart of his next two novels, *Double Indemnity* (1935) and *Serenade* (1937). While these first three novels form a unified trilogy of desire, *The Postman Always Rings Twice* stands by itself as the ur-text of the *roman noir*, for in it Cain successfully images a fragmented masculinity that is at the mercy of—that is, does not have mastery over—destructive and disobedient desires. Building upon Cain's vision of desires unmastered, Thompson and Goodis offer us heroes who know that desire leads to self-annihilation and who thus fight, above all else, to erase their desires. For Thompson's characters, however, the fight to erase desire is never successful for very long and, ultimately, Thompson's novels explode with desires gone wild, with men who destroy themselves (and, quite literally, the narratives they inhabit) because of their inability to master their obsessions. Whereas few of Thompson's heroes ever escape the self-destruction that eventually attends the pursuit of desire in the *roman noir*, Goodis's heroes do survive, but their survival is qualified because it depends upon being "a soft-mouthed nobody whose ambitions and goals aimed at exactly zero, . . . [at being a man whose] presence . . . meant nothing."[11] This kind of "living degree zero," living without desire, is Goodis's grim and bitter solution to the problem of desire raised by Cain in the earliest *romans noir*, a solution Chandler would have found profoundly distasteful (for Chandler, recall, the hero "is everything"; for Goodis, however, the hero is "nothing," "exactly zero"). Thus, if Cawelti is correct in claiming that the hardboiled detective novel reflects the "common fantasies" of masculinity—fantasies in which male desire for escape, security, vengeance, and domination are reassuringly fulfilled—then the *roman noir* reflects the "common nightmares" of masculinity—nightmares in which desire imprisons, fragments, dislocates, and overpowers any man foolish enough to possess and pursue it.

II.

In a particularly resonant passage in *Notes from Underground*, Dostoyevsky, speaking through his nameless protagonist, sums up Cain's vision of desire as well as any critic can or has: "I will admit that reason is a good thing. No argument about that. But reason is only reason, and it only satisfies man's rational requirements. Desire is the manifestation of life—of all of life—and it encompasses everything from reason down to scratching oneself. And although, when we're guided by our desires, life may often turn into a messy affair, it's still life and not a series of extractions of square roots."[12]

While Frank Chambers, the hero of *The Postman Always Rings Twice*, is not able to recognize and articulate his vision of desire as eloquently as Dostoyevsky's underground philosopher, his first-person narrative is, at its very core, a narrative of a life turned messy by the affairs of desire. Much the same could be said for the first-person narratives of *Double Indemnity* and *Serenade*. Appropriately, then, many critics have been quick to note that in Cain's fiction desire "encompasses everything." According to O'Brien, the matter is quite simple: "In Cain's books, desire is all there is."[13] For Joyce Carol Oates, the great lesson of Cain's fiction is that "the world extends no farther than the radius of one's desires."[14] Madden concurs, describing Cain's protagonists in such a way that we cannot help but note how desire defines everything they do: "High on sex, often apotheosized into home-brew mysticism, drugged on orgasmic optimism, and gorged on food, they set off from their caves, make the kill, and consummate the ritual with another orgy of sex and food."[15] Finally, Frank Krutnick is even more direct in his assertion that desire—a specifically sexual, but ultimately disruptive desire—is central to Cain's fiction. According to Krutnick, Cain's early tales "begin with the eruption of desire at the sight of the woman, an eruption that displaces the hero and locks him within a trajectory leading to transgression—most often through the crimes of adultery and murder, the murder of the woman's husband—and ultimately, to catastrophe." For Krutnick, Cain's novels provide us with a perfectly "frantic 'imaging' of male desire."[16]

When Frank Chambers is tossed off the back of a hay truck at the beginning of *The Postman Always Rings Twice*, he seems anything but frantic. As a lawyer will later say of Frank, he is the kind of guy who is always "knocking around . . . never doing any work, or even trying to do any."[17] However, despite his surface serenity, what Paul Skenazy calls his "aimless peace,"[18] Frank is a creature of passions, a man with a voracious appetite. When he wanders into the roadside cafe owned by Cora and her husband, Nick Papadakis, Frank orders "orange juice, corn flakes, fried eggs and bacon, enchilada, flapjacks, and coffee" (1) for breakfast. Unfortunately, Frank's appetites do not end here, for when he first spies Cora he desires to devour her as readily as he devours his breakfast: "Then I saw her. She had been out back, in the kitchen, but she came in to gather up my dishes. Except for the shape, she really wasn't any raving beauty, but she had a sulky look to her, and her lips stuck out in a way that made me want to mash them in for her" (2). It takes less than twenty-four hours for Frank to satisfy his hunger for Cora. When Nick leaves for Los Angeles the morning after Frank first lays eyes on Cora, the two of them are left alone for the first time. "I took her in my arms," Frank tells us, "and mashed my mouth up against her . . . 'Bite me! Bite me!' [she said]." Frank, of course, obliges: "I bit her. I sunk my teeth into her lips so deep I could feel the blood spurt into my mouth. It was running down her neck when I carried her upstairs" (9).

In this swiftly paced narrative, sexual desire quickly engenders a desire for violence (a desire, albeit, which is already implicit in the brutal sexual relationship between Frank and Cora). The lovers' first attempt to kill Nick Papadakis fails. Their second attempt, however, is successful. Frank and Cora stage a car accident, making it look as if they and Nick have inadvertently driven off the road and dropped fifty feet into a ravine. Of course, Nick is dead before Frank pushes the car into the ravine. In order to make it look as if they too plummeted down the ravine with Nick, Frank rips Cora's blouse, leaving her "wide open, from her throat to her belly" (46). To heighten even further the realism, Frank hits Cora in the eye as hard as he can. Both acts, however, generate sexual excitement. Quickly, desire gets the best of them. This desire literally "un-mans" Frank, for he describes himself as "some kind of animal" (46), and in the famous passage that ends the chapter, Cain makes a resonant connection between desire and self-destruction, a connection that is at the very heart of the *roman noir:*

Next thing I knew, I was down there with her, and we were staring in each other's eyes, and locked in each other's arms, and straining to get closer. Hell could have opened for me then, and it wouldn't have made any difference. I had to have her, if I hung for it.

I had her. (46)

After Frank has Cora, the local district attorney wants to have her as well, that is, have her tried for Nick's murder. He manages to coerce Frank into accusing Cora of the crime. When Cora discovers this, she in turn accuses Frank. The two look as if they are indeed going to hang for pursuing their desires until an unprincipled lawyer, playing one insurance company off of the other, manages to free them. Cora gets probation and $10,000 from her husband's insurance, and she and Frank try to return to the lives they have made for themselves.

With Nick dead, however, Cora and Frank no longer share the same desires. Nick wants to wait out Cora's six-month probation, sell the tavern, and leave town. At first, so does Cora, but after six months of solid business—people flock to the tavern to catch a glimpse of the woman who may have killed her husband—Cora wants to buy a beer license and expand the restaurant. Frank, however, wants no part of this scheme, and when Cora is away at her mother's funeral in Iowa, he closes up the business and heads to Mexico with another woman. Frank returns from Mexico before Cora herself returns from Iowa, but it is not long before Cora discovers that Frank has once again betrayed her.

Earlier in the novel, just after she receives her probation, Cora tells Frank, "We were up on a mountain [the night we killed Nick]. We were up so high, Frank. We had it all, out there, that night. . . . We had more than any two people in the world. And then we fell down. . . . Our mountain is gone" (87). The mountain, for Cora, is a space of fulfillment; it is both the place where she and Frank kill Nick and the place where she and Frank engage in their most passionate sex. For Cora, these two acts of desire are transcendent moments—they lift her "up so high"—and the mountain, her place of consummate desire, represents the moment when they "had it all," when they were the masters of themselves and their destinies (as she later tells Frank, "God kissed us on the brow that night," 88).

Now, however, after Cora learns of his betrayal in Mexico, Frank reinscribes her mountain in terms focusing not on the redeeming or transcendent qualities of their consummated passion but on its destructive and imprisoning dimensions. As the following passage suggests, Frank realizes that it is not they who master desire but desire that masters them: "We can kid ourself [sic] all we want to, and laugh about the money, and whoop about what a swell guy the devil is to be in bed with, but that's just where we are. . . . We're chained to each other, Cora. We thought we were on top of a mountain. That wasn't it. It's on top of us, and that's where it's been ever since that night" (111).

Chained to each other by their appetites for violence and sex, Frank and Cora now spend their evenings together in silence, plotting out in their minds how to kill each other. But they are offered one last chance for happiness, one last chance to get rid of the fear that has turned their love into hate. When Cora tells Nick that she is pregnant, Frank wants to marry her. Cora agrees, but she also wants Frank to make a deeper, more profound choice. She suggests that tomorrow, after they get married, they go to the beach. "You can kill me swimming," she tells Frank. "We'll go way out . . . and if you don't want me to come back, you don't have to let me" (113).

Frank doesn't kill her. As he swims out into the water with his bride, his desires change. He is no longer a man who needs to devour everything around him. As he swims back to shore, we see a different man, one who, while still possessing passion, now seems free of every destructive appetite and urge:

We started back, and on the way in I swam down. I went down nine feet. . . . I whipped my legs together and shot down further. . . . And with my ears ringing and that weight on my back and chest, it seemed to me that all the devilment, and meanness, and shiftlessness, and no-account stuff in my life had been pressed out and washed off, and I was already to start out with her again clean, and do like she said, have a new life. (114-15)

At this moment, as he surfaces from the water, Frank becomes an almost Chandleresque hero. In a world full of meanness, Frank, for the moment at least, is not himself mean. Like Chandler's Marlowe, Frank is not purged of all desire—he has not become a "eunuch." Rather, his desires are purified; he has come away "clean," thus avoiding the fate of the satyr as well as the eunuch. With his desires refashioned into a more acceptable hierarchy (he leaves all the "meanness" down in the water, bringing back to the surface only those desires that are "clean") Frank, like the baby in Cora's womb, is about to be born into a "new life," with, one senses, a new chance to pursue his desire for family and assume the honorable and exclusively masculine roles of husband and father.

But Cain's universe is one in which the pursuit of desire disables rather than enables an honorable masculinity. When Frank surfaces from his purifying dive, with all the devilment and meanness pressed out of him, Cora, treading water nearby, tells Frank that she feels "funny inside" (115). Both of them fear that she is miscarrying. As she fatigues, Frank must tow her to shore. Now, instead of desiring her death, he desires only to save the life of his wife and child. After getting her to the car, he speeds toward the nearest hospital. Caught behind a truck, Frank tries to pass it on the right. In his frantic pursuit to save that which he most desires, he does not see the culvert wall in time, and, as he tells us, "There was a crash, and everything went black" (115).

While in the water, Frank purifies his desires, becoming a seeker not of death but of a "new life" of love and family. But this new world, this "clean" world, quickly turns "black." In a further, equally cruel twist of fate, Frank is sentenced to hang for Cora's death. As Frank puts it, the district attorney "had it all figured out. We murdered the Greek to get the money, and then I married her, and murdered her so I could have it all" (117). Frank insists, however, that "I never really wanted anything, but her" (119). If this is true, then Frank's narrative represents his successful struggle to move beyond his earlier, less noble desires for power, money, and sex. At the end of the novel, so it seems, Frank has indeed cleansed himself and has indeed subordinated and mastered his base desires so that he might pursue the more noble desire of love.

But as he awaits his execution, Frank can no longer be certain that he is the master of his desires, and as he protests his mastery, we think that he does protest too much:

There's a guy in No. 7 that murdered his brother, and says he didn't really do it, his subconscious did it. I asked him what that meant, and he says you got two selves, one that you know about and the other that you don't know about, because it's subconscious. It shook me up. Did I really [kill Cora on purpose], and not know it? God Almighty, I can't believe that! I didn't do it! I loved her so, then, I tell you, that I would have died for her! To hell with the subconscious. I don't believe it. . . . You know what you're doing, and you do it. I didn't do it, I know that. That's what I'm going to tell her, if I ever see her again. (119)

At the end of *The Maltese Falcon,* Sam Spade knows what he is doing and why he is doing it. The same is not true for Frank Chambers, and it is this ambivalence over the mastery of desire that marks a key difference between the hardboiled detective novel and the *roman noir.* In the end, neither we nor Frank are certain of his desires, and Frank, without the certainty he needs, cannot, like Spade, construct an honorable hierarchy of motivations.

Ultimately, it matters not what Frank desired as he tried to pass the truck on the highway that afternoon. If, on the one hand, Frank was indeed trying to kill Cora, then he was unchanged and was once again pursuing an impure and insatiable desire, a desire he had to fulfill even if he had to hang for it. On the other hand, if Frank was no longer a mean man, if he was seeking to fulfill a set of purified desires, what then? The outcome is the same. In either case, Frank hangs for his desires. The fault, Cain seems to be telling us, lies not in the direction of Frank's desires, but in the fact that he desires at all. Whether acting out of meanness or out of love, out of his old devilment or out of baptismal newness, Frank is destroyed by his pursuit of desire. When, after his conviction, Frank claims "I never really wanted anything, but her," he may be wrong, but he has articulated the problem of desire at the very heart of the *roman noir.* The profound despair of this novel, the despair that Camus exploited so well in *The Stranger,* rests upon the unspoken assumption that even a single, simple desire—represented in a single, simple syntactical construction, "but her"—can have the most catastrophic implications for the construction of the self. Ultimately, Frank Chambers would have been better off if he could have just said "I never really wanted anything." His life, of course, would not have amounted to much, but then again his life would also not have destroyed so much. Such renunciation, although it would have allowed him to survive, would have also, on the other hand, deprived him of a more "complete" masculinity. Without desire, to be sure, he could never have assumed the honorable masculinity that attends a man's devotion to his wife and child, but at least he would not have been responsible for the death of that very same wife and child.

Operating as the generative text of the *roman noir*, *The Postman Always Rings Twice* gives articulation to the despair of masculine desire, a despair out of which a generation of popular novelists would fashion their frustrated and disturbing visions of fragmented and ineffectual masculinity. For Jim Thompson, this despair of desire leads his heroes into a violent and often psychopathic engagement with the world, toward a sense that if one possesses desire and desire engenders self-destruction, then one might as well get on with the business at hand, might as well play out the self-annihilation as swiftly and as violently as possible. For David Goodis, however, the self-destruction of masculine desire leads in the other direction. Instead of giving into the pull of desire and thus initiating the inevitable, Goodis's men try more diligently to erase that pull, exchanging, as it were, the despair of desire for the despair of nothingness. They seek the degree zero implicit in the revision of "I never really wanted anything, but her" to "I never really wanted anything," seeking as they do a place where "nothing could bother them, nothing at all."[19]

III.

When Jim Thompson died in 1977 at the age of seventy, all twenty-nine of his novels were out of print. Thus, in 1981, Geoffrey O'Brien was certainly justified in conferring upon Thompson the dubious title of "Most Neglected Hardboiled Writer."[20] Over the past decade, however, Thompson has swiftly arisen from the ashes of this neglect. In a 1990 issue of *Vanity Fair*, for instance, James Wolcott noted that with "three movie adaptations (with more being prepped), two forthcoming biographies, a series of paperback reissues—Jim Thompson is due to become the coolest dead writer in rotation."[21] Writing at the same time, crime-novelist Lawrence Block agreed: "Jim Thompson is a hot ticket these days. . . . Suddenly, he seems to be everybody's favorite writer."[22]

If, as Luc Sante argues, "Cain spawned a genre. The ingredients of compulsion, self-destruction, revenge, and blind chance awakened a kind of poetry in pulp writing,"[23] then, as Cain's offspring, Thompson took the poetry of pulp writing and pushed it to the discordant edges of madness and nightmare. According to Max Allan Collins, "Thompson is to Cain as Spillane is to Chandler: stronger, darker medicine, the violence and sex starkly, unapologetically depicted, the protagonist's mental state constantly verging on and often into psychosis. . . . Certainly anyone who finds Jim Cain unpleasant will, upon encountering Jim Thompson, rush for the exits immediately."[24]

Despite the differences in intensity between Thompson and Cain, the hero of almost any Thompson novel would benefit from the renunciation of desire encouraged by Cain in the closing pages of *The Postman Always Rings Twice*. In fact, several of Thompson's heroes believe they have indeed renounced desire, have indeed "never really wanted anything." Sheriff Nick Corey of *Pop. 1280* (1964) characterizes himself as "just a nothing doing nothing."[25] The only problem, however, is that the citizens of Pottsville, Texas, population 1,280, want Corey to do a better job of "sheriffin'" the county; they want him to do more than "just grinning and joking and looking the other way" (9). Because they want him to "do a little something" (9) instead of "doing nothing," Corey is forced to act, and he decides that whatever he wants to do he can do. So, when the town's two pimps, who have for a long time been causing Corey "a powerful sight of trouble" (9), continue to bother him, Corey concludes "something plumb drastic" (10) needs to be done. When he next meets the pimps they end up "in the river, each with a bullet spang between his eyes" (40). After this, Corey continues to kill whomever he pleases. The way he murders his lover's husband shows us that Pottsville would have been better off if it had just allowed Corey to continue on as "a nothing doing nothing," to continue living degree zero:

"The second thing I'm gonna do," I said, "is somethin' I should have done long ago. I'm gonna give you both barrels of this shotgun right in your stupid stinking guts." And I did it.

It didn't quite kill him, although he was dying fast. I wanted him to stay alive for a few seconds, so that he could appreciate the three or four good swift kicks I gave him. You might think it wasn't real nice to kick a dying man, and maybe it wasn't. But I'd been wanting to kick him for along time, and it just never had seemed safe until now. (68)

Nick Corey, like so many of Thompson's protagonists, is better off being a man without desire. Otherwise, given the opportunity to pursue some need or want, and in every novel they are presented with abundant opportunities, Thompson's protagonists cannot control themselves. Some of his heroes are, at heart, full of what Sheriff Lou Ford of *The Killer Inside Me* (1952) calls simply *"the sickness."*[26] Others, like Toddy Kent of *The Golden Gizmo* (1954), are "peaceful [men who] don't ask much but to be left alone and leave others alone," except that circumstances (usually in the form of a woman) keep them from following that "basic pattern."[27] Most of Thompson's heroes, however, experience the "two-way pull" of Clinton Brown, the emasculated war veteran of *The Nothing Man* (1954), a pull in which violent and often self-destructive desires compete with and win out over the impulse to leave well enough alone:

I was experiencing that peculiar two-way pull that had manifested itself with increasing frequency and intensity in recent months. It was a mixture of calm and disquiet, of resignation and frantically furious rejection. *Simultaneously I wanted to lash out at everything and do nothing about anything.* The logical result of the conflict should have been a stalemate, yet somehow it was not working out that way. The positive emotions, the impulse to act, were outgrowing the others. The negative ones, the calm and resignation, were exercising their restraining force not directly but at a tangent. (emphasis added)[28]

Nick Corey, strangely enough, is one of Thompson's luckiest heroes, for despite the fact that he gives in to his most psychopathic desires, gives into the "frantically furious" pull "to lash out at everything," he survives.[29] Other protagonists are not so fortunate and, for the most part, they meet brutal fates as a result of their pursuit of desire. When Ford, the easygoing but deeply disturbed sheriff of Central City, for the first time meets Joyce Lakeland, Central City's newest prostitute, he too, like Clinton Brown, is being pulled by disquieting desires. After she calls him a "son-of-a-bitch" for impersonating a client just to gain access to her trailer home, Ford experiences a welling of uncontrollable anger: "I had to get out of there. I knew what was going to happen if I didn't get out, and I knew I couldn't let it happen. I might kill her. It might bring *the sickness* back" (13). But Lou Ford cannot get out of there, and soon he is smacking her around her bedroom and tearing her clothes off. "I don't know how long it was before I stopped, before I came to my senses," Ford tells us afterward. "All I know is that my arm ached like hell and her rear end was one big bruise, and I was scared crazy—as scared as a man can get and go on living" (14).

Ford, however, does not go on living for long. His afternoon with Joyce Lakeland has indeed brought back *the sickness*. With his sickness tapped, Lou Ford, like Nick Corey, begins to stack up bodies, beating and killing whomever he pleases. Soon, of course, he leaves too many bodies behind and the police are on his trail. At the end of the novel he is alone in his kitchen, asking himself how come his "life doesn't depend on anything that makes sense" and wondering "where in the hell [he] got the idea it did" (184). Unable to find an answer, and unable to master his sickness, he methodically plans his own suicide. He goes into his basement with a "gallon bottle of alcohol and [a] box of tall candles" (185) and returns to his kitchen without them. As the basement beneath him slowly burns, he sips on coffee and smokes a cigarette, waiting for Joyce Lakeland and her police escort to show up at his house. Soon, his house is surrounded by police and, sitting at his kitchen table, playing with the knife he will use on Joyce when she shows up at his door, Lou Ford reveals his belief that his life has been nothing but one long drama of self-annihilation: "You wonder if you've done things right [in setting up your own suicide], so's there'll be nothing left of something that shouldn't ever have been, and you know everything has been done right. You know, because you planned this moment before eternity way back yonder someplace" (185). When he leaps out of his front door, sticking a blade between Joyce's ribs, the house suddenly bursts into timely flames and, Ford tells us, the "room exploded with shouts and yells, and I seemed to explode with it, yelling and laughing and . . . and . . ." (185).

Such apocalyptic endings are standard Thompson fare. No matter how much they want to fight the two-way pull that finally demands they pursue desire rather than remain as calm and resigned "nothing men," Thompson's heroes are driven by passions that explode their very being. Such passions turn Nick Corey into a deluded psychopath, one who thinks that he is the second coming of Christ, put on this earth to grant and take life as he pleases. For Lou Ford, desire, which can only be described as a sickness, leads to his self-destruction. He knows desire to be his enemy, but he cannot master it no matter how hard he tries. It is almost as if Thompson's heroes subconsciously desire their own deaths, which they see as the only way out of the two-way pull: If they cannot return to being "a nothing doing nothing," then at least they can welcome the "nothingness" of death.

This is true of Kid Collins in *After Dark, My Sweet* (1955). Collins, an ex-boxer and recent escapee from a mental hospital, seems to know little of what he wants, but he, unlike most Thompson protagonists, has a vague sense that he wants to do the right thing. Directionless, he hooks up with two small-time hoods and becomes involved in a botched kidnapping. When he realizes that he cannot escape prosecution for his crime, he tries to imagine a way in which the woman he loves, who coaxed him into the kidnapping in the first place, will escape prosecution. The only solution he can imagine is one in which he so terrifies this woman that she is forced into killing him to save her own life. When he threatens her and then leaves his gun within her reach, she aims the gun at the back of his head. "There was one shattering explosion," Collins tells us, "and I pitched forward against the creek bank. . . . And I stayed where I was, unable to turn my face pressed into the dirt. And that was the way it should be. . . . And this—this, what had happened, was, as it had to be."[30]

What Kid Collins gives up so willingly—his life—other protagonists have taken from them. At the end of *The Grifters* (1963), small-time con man Roy Dillon and his mother, Lilly, are at odds with one another. Lilly, having recently murdered Roy's lover (who was, in turn, trying to kill Lilly), needs Roy's money in order to make a clean getaway. Roy, however, wants to keep his money because he believes that this is best for his mother—it will be the only way she will stop her life of crime. Or at least this is what he initially believes he desires. Slowly he realizes that he wants to keep his money because of deeper, less noble motives. As a child,

Roy felt sexual longing for his mother (Lilly is only fourteen years older than he). For Roy, his youth was a *"time when he had known need or desire and been denied because the denial was good for him."*[31] Now, he realizes, if he can keep his money he can *"Keep her available"* (183), allowing him to perhaps fulfill the need that has been so long denied him. Lilly senses this, and begins to tease her son:

> "Roy . . . what if I told you I wasn't really your mother? That we weren't related?"
> "Huh!" He looked up startled. "Why, I—"
> "You'd like that, wouldn't you? Of course, you would. You don't need to tell me. Now, why would you like it Roy?"
> He gulped painfully, attempted a laugh of assumed nonchalance. Everything was getting out of hand. . . . The sudden awareness of his feelings, the sudden understanding of himself, all the terror and the joy and the desire held him thralled and wordless. (185)

When Lilly asks, "I want that money Roy. I've got to have it. Now, what do I have to do to get it?" (185), Roy cannot articulate his desire: "And how could he tell her? How say the unsayable?" (186). But he never has to say anything. As Roy is poised to ask for the one desire that has always been denied him—sexual possession of his mother—his mother—the very object of his desire—murders him. As Roy sits before her, taking a sip of water at her behest, Lilly, "her grip tight on the heavy purse, swung it with all her might. . . . A torrent splattered and splashed with red. . . . [Roy] rose up out of his chair, clutching at [his throat], and an ugly shard of glass oozed out between his fingers" (186). At the very moment when "desire held him thralled and wordless," Roy Dillon meets his death.

Discussing the conclusion of *The Killer Inside Me*, David Lehman notes that Thompson's novel "reaches a nihilistic orgasm."[32] Lehman's phrase is a disturbing but acutely accurate one that suggests both the consummation of desire and the nothingness and destruction at the very heart of that consummation—a suggestion that is central to Thompson's vision of desire. As with *The Killer Inside Me*, the conclusion of *The Grifters* is also marked by an explosion of violent nihilism. So too is the ending of *Savage Night* (1953), in which Charlie Bigger, like Roy Dillon, is destroyed by the very woman he most desires: "The axe flashed. My hand, my right hand, jumped and kind of leaped away from me, sliced off clean. And she swung again and all my left hand was gone but the thumb. . . . She was swinging wild. My right shoulder was hanging by a thread, and the spouting forearm dangled from it. And my scalp, my scalp and the left side of my face was dangling, and . . . and I didn't have a nose . . . or a chin . . . or. . . ."[33] The violent conclusion of *Savage Night* is surpassed only by the strangely brilliant final chapter of *A Hell of a Woman* (1954), in which, at the very end, Thompson splits his narrative in two (every other line is in italics). Thus, one of two endings are possible, both of them equally nihilistic. The protagonist, Frank Dillon, either commits suicide as he leaps out a window or is castrated by an unknown woman. We cannot know for certain which is his true fate. What we can know for certain, however, is that yet another one of Thompson's protagonists has been destroyed by his desire. In one of the two optional endings, just before he is about to be castrated, Frank characterizes his life as

a . . . terrible tragedy and whoever was responsible for it . . . ought to be jailed. Making a guy want what he . . . couldn't get. Making him so he couldn't get much, but . . . he'd want a lot. Laying it all out for him every place he . . . turned—the swell cars and clothes and places to live . . . never letting him have anything, but always making . . . him want. Making him feel like a bastard because he . . . didn't have what he couldn't get. Making him hate . . . himself, and if a guy hates himself how can he love . . . anyone else?[34]

Frank Dillon's frantic and apocalyptic vision of life is strikingly similar to the cool and resigned vision offered by the nameless philosopher in Dostoyevsky's *Notes from Underground*, for Frank Dillon would certainly agree that desire "encompasses everything from reason down to scratching oneself." Thompson's men, however, do more than scratch themselves and, in the end, desire does more than encompass everything—it destroys everything as well. Yes, Thompson's "heroes" may begin like Sheriff Nick Corey, wanting only to be "a nothing doing nothing," but the moment they begin to pursue their desires, begin to give into the two-way pull that forces them into action and away from the zero degree, they initiate a swift process of self-annihilation in which the scratching of an itch soon becomes the tearing away of the soul. Thompson's attitude about the self-annihilation that always attends the pursuit of desire is quite clear, especially if we recall the final words of Kid Collins in *After Dark, My Sweet:* Self-destruction "was the way it should be. . . . And this—this, what had happened, was, as it had to be" (130).

The pursuit of desire that drove Frank Chambers into a world where "everything went black," is echoed in the final pages of *Savage Night*, where Charlie Bigger, lying mutilated in his basement, is left with nothing but "The darkness and myself. . . . And the little that was left of me was going, faster and faster" (147). In fact, the image of Charlie Bigger being hacked to death by the woman he most desires may be Thompson at his most Thompsonesque, and it may serve as well as a shocking reminder of the fragmented and ineffectual masculinity imaged in the *roman noir*. In the basement with Charlie, we could not be any further away from the Chandleresque vision of heroic masculinity informing the hardboiled detective novel. In the mean world in which he lives, Charlie Bigger is both tarnished and afraid. And whereas he is certainly an "unusual man," he is not a "complete" one. If anything, he is an incomplete man, first missing his right hand, then his left hand, then his scalp, his nose, his chin. Nor is there anything redemptive about his tragedy, for as O'Brien notes, "Rarely has an American writer—especially a mass market writer like Thompson—portrayed such hopeless ugliness, so unadorned a dead end."[35] Ultimately, the dead end of Thompson's fiction rests upon his dead-end vision of desire. Unlike Chandler, who envisions desire as something hierarchical and thus potentially honorable, Thompson understands desire as something unsettling and, quite literally, emasculating, leading not to heroic self-definition but to inevitable self-destruction. This dead-end vision of desire marks nearly everything Thompson ever wrote and, according to one French critic, it secures his reputation as "le plus noir, le plus amer, le plus pessimiste de tous les auteurs des romans policiers américains."[36] It is no wonder, then, that biographer Michael J. McCauley characterizes Thompson's works as "razor-sharp, pocketsized trips into the void."[37]

Seeing man as a someone who "couldn't get much, but . . .

he'd want a lot" (*Hell of a Woman*, 181), Thompson perceived the masculine condition as not only encompassed by desire but also thwarted and imprisoned by it. A Thompsonesque hero wants to be a nothing man, but he is pulled by desires that demand fulfillment, quite often against his better judgment. These desires take that hero out of his zero degree of negation and into a dangerous landscape of desperate need, a condition that will make him feel not like, "to use a rather weathered phrase, a man of honor" (Chandler, "The Simple Art of Murder," 533), but like a "bastard because he . . . didn't have what he couldn't get" (Thompson, *Hell of a Woman*, 181). For David Goodis, however, the solution to this predicament was quite simple: rewrite the landscape so that if a man "didn't have what he couldn't get" it wouldn't matter to him anyway—wouldn't make him feel like a bastard—because, ultimately, he didn't want that much to begin with. Thus, if for Thompson man was someone who "couldn't get much . . . but he'd want a lot," then for Goodis man was someone who simply couldn't get much—the "wanting," as we shall soon see, was totally erased from the equation.

IV.

David Goodis's first novel, *Retreat from Oblivion* (1938), was his first and only work of "serious" fiction. Soon, he turned to the pulps. With his second novel, however, he rescued himself, albeit momentarily, from the "oblivion" suggested by the title of his first novel and his subsequent foray into pulp fiction. This second novel, *Dark Passage* (1946), was serialized in *The Saturday Evening Post* and Warner Brothers turned it into a feature film starring Humphrey Bogart and Lauren Bacall. Immediately thereafter signed on as a Warner Brothers staff writer, Goodis had unknowingly reached the peak of his fame. After a few more hardcover publications, he was consigned to the field of paperback originals. This consignment, however, although not to Goodis's economic advantage, benefitted him as an artist. O'Brien writes:

With the move to paperback originals, the style and content of his books changed radically. As if mirroring the failure of Goodis' higher-toned literary ambitions, the novels turned decisively toward the lower depths. From here on he would be the chronicler of skid row, and specifically of the man fallen from his social class. . . . In this fashion David Goodis, great literary artist turned street-corner hack writer, could tell his own story and ply his trade at the same time.[38]

Goodis's first paperback hero, James Cassidy of *Cassidy's Girl* (1951), is much akin to the violent and sexually passionate protagonists of Cain and Thompson. A one-time airline pilot and war-hero, Cassidy is now a down-and-out bus driver. Years ago, he lost his airline job when, upon take-off, his co-pilot, suffering "a sudden emotional collapse, the kind that gives no warning . . . and causes a man to break up as earth breaks up when a quake hits it," "turned on Cassidy, pulled him away from the controls, grabbed the controls, and sent the plane downward when it was less than a hundred feet in the air."[39] Cassidy, the only surviving crew member in a crash that took more than seventy lives, lost his wings when it was proven that he had been drinking the night before—which he had, but that had nothing to do with the crash.

A ruined man, Cassidy drifts from job to job. A victim of another man's loss of control, what Cassidy most cherishes about his bus-driving job is that "he was at the controls. That was the thing that mattered. That was what he needed. More than anything. He knew he had lost the ability to control Cassidy, and certainly he would never be able to control Mildred [his wife], but there was one thing left in this world that he could and would control. . . . It was a wonderful bus. Because it would do what he wanted it to do" (15). But, like a Thompsonesque hero, Cassidy is engaged in a two-way pull. As much as he needs and seeks control, Cassidy will often find himself "itching for a solid session of violence" (18), itching, as it were, for a release of his passions. He is married, in turn, to a woman whom he characterizes as "a harsh and biting and downright unbearable obsession" (5). At the beginning of the novel, as we watch him take sexual possession of his wife despite her indifference, we see Cassidy, like Frank Chambers, as a man mastered by his desires: "Very deep inside of him a warning voice told him to let go of her, to leave her alone. . . . [But he] wanted this and he was going to have it and there was no other matter involved. . . . And yet, although the knowledge of her indifference was almost a physical agony, the roaring fire inside him had far greater power, and the only thing he could do was surrender himself to it" (9–10).

Pulled in two directions—one for control, the other for release—Cassidy often frequents Lundy's, a local tavern, and there we soon discover yet another one of his obsessions: alcohol. One evening, he meets Doris, an emaciated, twenty-seven-year-old woman who shares, to an even greater degree, Cassidy's passion for drink. Unlike Cassidy, however, Doris has only this one passion, and nothing else, for the "look in her eyes was the dead look far beyond caring, beyond the inclination to care" (35). There is no roaring fire inside of her. Cassidy, however, decides that he wants to shake Doris out of her degree zero, out of her "beyond caring." Looking into her expressionless eyes, Cassidy "felt the kind of pain that one feels when seeing a crippled child. And all at once he felt an enormous desire to help Doris" (41). As he makes love to her, he insists that it "has nothing to do with lust. It was desire . . . his need to caress her, to give her something of his strength" (43). Cassidy's desire, then, will be Doris' salvation.

But Shealy, Lundy's resident philosopher, warns Cassidy that such desires are misplaced and, in fact, will destroy Doris. According to Shealy, the people who frequent Lundy's, a place of "no color, no gloss, no definite shape" (20), do not want their lives complicated: "The credo I hold is based on simple arithmetic, nothing more. We can all survive and get along if we can just add one and one and get two. . . . If you don't leave her alone she won't survive. . . . Doris has only one need; and that's whisky" (48). Shealy argues that "we dragged ourselves [down to Lundy's]. Wanting it. Knowing it was just what we wanted and we'd be comfortable . . . because there's no bumps" (48). When Cassidy says that such a "comfortable" life is "rotten" and that he is "getting out" (48), Shealy sighs: "The dreams again" (50).

But Cassidy, in a flash of Chandleresque chivalry, believes that there "really was something noble to live for" (56). And while he tries to "construct a better life for himself and for Doris" (54), Mildred, his wife, and Haney, her lover, make his life a living hell. One afternoon, Haney, drunk and desperate, buys a ticket on

Cassidy's bus. Haney wants Cassidy to crawl "like a worm" (79) back to Mildred so that Mildred can have the satisfaction of throwing Cassidy out. Haney hopes that this will get Mildred's mind back on him and off of Cassidy, who deserted her for Doris. When it becomes clear that Cassidy will do no such thing, Haney strikes him over the head with his flask, knocking Cassidy unconscious and causing the bus to roll over a steep embankment. Cassidy and Haney are thrown from the bus; the other twenty-six passengers die as the bus explodes into a ball of flame.

As Cassidy lies on the side of the road, half-unconscious, Haney pours whiskey down his throat. When the police arrive, Haney, the only witness, testifies that Cassidy was drunk, and so once again Cassidy is falsely accused of killing his passengers. When the police are momentarily distracted, Cassidy escapes and spends the evening making his way back to Doris' apartment. When he arrives there, however, she is not home; she is down at Lundy's drinking again. At this moment, Cassidy is struck by the futility of his dreams: Doris' absence "expressed something completely negative, a kind of dreary pessimism, telling him that no matter what moves he made, no matter what he tried to do, he just wouldn't get anywhere" (95). But he will not give up; he cannot accept this kind of negativism. With the help of Shealy, he plans to escape to South Africa aboard a ship, with Doris by his side. He sees everyone else in his world as those "who had long ago lost the vigor and the spine and the spark. But he, Cassidy, he hadn't lost it. . . . He would never lose it. It was the marvelous substance and fire and surging and as long as it was there, as long as it revolved and throbbed, there was a chance, there was hope" (109–10).

By novel's end, however, Cassidy must jettison this "marvelous substance" of hope, this "fire and surging" of desire for something better. Cassidy's epiphany marks a profound awareness that living degree zero is the proper posture of existence—that living without desire is what others want to do and it is what he must and should want for himself:

The moment of realization was almost tangible, like a page containing words of truth. Now he was able to understand the utter futility of his attempt to rescue Doris. There was no possibility of rescue. She didn't want to be rescued. . . . His pity for Doris had been the reflection of pity that he felt for himself. His need for Doris had been the need to find something worthwhile and gallant within himself. (154)

"The moment ended," Goodis writes, "and for Cassidy it meant the erasing of Doris" (154). The erasing of Doris, of course, means the erasing of desire. Unlike Chandler's chivalrous Marlowe, Goodis's defeated Cassidy cannot find something "worthwhile and gallant within himself," and thus, in turn, he can find little that is worth desiring. Cassidy does not want to be here in this world of erasure, this world without desire, but Goodis is telling us that this is where he must be. When earlier in the novel Cassidy tells Shealy, "I don't know what I believe. There's part of me says I shouldn't believe in anything," Shealy responds with a sentiment that is unmistakably that of the author: "That's the sensible way. . . . Just wake up every morning and whatever happens, let it happen. Because no matter what you do, it'll happen anyway. So ride with it. Let it take you . . . down. . . . No effort. No climbing. Just slide down and enjoy the trip" (101).

For Goodis, the "sensible way" is a life of "no effort," of "no climbing." Cassidy must learn this. So too must Hart, the protagonist of *Black Friday* (1954), who begins as a man who "knew how to run [from] the emptiness."[40] Frightened by the erasure of desire that threatens to strip his life of meaning and feeling, Hart seeks constant contact with the world, even if it is a painful contact, just so as to avoid the zero degree: "He slammed his fist against the tree and pain shot through his knuckles. Not enough pain. . . . He had to hurt himself more than this, make himself realize that he couldn't continue this [emptiness]. . . . He told himself that even if he had to break his hand he had to cure himself now" (7). In the final paragraph of the novel, however, Hart can no longer outrun the emptiness that is chasing him and, like Cassidy, he embraces the erasure of desire: "He was walking very slowly, not feeling the bite of the wind, not feeling anything. And later, turning the street corners, he didn't bother to look at the street signs. He had no idea where he was going and he didn't care" (129).

Where Hart and Cassidy end up, this is where the protagonist of *Street of No Return* (1954) begins. Like Cassidy and Hart, Whitey was at an earlier time a successful man. A famous night-club singer, Whitey hooks up with Cecelia, the common-law wife of a small-time gangster. The gangster tries to convince Whitey to leave Cecelia alone, but Whitey, in classic *roman noir* fashion, tells him, "I want her. . . . I can't give her up. Just can't do without her" (76). Whitey's desire leaves the gangster no choice, and he has Whitey beaten so badly that the singer's vocal chords are forever damaged. When Cecelia fails to call him while he is in the hospital, he realizes that what he most wants, what he "can't do without," no longer wants him. After this realization, "nothing mattered" (87). He gambles away his fortune, takes up drinking, and soon he finds himself, much to his liking, "Going down. One step at a time" (89).

When the novel opens, Whitey's "slow motion suicide" (88) has long been complete. For the past seven years, he has been living on Skid Row, and every day at dawn "he'd hit the street and join the early-morning parade that moved in no special direction, the dreary assemblage of stumble bums going this way and that way and getting nowhere" (91). This nowhere is right where Whitey wants to be, for he is "a little man lost in the emptiness of a drained bottle" (2), with "nothing in his pockets and nothing in his eyes" (3). When a riot breaks out in the opening pages of the novel, "Whitey's face showed no interest at all. He wasn't even listening to the hectic noises coming from three blocks south" (6). One of Whitey's wino buddies bemoans this riot because it reminds him that "Skid Row wasn't really the hiding place it was supposed to be. . . . [Down on Skid Row, you] tried to keep away from contact with the world but somehow or other the world always made contact. The world tossed the bait and tossed it again and again, kept tossing it to get a nibble, and sooner or later the hook was taken and the line reeled in" (7).

The secret, this wino believes, is to "play it Whitey's way and not let it touch him, let nothing touch him" (9). Resist the hook of desire that the world keeps tossing at you, don't take the bait and be reeled in by wants and needs—according to the wino, this is the only way to survive. Unfortunately, Whitey, who is so good at not letting the world touch him, sees something on the other side of the street, something that forces him into contact with the world. Reeled into the "Hellhole," the place of the rioting, Whitey begins his curious odyssey. In the course of his evening in the "Hellhole," Whitey confronts the people who beat him long ago and exacts revenge upon them by foiling their plans to foment a larger, more disastrous race-riot. He even meets Cecelia again, and she is still hooked up with her gangster. He toys with the idea of trying to take her back, but he realizes that he does not want her, or anything else, bad enough.

Through it all, Whitey retains his sense of nothingness, and while the world makes contact with him, he is always aware that what he wants and seeks most is to live degree zero, to live without ambition or desire. At the beginning of Whitey's evening in the "Hellhole," an elderly black man tries to convince Whitey that he must have something to live for:

> Jones said, "You gotta care. You gotta drill it into yourself, you got to have something to live for."
> "Like what?" [Whitey] asked in the cracked whisper that always reminded him it was a matter of no hope, no soap, nothing at all.
> But the old man was still in there trying. And saying, "Like looking for an answer. No matter what the question is, there's always an answer."
> "Sure," he agreed, grinning again. "In this case, it's strictly zero."
> "It's never zero," the old man said. "Not while you're able to breathe."
> "I'm tired of breathing." (51)

When Whitey gets back to his corner at the end of the evening, he has not come up with anything to live for. For Whitey "the answer" is still "strictly zero." When his two wino buddies ask him where he has been and what has happened to him, "Whitey shrugged and didn't say anything" (166) because, in a way, nothing has happened to him. In his discussion of the novel, O'Brien concludes that Whitey "wanders off and comes back 175 pages later . . . only to find that all he really wants to do is go back to [his] corner" on Skid Row.[41]

The novel closes with Goodis's vision of survival, his belief that men need to live in a perpetual state of dreams deferred and desires erased in order to endure:

> The three of them walked across the street. They sat down on the pavement with their backs against the wall of the flophouse. The pavement was terribly cold and the wet wind from the river came blasting into their faces. But it didn't bother them. They sat there passing the bottle, and there was nothing that could bother them, nothing at all. (166)

Like Cassidy and Hart, Whitey ends up in a world where nothing
bothers him, where nothing matters. Unlike Cassidy and Hart,
however, this is the very place where Whitey begins. If *Cassidy's
Girl* and *Black Friday* enact a movement from desire to the erasure
of desire, then *Street of No Return* enacts no movement at all—
Whitey never gets beyond the zero degree.

Shoot the Piano Player (1956), however, is a fusion of these two
structures, for in it Goodis creates an existential odyssey in which
his hero, Eddie Lynn, moves from wanting nothing to wanting
something and back to wanting nothing once again.[42] Eddie begins as a man with "no debts or obligations" (5), "a soft-eyed, soft-
mouthed nobody whose ambitions and goals aimed at exactly
zero" (24). Even his smile is "something neutral. . . . It was aimed
very far out there beyond all tangible targets" (24). Like Goodis's
other heroes, Eddie is running from his past. Eddie was once a
world-famous concert pianist, but his career fell apart when his
wife, because of his neglect, took her own life. When the novel
opens, Eddie is playing piano in a two-bit bar. The music he
makes symbolizes the state of his soul: "The music went on, the
rhythm unbroken. It was a soft, easygoing rhythm, somewhat
plaintive and dreamy, a stream of pleasant sound that seemed to
be saying, Nothing matters" (4). A complex set of circumstances
and coincidences shake Eddie out of his easygoing rhythm of nothingness, and soon he finds himself drawn into a world of violence
and, much to his disbelief, love. At the end of the novel, however,
we find him right back where he started, with his "fingers caressing the keyboard" (156). And while the crowd at the bar urges him
to "put some life into this joint" (156), we sense that Eddie's
return to the piano marks his return to a life "aimed at exactly
zero." The music will go on, the rhythm will be unbroken, and
Eddie, like the author who created him, will continue to produce
the "pleasant sound" that says "Nothing matters."

V.

Frank Chambers awaiting his execution, uncertain about the
source and direction of his desires; Charlie Bigger crawling about
in a dirt basement, what little there is left of him "going, faster

and faster"; James Cassidy realizing that "no matter what moves he made, no matter what he tried to do, he just wouldn't get anywhere": These are the images of masculinity inscribed in the *roman noir*, images reflecting not the common fantasies of masculine prowess and domination but the common nightmares of impotence and ineffectuality. If, as Stephano Tani has suggested, "the mythic private detective conceived of by such writers as Dashiell Hammett and Raymond Chandler . . . [is] a creature capable of dealing efficiently with a disorderly and dangerous world,"[43] then the less-than-mythic "hero" conceived of by those other hardboiled novelists—Cain, Thompson, and Goodis—is the very nexus of danger and disorder. Instead of being defined by his ability to deal efficiently with the world—or, as we have stated the case here, being defined by his ability to deal efficiently with his contentious desires—the hero of the *roman noir* is destroyed by his very inability to do so. Lacking a Chandleresque mastery of desire, the hero of the *roman noir* has but two options. He can continue to pursue his desire until he enacts an inevitable self-annihilation, or he can embrace the zero degree and trade in self-annihilation for self-erasure. In either case, the hero is un-manned, becoming less and less like the "everything" Chandler tells us a hero must be, and more and more like, as Thompson reminds us, a "something that shouldn't ever have been." But such is the life, such is the nothingness, on the mean streets of the *roman noir*.

Notes

1. Raymond Chandler, "The Simple Art of Murder," in *The Simple Art of Murder* (Norton: New York, 1968), 533.
2. George Grella, "Murder and the Mean Streets," *Contempora* 1 (March 1970): 8.
3. John G. Cawelti, *Adventure, Mystery and Romance: Formula Stories as Art and Popular Culture* (Chicago: Univ. of Chicago Press, 1976), 151.
4. David Madden, *James M. Cain* (Boston: Twayne, 1970), 22.
5. Geoffrey O'Brien, *Hardboiled America: The Lurid Years of Paperbacks* (New York: Van Nostrand Reinhold, 1981), 68.
6. O'Brien, *Hardboiled America*, 77.

7. Cawelti, *Adventure, Mystery and Romance,* 160.
8. Dashiell Hammett, *The Novels of Dashiell Hammett* (New York: Knopf, 1965), 438.
9. Chandler, "The Simple Art of Murder," 533.
10. Chandler, "The Simple Art of Murder," 533.
11. David Goodis, *Shoot the Piano Player* (Berkeley: Black Lizard, 1987), 24.
12. Fyodor Dostoyevsky, *Notes from Underground,* trans. Andrew R. Mac-Andrew (New York: Signet Classic, 1961), 112.
13. O'Brien, *Hardboiled America,* 73.
14. Joyce Carol Oates, "Man under Sentence of Death: The Novels of James M. Cain," in *Tough Guy Writers of the Thirties,* ed. David Madden (Carbondale: Southern Illinois Univ. Press, 1968), 111.
15. Madden, *James M. Cain,* 66.
16. Frank Krutnick, "Desire, Transgression, and James M. Cain," *Screen* 23 (1982): 34.
17. James M. Cain, *The Postman Always Rings Twice* (New York: Vintage, 1978), 58.
18. Paul Skenazy, *James M. Cain* (New York: Ungar, 1989), 20.
19. David Goodis, *Street of No Return* (Berkeley: Black Lizard, 1987), 166.
20. O'Brien, *Hardboiled America,* 120.
21. James Wolcott, "Dead Cool," *Vanity Fair* (July 1990): 20.
22. Lawrence Block, "A Tale of Pulp and Passion: The Jim Thompson Revival," *New York Times Book Review,* 14 October 1990, 37.
23. Luc Sante, "The Gentrification of Crime," *New York Review of Books,* 28 March 1985, 18.
24. Max Allan Collins, "Jim Thompson: The Killers Inside Him," in *Murder Off the Rack: Critical Studies of Ten Paperback Masters,* ed. Jon L. Breen and Martin Harry Greenberg (Metuchen, NJ: Scarecrow Press, 1989), 38.
25. Jim Thompson, *Pop. 1280* (Berkeley: Black Lizard, 1984), 9.
26. Jim Thompson, *The Killer Inside Me* (New York: Quill, 1983), 13.
27. Jim Thompson, *The Golden Gizmo* (New York: Mysterious Press, 1989), 71.
28. Jim Thompson, *The Nothing Man* (New York: Mysterious Press, 1988), 10.
29. As Michael J. McCauley has discovered, however, Thompson's original manuscript suggested a different fate for Corey. The published novel ends with the following paragraph: "So here it is, Buck, here's my decision. I thought and I thought and then I thought some more, and I finally came to my decision. I decided I don't know no more now what to do than if I was just another lousy human bein'!" Thompson's manuscript version ends with the following lines, which Thompson scratched out with a pen: "I whirled around, drawing my

gun. We both fired at the same time." See Michael J. McCauley, *Jim Thompson: Sleep with the Devil* (New York: Mysterious Press, 1991), 243.

30. Jim Thompson, *After Dark, My Sweet* (Berkeley: Black Lizard, 1986), 130.
31. Jim Thompson, *The Grifters* (Berkeley: Black Lizard, 1985), 183.
32. David Lehman, *The Perfect Murder: A Study of Detective Fiction* (New York: Free Press, 1989), 63.
33. Jim Thompson, *Savage Night* (Berkeley: Black Lizard, 1985), 146.
34. Jim Thompson, *A Hell of a Woman* (Berkeley: Black Lizard, 1984), 181.
35. Geoffrey O'Brien, "Jim Thompson, Dimestore Dostoevsky," afterword to *Savage Night* (Berkeley: Black Lizard, 1985), 154.
36. Noel Simisolo, "Notes sur le film noir," *Cinema* 223 (July 1977): 102.
37. McCauley, *Jim Thompson*, 136.
38. Geoffrey O'Brien, "Introduction," in *Cassidy's Girl* (Berkeley: Black Lizard, 1987), ix.
39. David Goodis, *Cassidy's Girl* (Berkeley: Black Lizard, 1987), 12–13.
40. David Goodis, *Black Friday* (Berkeley: Black Lizard, 1987), 7.
41. Geoffrey O'Brien, "Introduction," in *Street of No Return* (Berkeley: Black Lizard, 1987), xii.
42. *Shoot the Piano Player* was originally published under the title *Down There*. When the novel was republished by Black Lizard Press in 1987, they opted to use a revised title, which is the English translation of the Serie Noire translation *(Tirez sur le pianiste)* of *Down There*. *Shoot the Piano Player* has become the accepted title of the novel because of its association with Francois Truffaut's 1960 film *Tirez sur le pianiste*.
43. Stephano Tani, *The Doomed Detective* (Carbondale: Southern Illinois Univ. Press, 1984), xi.

8

Fighting Words: The Talk of Men at War in *The Red Badge of Courage*

Alfred Habegger

Much of Stephen Crane's work, especially his perplexing novel *The Red Badge of Courage*, constitutes an intense inquiry, simultaneously sardonic and passionately involved, into what it means to negotiate the transition from youth to manhood. From the moment Crane introduces his main character, Henry Fleming, as "a youthful private," our attention is directed to his innocence, the private fears of battle that he dare not utter, and his anxiety at not measuring up to the standards of courage and performance he is afraid his fellow soldiers take for granted. Clearly introduced as someone about to be tested in combat, the youth passes through a cascading sequence of extreme experiences and states of mind, ranging from elation at repulsing the enemy's charge to panic-stricken flight and a strenuous effort to avoid seeing himself as a coward. Rather than encouraging us to share the youth's point of view, Crane's narrator sneeringly calls attention to the callowness of his daydreams and self-exculpating rationalizations, particularly when he is wandering in isolation. Once he is back with his regiment, the youth's initiatory experience culminates in "the enthusiasm of unselfishness" as he participates in a frenzied charge, which the narrator calls, almost at one and the same time, mad, savage, and sublime. At the end, though the youth is troubled by his two desertions—of his regiment and of a dying soldier who had tried to assist him—he manages to feel more comfortable about himself. In addition, his "tupenny fury"[1] at the heavens has not only been dispelled, but he feels convinced that, in the nature of things, he will be looked after:

With this conviction came a store of assurance. He felt a quiet manhood, non-assertive but of sturdy and strong blood. He knew that he would no more quail before his guides wherever they should point. He had been to touch the great death and found that, after all, it was but the great death and was for others. He was a man.

Those readers who emphasize the irony with which the youth is regarded, and who tend to prefer the manuscript-based edition of the novel, read the "quiet manhood" passage as the height of sarcasm. For them, the youth's conviction that the great death "was for others" is a sign he has not succeeded in growing up.[2] On the other hand, those who feel the youth has completed the passage into manhood (with whatever qualifications) are uneasy about the quoted phrase, which was in fact dropped in the first (Appleton) edition.[3] "And was for others": These four words are like a rude interruption in the ennobling ceremonial language climaxing in the terse assertion, "He was a man."

The Red Badge turns out to be a test not just of Henry but of us as readers. We too are in danger, either of being lulled by the resonant organ tones of the "he was a man" paragraph or of encasing ourselves in a bristling and prophylactic irony. The problem is to reach an understanding of the changes the youth has undergone. In some ways he *has* improved. He is less anxious and defensive. He has attained the inner stability required of an effective soldier. He has learned how to take orders without quailing, and he no longer dreams of becoming a heroic leader. Given the great appeal of this foolish dream, the young man's achievement deserves respect. But it is an achievement that comes at a high cost—a loss of individuality and an illusory sense of being the darling of the universe. Fleming has learned how to follow, how to work with others, how to be a strong and sturdy member of his outfit, but these adjustments seem to entail the comforting illusion that there is a great friendliness out there. The passage says that to become a man is to become one with a group in a rather thoroughgoing sense: you don't speak up, you don't make a fool of yourself any longer, you do what you've got to do, and you've got the heavens on your side. It is all summed up in the honorific cliché, "quiet manhood," which I would imagine was a cliché in 1895.

But why is manhood *quiet? The Red Badge* is about, not grace, but silence under pressure—about the need felt by men fighting for their lives to refrain from expressing themselves and to stifle other men's more open self-expression. Crane was profoundly concerned with the competing claims of individual self-assertion and solidarity with a team. In *The Red Badge* he undertook an exploration of the costs and rewards of turning one's back on the team, and the costs and rewards of merging with it. One of the discoveries Fleming makes is that he is more afraid of being isolated from his group than of facing combat as a part of it. To be engaged in a joint battle for survival is to undergo an extreme test of the value of individual self-expression. You're going to have to learn to button up, to keep to yourself much of what you think, if you want to have the group's respect and get out alive. How much do you suppress? If learning how to become a nonassertive but effective member of a fighting team is what becoming a man is all about, then, judging from *The Red Badge*, there is good reason to feel uneasy about that hard-won quietness.

One of the reasons Crane is of interest is that the uneasiness not only pervades his writing but flagrantly calls attention to itself in his style. His bitter intensity, the conspicuously sardonic tone, and the strained diction emphatically proclaim that he is not one with Henry and the other fighting men. Yet few writers have shown such obsessive interest in the pleasures and pains of being on a fighting team (Crane himself was an expert baseball player). It is the writer's own radical instability (*his* Civil War) that drives readers to try to reach an integrated understanding of his only important novel. What I have in mind is a thematic interpretation of *The Red Badge* that neither explains away its disharmonies nor ignores the existence of different textual versions.

I.

To see what is at issue in Crane's treatment of men's reluctance or willingness to express themselves, we must pay particular attention to those scenes in which a band of men respond to an individual's loose speech. This kind of scene, which frequently reappears in Crane's work, is a powerful and defining moment for him. I would like to look at one such scene in "The Open Boat" before considering what we can learn from the characters' speech in *The Red Badge.*

Survival through solidarity is perhaps the most important lesson learned by the correspondent in "The Open Boat." Well before the conclusion of the story, this character, who is clearly a version of the author (Crane had already partly exploited the adventure in a syndicated story),[4] realizes that the experience of selfless mutual assistance is the best thing that has ever happened to him. But of course he does not express this to the three other men. Throughout the story he and they are all suitably laconic. There is one moment, however, where they all break into excited and un-self-conscious speech. At this moment the author's narrative method also changes.

As the castaways observe and comment on the tantalizing movements of a group on a beach, Crane shifts to a very intriguing sort of direct discourse. The speakers are not identified; the speeches seem much more unpremeditated than the rest of what gets uttered on the tiny dinghy; and the conversation, if this is the correct word, seems to represent a group thinking out loud rather than four individual speakers voicing their separate thoughts. Each line of dialogue (again, the term is not quite right) responds to the preceding lines, yet the attention of all four men is not on one another but on people who are obviously out of earshot. The prevailing decorum that rules self-expression on the boat has been set aside, with great relief, and the men happily enter into a cascade of eager collective commentary, a kind of prose choral ode that slowly shifts in tone from excited hope to sullen resentment. The latter feeling is directed at the man on shore whose attention-getting signal, the whirled jacket, remains maddeningly indecipherable, and of course ineffective. At the time banners and hand positions were widely used to convey messages over great distances or loud noises. This man is a loose speaker, as one of the shipwrecked men concludes: "No! He thinks we're fishing. Just giving us a merry hand. See? Ah, there, Willie."[5]

Those three last words have not drawn comment, even though their meaning seems no clearer than that of the rotated garment. Nearly everyone whom I have approached for an explanation has told me that the speaker is addressing Billie the oiler. When I proposed a query about the passage to a respected journal devoted to the elucidation of American speech, I received the same clarification from the editor:

> Since *Willie* is an alternative diminutive for *William* isn't it most reasonable to assume that "Willie" is a vocative address to Billie the oiler? Also, my memory is that Crane was pretty sloppy about details; even if he wasn't thinking of the "Willie" as a variant of "Billie," he may well have been thinking of the same character. In any case, for one of the men to call Billie "Willie" would be a perfectly natural thing, it seems to me.

This, evidently the "natural" explanation, is unsatisfactory for many reasons. In my own experience of American speech, "Billie" and "Willie" are not at all interchangeable. Within the scene, not only the speakers' names but their very identities are unguessable: so why is one of them now singled out as a *listener?* Why would the speaker of the three mysterious words suddenly abandon ordinary functional speech, and why would he do so in addressing a *working man?* Surely, we may presume that Billie already has his eye on the shore. There is no need to say "Behold!" to this man.

The mysterious exclamation must mean something well beyond the signification of the individual words. If we look at an essay written fifty years later by one of the masters of American speech, "The Secret Life of James Thurber," the general meaning of the phrase becomes apparent. This sketch, a fine put-down of Salvador Dali, exposed the vain pretensions of the artist's memoir of childhood by contrasting it with Thurber's own homely upbringing in the Midwest. Dali had known girls named Galuchka and Dullita and recollected the comforts of his mother's womb. Thurber's first memory was of accompanying his "father to a polling booth in Columbus, Ohio, where he voted for William McKinley." The only romance in Thurber's childhood came from his fascination with idioms not to be taken literally—skeleton key, leaving town under a cloud, crying one's heart out, all ears. In his conclusion, after having vindicated his "secret world of idiom" in the face of Dali's affected glamour, Thurber taunted his rival with the idiom that was now (in 1943) as antiquated and homely as Thurber's boyhood in Columbus—"Ah there, Salvador!"[6]

Evidently, at one time "Ah there" or "Ah, there, Willie" was an immediately recognizable formula expressing derision and defiance. I am not sure whether "Willie," by itself an insulting term for a homosexual man, a "Willie-boy," was part of the phrase. Neither do I know just when it was in vogue, how it got started, or even precisely what it meant. It may have served as a challenge to fight, a taunt directed at someone not considered a proper man, a victorious crowing at a rival, or something else. Perhaps it was accompanied by a gesture or movement that could not be alluded to in print. (This might explain why a distinguished expert on American speech is not familiar with the phrase.) But it was definitely an expression of rude, personal defiance. That is why the phrase forms the culminating moment of the men's excited commentary on the mystifying signal from shore. "Ah, there, Willie" epitomizes Crane's great interest in representing hoots, jeers, catcalls, threats, surly challenges, and similar utterances. But it was not just the colloquial expression of insults that caught his ear. What primarily concerned him were the social and moral aspects of jeering speech. Rude put-downs were worth recording because they articulated one of the most important means by which groups of men define, defend, and maintain themselves.

What makes Crane complicated and interesting is that he doesn't automatically say the group is always in the wrong whenever it declares a nonmember to be an outcast or a deviant. In "The Open Boat," where the group is itself in the outcast position and we as readers are made to feel that we are in the same boat, the man on shore really does look like a fool who deserves to be insulted. (But then, thinking of the gay-bashing possibly implied by "Willie," one feels uneasy.) Another story, "The Blue Hotel," is a profound investigation of the social process by which a man is defined/defines himself as a pariah. It is characteristic of Crane that this individual, a ham-handed and suspicious Swede, belongs to an ethnic group reputed not to understand the tonal intricacies (in humor, insult, tall tales) of American language. The question of responsibility, raised by two characters at the end of the story, cannot be solved precisely because the operative dynamics are sociological. And yet the story also insists that the question of responsibility is not to be evaded, as the cowboy would like. It's the reader who is left to worry about the problem.

Leaving the reader to his or her anxiety, let us now turn to Crane's most sustained exploration of the relation between a beleaguered group and the disdained outsider, *The Red Badge of Courage*, whose very title, we note, designates an insignia of attested manhood.

II.

In discussing the representation of speech in this novel,[7] I will not be concerned with talk that is metaphorical rather than literal— "the courageous words of the artillery and the spiteful sentences of the musketry." Neither will I have much to say about the many passages in which Henry Fleming's unarticulated thoughts are rendered in language and imagery he himself would not have used. "Minds, he said, were not made all with one stamp and colored green" (54). "He had been out among the dragons, he said" (72). The diction, the absence of quotation marks, and the familiarity of the narrative convention these sentences follow all announce that "said" does not mean "spoke." (Tacit though the convention may be, Crane himself called attention to it in one sentence: "But [Henry] said, *in substance*, to himself that if the earth and the moon were about to clash, many persons would doubtless plan to get upon roofs to witness the collision," 38; italics mine.) I am confining my attention to those passages that represent *spoken* language, whether that language is recorded in direct discourse or summarized by Crane in indirect discourse.

Although I will also ignore the much-discussed problem of *dialect*, using the term to refer to the presentation of regional or uncultivated speech through nonstandard orthography, it will be necessary to comment briefly on the generalized countrified traditionalism of the soldiers' talk. Some of their statements—"Well, I

swan" (104), "I'm a gone coon" (21), "Be keerful, honey, you'll be
a-ketchin' flies" (41)—probably had an old-timey feel for Crane's
first readers. Perhaps the same was true for "kit-an'-boodle" (8,
68), "jim-hickey" (96), "chin-music" (77), "skedaddle" (14, 16),
"fresh fish" (7), "fight like hell-roosters" (75), and "smart as a steel
trap" (47). Most of the mild oaths and curses probably had an old-
fashioned flavor by 1895—"make way, dickens [i.e., devil] take it
all" (40), "by ginger [i.e., Jesus]" (62), "Great Jerusalem" (63).
That Crane was able to introduce undisguised profanity into the
next-to-last charge—"Where in hell yeh goin' " and "Gawd damn
their souls" (89)—suggests the various euphemistic oaths were
not simply an evasive concession to standards of taste. They also
contributed to the general representation of how the 1890s
thought the 1860s spoke.

The character with the strongest rural twang is the tattered
man, whose speech—"a reg'lar jim-dandy" (46), "there's a bat'try
comin' helitywhoop" (44), "first thing that feller knowed he was
dead" (47)—shows none of Henry's anxiety at being taken for a
greenhorn. Even so, as the last quotation shows, humor and irony
are well within the tattered man's range:

"Oh, I'm not goin' t' die yit. There too much dependin' on me fer me t' die
yit. No, sir! Nary die! I can't! Ye'd oughta see th' swad a' chil'ren I've got,
an' all like that."
   The youth glancing at his companion could see by the shadow of a
smile that he was making some kind of fun. (47)

Here the bitter countrified drollery with which Crane's yokel
speaks is beyond Henry's appreciation.

One could cite a few other expressions that may have struck
readers in 1895 as colorful and old-fashioned—"a hull string of
rifle-pits" (22), "sore feet an' damn' short rations" (23), "could
tear th' stomach outa this war" (80, 106), "sech stomachs aint a-
lastin' long" (7), "Gee-rod [Jesus God], how we will thump 'em"
(14). Framed by the narrator's own terse, up-to-date, and highly
individualized prose, these and other locutions and speeches
helped give the soldiers' talk a slightly quaint, historical feel. The
novel had an overwhelming historical authenticity for readers,
not because it revived the history of battles and leaders and offi-

cial rhetoric, but because it revived, or seemed to revive, the unofficial voices and the unexpressed experiences. The book seemed to disclose what went on *behind*—and in this sense resembles the new social history of our own time (which also uses smoke and mirrors at times). It was the *illusion* of factual excavation and reconstitution that Crane was apparently after. The glaring disparities between his language as narrator and the way his characters speak helped turn the trick.

To single out the more colorful speeches for attention, however, is to convey a misleading impression of Crane's soldiers' talk, which is flat and inexpressive and on the whole rather dull. "Billie—keep off m' feet. Yeh run—like a cow" (16). We're allus bein' chased around like rats. It makes me sick" (77). "Mebbe yeh think yeh fit th' hull battle yestirday, Flemin'." "Why, no, . . . I don't think I fit th' hull battle yestirday" (76). A general, elated that the center of his line has held, repetitiously gloats, "Yes—by Heavens—they have! . . . Yes, by Heavens, they've held 'im! They've held 'im" (34). A sort of shapeless ordinariness characterizes the language of all the speakers, ranging from the garrulous cheery-voiced man who guides Henry to his regiment to tongue-tied Henry himself.

In fact, rather than trying to make his characters sound interesting, Crane deliberately spotlights their inexpressiveness. Again and again he shows how poorly their words match their thoughts and feelings. After Henry's regiment has repulsed the first charge, he preens himself on having lived up to his ideals; all he says, however, is "Gee, aint it hot, hay?" (30). When he seems "about to deliver a philippic" (one of the narrator's many references to classical oratory), he can only say, "Hell—" (45–46). His intense effort to deliver a "rallying speech" only produces "Why—why—what—what's th' matter?" (57).[8]

It is striking how often what we hear the characters saying doesn't match in interest what we are told about their speeches. When a young girl prevents a fat soldier from stealing her horse, we hear the men saying "Gin' him thunder" and "Hit him with a stick," but the "crows and cat-calls" (12–13) that assail him when he runs off are not reported. When "a black procession of curious oaths" comes from Jim Conklin's lips, we hear nothing but another man's not very interesting questions: "Well, why don't they support us? Why don't they send supports? Do they think—" (27). In Chapter 1, it is reported that Jim Conklin and Wilson "had a rapid altercation, in which they fastened upon each other various strange epithets"; the only speeches that get reported, however, are on the order of "Oh, you think you know—" and "Huh" (9). Similarly, there is often a disparity between the claimed and the apparent tone in which speeches are delivered. When we are informed that Henry "yells in a savage voice," the spoken words hardly live up to this advance billing: "Well, yeh needn't git mad about it" (15). The cumulative impression is that, although there may be interesting language somewhere, practically everything *we* overhear is marked by an all-pervading dullness.

This flagrant inarticulateness, so pervasive and obvious in the novel, of course contributes to its realism of speech, but, more important, it contributes to an ambitious inquiry into the social and moral constraints on self-expression. From the second paragraph on, Crane makes it clear that unrestrained speech carries real risks. In fact, it is an incautious speech that gets the story moving: A soldier identified at first only as tall returns to camp "swelled with a tale" to the effect that the army is about to move. He is immediately contradicted by a sulking soldier who is tagged with the epithet "loud." Before long the two characters are given names, Jim Conklin and Wilson, and as the narrative develops, each one's changing habits of speech reflect what he has learned in battle. For now, though, they are only two different kinds of loose speakers, an expansive tall-talker and a hectoring loud-mouth.

At this early stage Conklin is another version of the jacket-whirling man on shore in "The Open Boat," whose signalling turns out to be without significance. Jim carries a garment that he waves "banner-like," and he adopts "the important air of a herald." When he speaks, it is "pompously" and "with a mighty emphasis" (1, 9). He seems to be the sort who is never at a loss for answers, as when he produces "a heavy explanation" (19) of troop movements: "I s'pose we must go reconnoiterin' 'round th' kentry jest t' keep 'em from gittin' too clost, or t'develope'm, or something" (20). The sentence makes it clear that this great windbag doesn't know the meaning of *reconnoiter* or the technical military sense of *develop.*

Later, after Conklin has sustained a mortal wound in the abdomen, he no longer talks like a blowhard. When he says to Henry, "I thought mebbe yeh got keeled over. There's been thunder t' pay t'day. I was worryin' about it a good deal" (42–43), his words ring pathetically true. His newfound gift for honest speech seems connected, paradoxically, to his effort to conceal his mortal wound. There is a grim humor, in fact, in the revelation that his abdomen has the appearance of being "chewed by wolves" (45). Crane, always aware of parallels with ancient Greece, wants us to recall the Spartan boy who was chewed to death by a fox hidden under his cloak. Conklin now knows how to govern his tongue, having learned Laconic speech the hard way. Wilson also develops for the better as a result of his combat experience. Although he begins by ordering Conklin to shut up, he soon learns to express himself more gently. What changes him is the knowledge that others, Henry in particular, have witnessed his fear and cowardice. Wilson's secret is out, and with it his loud defensiveness. His comrades are still liable to be "stung" by "language," but Wilson can no longer be "pricked" by the "little words" that "other men aimed at him" like bullets (68). This invulnerability is what chiefly distinguishes him from Henry, who remains fearful that his shameful acts will come to light. Henry's "tender flesh" is repeatedly "stung" (93) by taunts, and when he and Wilson hear themselves dismissed as "mule-driver" and "mud-digger" by an officer, it is Henry alone who sustains a wound: "arrows of scorn . . . had buried themselves in his heart" (100). Ironically, Wilson has acquired his armored immunity by rashly disclosing his fear of combat. Henry, by contrast, feels compelled by the accidents of war and his own moral weakness to conceal his desertion of the regiment and of the tattered soldier.

Thus, as far as the capacity to speak moral and emotional truth is concerned, Henry develops in an opposite way from Conklin and Wilson. At first the loud talk of these two men masks their real fears. Then they learn to express themselves: "I was worryin' about it a good deal." Henry, on the other hand, remains alternately tongue-tied and dishonest. At the beginning he does not dare give voice to his "outcry" (19) that the stupid generals are marching the men into ambush. Near the end, recalling his shameful treatment of the tattered man, he can only utter "a cry of sharp irritation and agony" followed by a covering "outburst of crimson oaths" (107). In the few instances when his tongue seems unloosed his speech is notably hollow, as when he finally expresses the thoughts that have been on his mind from the beginning and delivers "a long and intricate denunciation of the commander" (75). Such talk is foolish as well as dangerous, and he lapses back into his uneasy state of silence after being "pierced" by the "words" of a "sarcastic" voice (76). What we follow in *The Red Badge* is an account of incomplete development, an explanation, partly moral and partly circumstantial, of how a youth loses the capacity to express himself in speech. He grows up to be the kind of man who is chronically unable to speak his mind.

To say that Henry's development is incomplete is not, however, to say that he remains unchanged, as he does succeed in losing the callow daydreams, fantasies, and aspirations that are a product of his untested egotism. In some of the longer passages that were dropped from the manuscript, Henry's lofty philosophizing allows him to feel great disdain for those who do not see how nature tricks men into the risky pursuit of glory. Wandering alone away from his outfit, unable to endure the prospect of being turned into a "slang-phrase" at whom others "crowed and cackled," he sees himself alone on "the bitter pinnacle of his wisdom." He feels called to become the "prophet of a world-reconstruction." "Far down in the untouched depths of his being, among the hidden currents of his soul, he saw born a voice." This voice, grandiloquent and self-honoring, never finds an occasion to express itself in speech, for once Fleming is safely back with his regiment he begins to distance himself from his "foolish compositions." (The manuscript presents Henry as a bad writer—and thus an alternative version of the author—much more so than does the Appleton edition.) In the end he feels contempt for these "earlier gospels" and is glad to know he does not have to be a prophet: "he would no more stand upon places high and false, and denounce the distant planets." As one who has not only survived but who has shown himself capable of heroic deeds in battle, he feels "a large sympathy for the machinery of the universe." The universe is on his side after all, and it is this comforting conviction that introduces the quiet manhood paragraph.[9] He is somehow at one with the powers that be: this is the illusion on which his manhood is founded. He has grown up to the extent that he has renounced the megalomania of lonely and unhappy adolescence. But he is very far from the correspondent's wisdom at the end of "The Open Boat."

Because Wilson develops in such a different way from Henry, it is a serious mistake to take Henry's maturation as universal and inevitable. Some readers have made *The Red Badge* out to be a systemic account of war or struggle or language. In fact, it is close to being a traditional narrative of an individual's moral and social *bildung*.[10] One of its traditional elements is its use of significant contrasts that establish a context for judging the central character. The chapter in which Henry returns Wilson's packet of letters makes the key differences clear. This packet, like Wilson's original "melancholy oration" (one of the novel's countless references to forms of studied speech), constitutes a "small weapon" in Henry's hands. To use this weapon would be "to knock his friend on the head" (70–71). Henry imagines he is acting with magnanimous forbearance by saying nothing about the letters, but in actual fact he is humiliating his friend by extorting an embarrassing speech from him. In effect he has wounded Wilson on the head, so that "dark, prickling blood had flushed into his cheeks and brow." Wilson now has his own red badge, except that his shame is public in a way that Henry's will never be. Simultaneously, Henry quietly enjoys a daydream about "the stories of war" (73) he will tell his mother and the schoolgirl back home. The contrast is richly significant: while Wilson makes himself engage in a painful act of communication, Henry indulges a solitary fantasy about the self-flattering speeches he will make elsewhere. The scene brilliantly exposes the evasions of "quiet manhood."

It is surprising how many soldiers are wounded in the head in Crane's novel, and how often their head injuries are linked to the capacity for speech. When the babbling man is grazed on the head by a bullet, he responds by saying, "Oh" (28). Another man has his jaw supports shot away, "disclosing in the wide cavern of his mouth, a pulsing mass of blood and teeth. And, with it all, he made attempts to cry out. In his endeavor there was a dreadful earnestness as if he conceived that one great shriek would make him well" (100). The tattered man apparently gets his mortal wound after a friend, Tom Jamison, blurts out that his head is bleeding. Another man in the tattered man's regiment dies after being shot "plum in the head":

Everybody yelled out t' 'im: 'Hurt, John? Are yeh hurt much?' 'No,' ses he. He looked kinder surprised an' he went on tellin' 'em how he felt. He sed he didn't feel nothin'. But, by dad, th' first thing that feller knowed he was dead. . . . So, yeh wanta watch out. Yeh might have *some queer kind 'a hurt yerself.* (47; italics mine)

Finally there is the cheery-voiced man's comrade, Jack, who answers a stranger's question at the wrong time:

"Say, where's th' road t' th' river?" An' Jack, he never paid no attention an' th' feller kept on a-peckin' at his elbow an' sayin': "Say, where's th' road t' th' river?" Jack was a-lookin' ahead all th' time tryin' t' see th' Johnnies comin' through th' woods an' he never paid no attention t' this big fat feller fer a long time but at last he turned 'round an' he ses: "Ah, go t' hell an' find th' road t' th' river." An' jest then a shot slapped him bang on th' side th' head. (61)

In all these accounts there is an association between a terrible head wound and the articulation of thought through speech. Whether to speak up and what to say are extremely delicate questions in combat. How you resolve them may well determine whether you emerge dead or alive.

Henry himself is struck and injured on the crown of his head while confusedly attempting to declare himself, though whether he is trying "to make a rallying speech, to sing a battle-hymn," or simply to ask a question is not clear: " 'Why—Why—' stammered the youth struggling with his balking tongue." What counts is that he gets his wound while struggling unsuccessfully to express his thoughts, and, strangely, from then on his red badge marks a permanent incapacity to speak the truth about his experience in war. The tattered man has it right: Henry has sustained "some queer kind 'a hurt" in his ability to communicate through speech. *The Red Badge* is the circumstantial account of an odd injury to the central character's capacity to utter moral truth about himself.

Because we cannot know exactly what goes on in the minds of the other soldiers, it is difficult to say whether they share Henry's systematic untruth. (The question is similar to the one that bothers Henry in Chapter 1.) But there are certain features of the narrative that invite us to see him as representative of a large class of men, though not of all men. He is identified as "the youth," first of all, and the deceptive silence that characterizes him at the end seems to be the new order of the day. Significantly, the final instances of direct discourse in the novel are all rude put-downs intended to reduce others to silence:

"Oh, shet yer mouth."
"You make me sick."
"G'home, yeh fool." (107–8)

The Appleton edition kept only the first of these, the command to shut one's mouth. This and the two following commands, and also the immediately preceding speeches, all by unnamed members of the regiment, are placed within the frame of Henry's agonized reflections on his abandonment of the tattered man. Evidently, the other men also feel it is best not to engage in public postmortems. Indirectly, they are telling Henry to keep his shame to himself. Confession would be sickening. The way to be a man among men is to refrain from telling what you have done or how you feel about it.

Wilson is the significant exception. The concluding exchanges between him and Henry imply that Wilson has become an outsider by virtue of his newly developed ability to talk. Like Crane's own father (whose profession was defined by formalized talk, that is, the sermon), Wilson is now "a dog-hanged parson" (77). One particular exchange establishes the final positions of the two young men relative to speech. "Well, Henry, I guess this is good-bye-John," says Wilson, and Henry answers, "Oh, shet up, yeh damn' fool" (91). Wilson's speech is not notably mawkish or embarrassing. Indeed, his use of a humorous colloquialism serves to keep his sentiment at a safe enough distance. Even so, Henry orders him to cease speaking, in this way expressing his solidarity with the final sentiment of the other men: whatever it is you have to say, keep it to yourself.

One of the most horrifying moments in the novel occurs when Jimmie Rogers, mortally wounded, is noticed by his fellows:

When their eyes first encountered him there was a sudden halt as if they feared to go near. He was thrashing about in the grass, twisting his shuddering body into many strange postures. He was screaming loudly. This instant's hesitation seemed to fill him with a tremendous, fantastic contempt and he damned them in shrieked sentences. (81–82)

A very minor character, Jimmie is forgotten as the battle continues. In the final chapter, however, in a passage excised from the Appleton edition, Wilson remembers him:

[H]e suddenly gestured and said: "Good Lord!"
"What?" asked the youth.
"Good Lord!" repeated his friend. "Yeh know Jimmie Rogers? Well, he—gosh, when he was hurt I started t' git some water fer'im an', thunder, I aint seen'im from that time 'til this. I clean forgot what I—say, has anybody seen Jimmie Rogers?"
"Seen'im? No! He's dead," they told him.
His friend swore. (106)

Before being deleted, this passage served to interrupt a sequence in which Henry reflects on his performance and seeks to overcome his sense of private shame. Just before the passage Henry struggles "to marshall" (106) his acts and make them "march" (106) in front of him. There follows the transition to Wilson's act of recollection: "His friend, too, seemed engaged with some retrospection" (106). Then, immediately after the Jimmie Rogers passage, our attention is called to the contrast between Wilson's act of memory and the triumphal procession that Henry is privately staging for his own benefit: "But the youth, regarding his procession of memory, felt gleeful and unregretting, for, in it, his public deeds were paraded in great and shining prominence," (106) figuratively marching "in wide purple and gold" (106) and culminating in a glorious "coronation" (106). There is an obvious contrast between Wilson's public act of recollection and the private march of triumph Henry indulges in.

Curiously, the difference between Wilson's and Henry's ways of recalling scenes of battle matches the difference between the manuscript and the Appleton edition. In suppressing the imagery of the triumphant procession along with Wilson's recollection of Jimmie Rogers (and in combination with other deletions), the latter version largely prevents us from getting a purchase on Henry's self-deceptions. Indeed, Crane even added a final sentence that closely parallels the self-flattering coronation: "Over the river a golden ray of sun came through the hosts of leaden rain clouds." In replacing the private and ironic coronation with an external and quasi divine endorsement of Henry's new faith and confidence, Crane in effect rewrote the ending *as Henry might have written it.* The private self-solacing deception in the manuscript becomes objective reality in the version of the novel that all readers regarded as authoritative until 1982, when Binder's edition first became available.

It is not necessary to explain such major alterations in the text and meaning of the novel by blaming them on Crane's editor or publisher.[11] The fact that the altered sense of the last chapter is so closely entangled with the questions at issue in the book suggests that Crane himself may well have been responsible. Belonging to a band of men was no less vital for him than was the need to go off on one's own, whether in a social or philosophical sense. *The Red Badge* emerged from a battle waged within himself, and the battle was still being fought as he moved from the manuscript to the version finally brought out by Appleton.

The instability in Crane is epitomized by a curious opposition between the way *The Red Badge* (both editions in this case) and "The Open Boat" treat the sort of scene in which a man becomes the butt of others' derisive laughter. In Henry's eyes, the worst social injury a man can sustain is to be turned into a "slang-phrase" by another man uttering "a humorous remark in a low tone" (54) to a group of men. After alternating between an incommunicable anxiety about his proven treachery and a sense of satisfaction at his public image, Henry joins the group whose identifying speech-act is the silencing jeer directed at the outsider. Wilson, however, seems to be well on his way to becoming the butt of someone's "Ah, there, Willie." We have very different feelings for the man who painfully acquires a decent kind of honesty in *The Red Badge* and for the loose signaler of "The Open Boat."

Yet, as the similarity in their names suggest, it would not be completely absurd to see them as the same man. But if they are the same man, then Crane himself must have been two very different men.

Notes

1. The quotation comes from the end of Chapter 10 of Henry Binder's edition (New York: Norton, 1982). Based on the manuscript, this edition gives considerably more attention to the pessimistic philosophy Henry Fleming indulges in while isolated from his regiment. The passages, later excised, in which he mentally labors on his new "gospels" originally constituted the conclusions of Chapters 10 and 15 (Chapter 14 in the Appleton edition), a long section in the middle of Chapter 16 (Chapter 15), and all of Chapter 12. These segments are repetitious and overwritten and are narrated with heavy sarcasm, and it is understandable that they would have been dropped. Unfortunately, they are necessary in order to make sense of certain key passages in the concluding chapter, as Hershel Parker was the first to notice. For that reason alone, my text is the one first assembled by Binder. The virtue of this text is that it gives us an idea of what the author originally had in mind in composing the novel. But there will never be an adequate final text.

   Space and time forbid any consideration of the third version of the novel, the abridgement published by a newspaper syndicate, which emphasized action over reflection and concluded with the successful capture of the rebel colors.
2. See Henry Binder, "*The Red Badge of Courage* Nobody Knows," in Stephen Crane, *The Red Badge of Courage,* ed. Henry Binder (New York: Avon, 1987), 150.
3. See Donald Pizer, " '*The Red Badge of Courage* Nobody Knows': A Brief Rejoinder," *Studies in the Novel* 11 (Spring 1979): 77–81, and "*The Red Badge of Courage:* Text, Theme, and Form," *South Atlantic Quarterly* 84 (Summer 1985): 302–13.
4. "Stephen Crane's Own Story," in *Prose and Poetry* (New York: Library of America, 1984), 875–84.
5. Stephen Crane, *Prose and Poetry* (New York: Library of America, 1984), 897.
6. James Thurber, "The Secret Life of James Thurber," *New Yorker* 19 (27 February 1943): 15–17.
7. Of those who have considered the representation of speech in the novel, W. M. Frohock, "*The Red Badge* and the Limits of Parody,"

Southern Review 6 (1970): 137–48, comments on Crane's use of free indirect discourse and Fleming's "bucolic" speech. Robert L. Hough, "Crane's Henry Fleming: Speech and Vision," *Forum* (Houston) 3 (1962): 41–42, shows that the inconsistencies in Crane's reproduction of Fleming's colloquial speech testify to Crane's lack of interest in the accurate recording of actual talk. I wish to thank Donald Pizer for calling these articles to my attention and for providing the impetus to pay closer attention to Crane.

8. See Amy Kaplan's treatment of the inadequacy of storytelling in "The Spectacle of War in Crane's Revision of History," *New Essays on the Red Badge of Courage,* ed. Lee Clark Mitchell (Cambridge: Cambridge University Press, 1986), 91–94.

9. Hershel Parker first pointed out that the deletion of the two paragraphs preceding the sentence, "With this conviction came a store of assurance," removes the referent of "this conviction."

10. For a recent example, see Christine Brooke-Rose's deconstructive reading, which maintains that *"The hero/the monster, running to/running from, separation/membership,* and *spectator/spectacle* . . . are intertwined with each other and caught up in the opposition that subsumes them-that of *courage/cowardice"* ("Ill Logics of Irony," in *New Essays on The Red Badge of Courage,* ed. Lee Clark Mitchell [Cambridge: Cambridge University Press, 1986], 129). This essay relies on Paul de Man's claim that "a narrative endlessly tells the story of its own denominational aberration" (141). Brooke-Rose's dependence on a thinker known to have concealed his Nazi collaborationism in order to construct her argument that Fleming's cowardice and savagery are exemplary for all men ravages her claim that the distinction between cowardice and courage may be safely collapsed.

11. In any case this argument has not held up to critical scrutiny. See James Colvert, "Crane, Hitchcock, and the Binder Edition of *The Red Badge of Courage,"* in *Critical Essays on Stephen Crane's Red Badge of Courage* (Boston: G. K. Hall, 1990), 238–63.

9

The Ambiguous Outlaw: John Rechy and Complicitous Homotextuality

Rafael Pérez-Torres

The Sexual Outlaw: A Documentary represents John Rechy's most overtly political novel. Although this is not a terribly interesting fact in and of itself, the text (first published in 1977) does represent for gay liberation an early and aggressive assertion of the lessons learned from the women's movement: the personal is political. Asserting this view, the book simultaneously complicates it by revealing the potentially contradictory politics of personal liberation.

The novel concerns itself with the actions of a socially marginal but sexually liberated figure as he moves through the decaying urban landscape of our postindustrial age. The protagonist—a semicomposite, semiautobiographical character named Jim—engages in a weekend "sex hunt" in and around the environs of a pre-AIDS Los Angeles sometime around the mid-1970s. Jim stands as a pastless and sexually tireless everyman who forms the moral and ethical center of the novel. He represents the image of male sexuality common to almost all of Rechy's other novels: the hustling homosexual whose actions not only address his own sexual desire, but represent a challenge to the rigid oppression of heterosexual society. Restlessly wandering the peripheries of society, the male hustler becomes for Rechy a sexual shock troop meant to disrupt and sabotage the heterosexual world. The male hustler forms a disruptive and liberating force against the repressive and rigid social order, against its narrowly defined heterosexual identity, against the social complacency and passivity that this identity engenders. His promiscuity challenges the unexamined pieties and platitudes of the repressive heterosocial world.[1]

The Sexual Outlaw thus offers a topology of homosexual masculinity, one that ostensibly maps practices of liberation and self-empowerment for a new, postrepressive age. The narrative posits an image of the homosexual hustler as a matrix of social disruption, agent and agitator for a "minority" cause, model of sexual animal *cum* revolutionary hero.

Rechy's representation of male identity as sexual outlaw emerges out of the contradictions rife within heterosocial order. The actions of the hustler—ostensibly liberating sexual practices comprised of public, anonymous sex antithetical to monogamy— position the outlaw in a tentative and limited relationship to the rest of society. The anonymity with which he performs his acts of sexual rebellion, the deserted urban terrain he claims as his own geography, serve to reinscribe the marginalization of the sexual outlaw. This marginalization is manifested most clearly by the silent codes which the hustler uses to communicate. Indeed, were it not for Rechy's text, the world it describes would remain a demimonde beyond the horizon of heterosocial vision.

More significantly, the novel reveals how the hustler can never fully reject society's repressions, contradictions, and hypocrisies. Beyond the reassertion of the homosexual as marginal, the sexual outlaw in Rechy's work embodies many of the contradictions and failures that characterize heterosociety. Conflicting modes of sociosexual organization—liberated revolutionary, entrapped sexual invert—come within the text to comprise the protagonist's identity. The homosexual hustler is constituted by the very repressive and delimiting social practices against which his own acts of erotic liberation battle. Homosexual and heterosexual practices meet in the outlaw to form an irresolvable tension. The tension becomes particularly tangible at those points where the narrative shows the hustler's sexual choreography to mirror the straight world's preoccupation with dominance and submission. Jim is compelled to power, selling his alluring body. Proving his worth by demanding money for sex, he places himself within both erotic and capital economies based in heterosocial order.

In textualizing the sexual outlaw, *The Sexual Outlaw* comes to embody numerous tensions that disrupt the semantic and semiotic order of the text. The novel valorizes a field of sexual play that seeks to trigger a form of revolt and liberation. The physical elements of this sexual play—symbolically charged clothing, actions, signals, looks—form the "silent" language of an erotic discourse that, textualized in Rechy's novel, seeks to overthrow the repressive discourses of identity imposed by heterosocial order. The "voicing" of a "silent" discourse marks one level of tension at work in *The Sexual Outlaw*. A second tension emerges at the discursive level where the homoerotic within Rechy's text, by inverting notions of heterosocial identity, unwittingly submits to them as well. Rechy's narrative seeks to construct a resistant discourse of homosexual liberation, to create, if you will, a heroic homotextuality. This homotextuality reveals the contradictions inherent both in the heterosocial world against which it speaks and in the homorevolutionary activity it champions. However, a fruitful analysis of this text cannot simply lay bare the novel's ideological enslavement to heterosocial order. While its homotextuality reinscribes elements of heterosocial order, the novel simultaneously disrupts narrative order by placing irresolvable contradictions in play. By evoking the binary structure that bolsters heterosocial order, *The Sexual Outlaw* not only inverts that binary structure but—by revealing its contradictions, contributes to its destruction.

I. The Split Narrative

The breakdown of binaries begins with the bifurcated structure of the novel. *The Sexual Outlaw* oscillates between neatly separated passages of realistic description and essayistic meditations. The descriptive passages offer in (porno)graphic detail an account of the novel's "outlaw" world. Their position as social outsider allows homosexual hustlers a critical perspective on the repressive and conformist practices of heterosocial order. Homosexuality, as defined by this order, is stigmatized, persecuted, labelled a

"deviate practice." Against these negative constructions of homosexuality, the descriptive narrative represents the revolutionary
function of the sexual outlaw.

The subtitle of the book, a documentary, underscores the function of the narrative as critical exposé. The work explores the
sexual activities of a marginal group whose actions question and
undermine heterosocial practices, practices that repressively define sexual identity in the service of social organization.[2] Sexual
outlaws disrupt and destroy the operations of the heterosocial
world by questioning the monological bases of its order: monogamy, reproduction, duality, stability, closure. The incessant repetition of almost identical sexual encounters detailed by these descriptive passages suggests the potentially endless lack of closure
inherent in the hustler's movement from one sexual partner to another.

These (porno)graphic passages alternate with meditative "essays" that form the other half of the novel's bifurcated structure.
These essays range through time and place and incorporate many
different narrative forms and diverse public discourses. Part interview, part public speech, part movie montage, part meditation on
gay culture, part reminiscence, these sections are mediated
through and unified by an authorial voice. This voice draws together the various heterosocial voices that comment on and react
to homosexuality: newspaper clippings about police harassment
of gays, reports by religious and psychiatric organizations on homosexuality as evidence of moral or psychic transgression, real
and imaginary audience reaction to the narrator's speeches about
the gay world. These sections articulate a number of social attitudes toward homosexuality. The social discourses, then, serve as
a multivocalic commentary on the outlaw's liberating practice of
endless desire described in the erotic section. Rechy notes in the
introduction that he, indeed, wrote the descriptive passages first,
later inserting the essays at points he had marked in the manuscript. The descriptive sections serve as the erotic "center" that
the "marginal" meditative passages and their evocation of social
discourses critique and amplify.

One process of inversion emerges as the novel reverses sociocul-
tural reality. Homotextuality—the discourse of homosexual liber-

ation—is inscribed as the center of the narrative structure. The historical "center"—heterosocial order evoked by the meditative sections—becomes the novelistic "margin" whereas the homosexual Other forms the narrative core of *The Sexual Outlaw*. Thus two asymmetrical regions come to define the novel: a unitary, closed, "silent" homosexual discourse sliced through by a multiplicitous, open, "voiced" social discourse.

M. M. Bakhtin's (1981) formalist model of novelistic discourse is illustrative here. He argues that a "unitary language" (monoglossia) is a system of linguistic norms that struggles to overcome the multiplicity of meaning (heteroglossia) linguistic utterances evoke. This monoglossic system is "conceived as ideologically saturated, language as a world view, even as a concrete opinion, insuring a *maximum* of mutual understanding in all spheres of ideological life" (271). The erotic passages in Rechy's narrative are written both as a documentary description of a particular sexual world and as an "ideologically saturated" world view that informs the novel's polemic. The meditative passages, by contrast, incorporate voices questioning both the revolutionary potential of the sexual outlaw as well as the society seeking to persecute him.[3]

The unitary erotic relies on the multiplicitous heterosocial in order to find a "public" voice. Without the meditative and reflective social narrative, the erotic discourse of the male hustler would remain enclosed within a descriptive but isolated narrative. One unfamiliar with the critical and rebellious intent of the sexual outlaw—indeed, one would suspect, the majority of Rechy's reading audience—would remain wholly "outside" the narrative able to perceive only repetitive and (porno)graphic descriptions of homosexual intercourse. The rebellious note would remain unheard by those uninitiated in the hustlers' "silent" language—the elaborate choreography of clothes and signals and movements carefully detailed in the descriptive passages. The presence of the social narrative within the novel as commentary on and explanation of the erotic narrative positions both the homorevolutionary and the heterosocial arenas in a mutually reliant discursive relationship.

The narrative structure thus evokes the compromised position of the sexual outlaw as standing both within and without various social orders. The narrator, by contrast, wants to position the hustler fully outside the systems of heterosocial control. His is a tenuous, doubly marginalized position: "Existing on the fringes of the gay world, male hustlers have always been dual outsiders, outlaws from the main society, and outcasts within the main gay world of hostile non-payers and non-sellers. Desired abundantly, and envied, they are nonetheless the least cared about."[4] This position of double marginality affords the narrative of *The Sexual Outlaw* a unique and powerful critical position. In order for this position of power to be made manifest, however, the silent and hidden erotic discourse must be made public through the multivocalic narrative. Hence, whereas a strict structural separation exists between the public voices of the essays and the erotic discourse of the descriptive passages, each simultaneously reflects upon and filters the contents of the other through its own lens. The revolutionary and the repressive within *The Sexual Outlaw* become not merely inversions, negative evocations of the other. They are fully reliant and dynamic players in the homotextuality of the novel, the articulation of a male homosexual revolutionary identity.

The sense of slippage exemplified by a homorevolutionary identity attempting to stand fully outside a heterosocial order comes to the fore as the narrative emphasizes its use of realist techniques. The erotic passages evoke a literary realism, an attempt to represent a specific reality as it is lived. Rechy notes in his 1984 preface to the book that he conceived of his work as a "prose documentary." The attempt at *cinema verité* is evident in the stark ("black-and-white" Rechy calls it) imagery used to describe the sex-hunt undertaken by Jim. Rechy explains that in these sections he "wanted to create characters, including the protagonist, who might be defined 'fully'--by *inference*—only through their sexual journeys" (16). These sections of the novel describe a movement through a sexual "underworld" marked by its repetitious cycle of desire, pursuit, contact, fulfillment, and renewed desire.

The episodic quality of these descriptions stands for narrative development. "Although there is a protagonist whom the book follows intimately, minute by recorded minute for a full weekend, there is no strict plot," remarks Rechy (16). A rigidly structured sequence of erotic description replaces a sense of narrative development based upon the dynamic growth and change of the protagonist. With the exception of a few flashbacks (passages unambiguously marked "FLASHBACK" in the text), the sex scenes in the novel form a strictly chronological sequence. The passage of time marked rigorously throughout these portions of the narrative inform the reader if a particular action occurs at 6:22 P.M. or 3:07 A.M. Time becomes the principal mode of organization and lends a controlling structure to the otherwise repetitive present-tense descriptions of sodomy, fellatio, and mutual masturbation. As one scene follows another, the narrative enforces a strict temporal order. It does not, however, truly evoke a realist narrative.

The sexual descriptions, realistic as they may seem, do not move simply toward documentary expression. They form a discourse marked by unresolved desires, allowing the reader to trace strata of contradictions and conflicts. Rechy's narrative as an account in the late 1970s of a post-sexual revolution, post-gay liberation, postmodern, post-1960s social world helps locate the complexities involved in social change and political revolution. One formal constellation of this complexity—and the point at which the realist aesthetic of the novel slips into a hyperrealism—develops at the level of character psychology.

As Rechy explains in his introduction, the characters that people Jim's rebellious sexual journey are fully defined by that journey. The bourgeois individual disappears, and the male hustler stands as a figure fully traversed by social discourses—the historical, social, and moral strictures used by heterosocial order to define the individual and against which the hustler stands. While he revels in the sexual urgency of his actions, the identity of the hustler is based on the delimiting social and historical orders he resists. His is a libidinal utopia found at the margins but also, dialectically, composed of the central discursive trajectories of society's order. He stands at a point where not just the sense of the inside and the outside of individual identity blur, but where the limits of political and sexual constituencies disappear. The hustler within an ostensibly realist narrative becomes a figure fully comprised of language. The novel thus does not sustain the illusion of a realistic discourse. Fully defined by his sexual journey, the hustler represents not a rounded individual but a hyper-real figure where the contradictions of the social world come to the fore.

The gay cruising world becomes a mirror of heterosexual norms. Jim hustles for money by playing the ultra—masculine street-tough: "He's wearing Levi's and cowboy boots, no shirt. Sunglasses" (38). Making sexual connections for money, "he will most often pretend to be 'straight'—uncomfortably rationalizing the subterfuge by reminding himself that those attracted to him will usually—though certainly not always—want him to be that, like the others of his breed"(39). As top man, Jim assumes the role of the quintessential heterosexual male, appropriating the image and exaggerating it as if in a funhouse mirror. Often bodybuilders (like the narrator, the author, and the fictional Jim) and male hustlers assume both the physique and the costume—Levi's, boots, sleeveless shirts—of macho masculinity. The hustler appropriates and reflects back to masculine society a version of its own (ideal) sexual self-image.

The ultra-feminine transvestites and transsexuals represent the binary opposite to the ultra-masculine male-hustlers: "At Highland and Hollywood, the queens, awesome, defiant Amazons, are assuming their stations. The white queens are bleached and pale, the black ones shiny and purple. Extravagant in short skirts, bouffant hairdos, luminous unreal mouths and eyes. The transsexuals are haughty in their new credentials" (39). Both the queens and the hustlers assume exaggerated versions of the sexual roles circumscribed by heterosocial order. The contradictions of the gay street world are magnifications of the contradictions running through this order. A problem with the straight world, the narrative argues, is that it denies a dialectic between the masculine and feminine principles of human identity. This denial forms one basis for the split in the outlaw world Rechy's novel serves to describe.

The meditative sections of the novel criticize writers who ceaselessly flaunt their masculinity, calling them "screaming heterosexuals" and "male impersonators." The narrative seeks to redress and subvert the sense of *machismo* and homophobia found in the works of Ernest Hemingway, the "hairy godfather of heterosexual writers," and the sexual anxiety and violence invoked by the

"Tarzan-howling" Norman Mailer (195). The narrator suggests that the writers who have created the most fulfilling work—Shakespeare, Joyce, Lawrence, Proust, Genet, Burroughs—are those artists who most fully accept and integrate the "female grace" and the "male strength" of their psyches. Which is to say that the narrator values those writers who seem to challenge most successfully the binary construction of "feminine" and "masculine."

One would be terribly hard pressed, however, to find some "female grace" evident in either the graphic descriptions of the erotic narrative or the outraged authorial voice of the social narrative. Instead, the novel celebrates the power the hustler exerts over his small domain: "There is a terrific, terrible excitement in getting paid by another man for sex. A great psychological release, a feeling that this is where real sexual power lies—not only to be desired by one's own sex but to be paid for being desired, and if one chooses that strict role, not to reciprocate in those encounters, a feeling of emotional detachment as freedom—these are some of the lures . . ." (153). The narrative valorizes an image of traditional heterosexual masculinity and attitudes toward sex that involve control, detachment, freedom.

This power, ironically, often leads Jim into a position of impotence. Though excited, he will not reciprocate a sexual act unless his partner is extremely handsome. Neither will he ever initiate a sexual act: "Two beautiful male bodies lie side by side naked. . . . Used to being pursued, each waits for the other to advance first. . . . Looking away from each other, both dress hurriedly, each cut deeply by regret they did not connect" (65); "Jim wants the man to blow him first, and the man wants Jim to do it first. They separate quickly" (265). Jim's quest for power traps him in impotence, just as his domination over sexual partners leads him to a reliance upon another partner in order to affirm his power. He must be pursued as an object of desire. Repeatedly, the narrative makes evident the conflicted position of the sexual outlaw who, attempting to escape the repression and boundaries of the heterosocial world, runs again and again straight into its contradictions.

Although the narrative attempts to position the male hustler as a doubly marginal figure, it reveals him to stand both within and without heterosocial systems. His inversion of heterosexual roles is at once subversive and critical as well as imitative and conformist. The revolutionary intent of both the novel and its protagonist becomes defused as the hustler is shown to assume a reactive and thus dependent position to the center.

The interplay between silence and voice underscores this sense of dependence. The language of the hustling world—"spoken" through posture, costume, and look—represents a form of "silent" language. After his early encounters by the pier, on the beach, in the restroom, Jim realizes he has "spoken not a word to anyone today. Not one" (34). Most of the communication described in the narrative occurs through the use of gesture ("from behind blue-tinted sunglasses, he surveys those gathered here, intercepts looks—but he moves along the sand toward the ocean," 23), through sexual position ("swiftly turning his body around, torso bending forward, back to Jim, the naked youngman parts his own buttocks," 26), or through clothing ("men lie singly in that parabola of sand—the more committed in brief bikinis, or almost naked—genitals sheltered only by bunched trunks," 23). The silence, along with its suggestion of near religious commitment and sacrifice—a vow of silence—stands in contradistinction to the form the novel assumes as a publicly "voiced" disclosure of the "silent" homorevolutionary world.

The silence essential to Rechy's homosexual discourse stands in contrast to and is only made manifest by the public voices of the socially discursive sections. Which is to say, the (silent) homosexual discourse only exists in Rechy's narrative when made present by the (voiced) public language of various other discourses—a novelistic discourse, a documentary discourse, a journalistic discourse, a media discourse. The form the novel takes betrays its vision of homosexuality as a singular and impenetrable margin. The bifurcated narrative articulates a homosexual/political practice dependent upon the very social strictures against and apart from which the novel's sense of a (true) homorevolutionary identity seeks to exist.

II. Marginal Masculine Identity

The Sexual Outlaw does not just represent a story of failed rebellion. Rather, the text betrays an incessant doubling whereby the discourses of liberation and repression are ever revealing the duplicity of the other. In his studied macho posturing, in his overt strategizing for domination and power, Jim plays out a heightened image of male heterosocial dominance. Simultaneously, the narrative finds in the male hustling arena a passive-aggressive role traditionally ascribed to women within male-dominated society. Working-out incessantly in order to be desirable, passively attracting the attention of others, Jim stands as the physical manifestation of idealized manliness. He behaves, however, by a code associated with a most prim and passive form of female behavior. He must always be the object of the chase. He must never initiate contact with another man. He must always allow the other to call his attention first: "Jim sees an obvious bodybuilder. The attraction and the competition are instantly stirred. Jim is prepared to ignore the other. But the other pauses. Jim looks back. With a nod, the other invites Jim into his cubicle" (265). Jim positions himself as the center of attention, an object of worship, the focus of desire.

Pushed by the pressures of heterosocial order to remain marginal, the hustlers lay claim to abandoned public spaces as their geosexual terrain. The discourses of the heterosocial mark this rebellious claim to geographical space as much as it marks the construction of the homorevolutionary self. The sexual outlaw plays within a field bounded by the unmerciful laws behind a form of social darwinism. The struggle to survive in the heterosocial arena is carried over into the homoerotic realm of supposed liberation. Those who are old or ugly do not survive in the game of the sex hunt: "In the shadows an unattractive man is jerking off; everyone walks by, ignoring him" (75); "an unattractive loose-fleshed old man lies there naked, his hand on his spent groin. Abandoned and desperate and alone—one of the many lingering, ubiquitous, wasted, judging ghosts in the gay world. Jim avoids him" (114); "beyond the cave of the tunnel he passes a forlorn old man, waiting, alone, ignored, wasted; waiting for anybody" (203).

These lonely images stand at the fringe of the outlaw arena, denied the right to play the hunt due to their advanced age and degenerating physical appearance. The irony of Rechy's use of the term "gay world" becomes uncomfortably apparent.

The narrative thus explores the problems engendered by a practice of complicitous rebellion, one simultaneously revolutionary and restrictive. The narrative voice speaks of a sexual revolution embodied by the spirit and actions of the sexual outlaws:

What kind of revolution is it that ends when one *looks* old, at least for most? What kind of revolution is it in which some of the revolutionaries must look beautiful? What kind of revolution is it in which the revolutionaries slaughter each other, in the sexual arenas and in the ritual of S & M?

We're fighting on two fronts—one on the streets, the other inside. (285–86)

The "outside" street fight of the sexual guerrillas, amid the broken buildings of the urban wasteland and the open terrain of beach and park, stands at the point where the repressive propriety of heterosocial order proves impotent. The hustling choreography continues despite repeated repressive measures taken by the police and other state authorities. The "inside" fight, the moral imperative to overcome personal prejudice and self-hatred, occurs within a discussion of homosexual identity. The narrative suggests that an idealized vision of youth and beauty informs and infuses notions of identity and desirability. Other outlaws reject individuals unfortunate enough to be old or unappealing, and this in turn can lead to a terrible self-hatred:

Jim faces a drunkenly swaying youngman. Not particularly attractive, the type he would not reciprocate with. Depression crowds the youngman's thin face. Jim doesn't recognize him even vaguely. . . . "You make yourself available," the drunken voice goes on tearing at the silence of the paused choreography. The shadows do not move, the spell locked. "You walk around showing off your body. You didn't even touch me, just wanted me to lick *your* body. Well, I have a body too!" (283)

The confrontation violates the hustler choreography, disturbs the "stirless dark silence," and assaults the "rigid silence" of the hunt. The moment allows the text to examine the cost of the hustler's identity: "In an unwelcome moment the ugly carnage of the sex-hunt gapes at Jim—his part in it" (284). The sex hunt exacts a demanding toll, and the narrative suggests that the erotic discourse of liberation to which the sexual outlaw lays claim carries with it a repressive charge as well. The contradictions of his simultaneously revolutionary and repressive intent inextricably bind the identity of the sex hunter and the resistant intent of the novel. *The Sexual Outlaw* functions as a complicitous critique. It examines the repressive function of heterosocial order and signals the inextricable connection between that order and the homorevolutionary outlaw. In addition, it scrutinizes those repressive practices that to some degree are independent of heterosocial order. The emancipatory outlaw function described by the narrative— the homotextuality—reveals the homosexual hustler occupying a complex marginal space, one simultaneously reliant upon and resistant to central discourses of sexual identity, one implicated in a dual movement of liberation and self-repression.

Rechy's novel thus raises the specter of a complicated and compromised resistant identity. The narrative's bifurcated structure and construction of interpenetrating heterosexual and homosexual social practices mark the contradictions the text finds inscribed in the protagonist's identity. Moreover, the text suggests that repressive practices in the gay world are at moments more than manifestations of a contradictory heterosocial order. The novel thus allows one to move away from the scrutiny of textual form and individual identity toward the exploration of a complex and resistant group identity marked by a sense of conflict and capitulation, resistance and repression.

The sections of social commentary throughout the text—the "public" half of the split narrative—indicate that North American gays in the late 1970s have come to assume a "minority" consciousness. Group identity, predicated upon notions of solidarity as a stand against the oppressive attitude of the majority society, can bolster self-esteem and self-identity while simultaneously silencing critical voices. As the narrator notes: "For a gay person to criticize any aspect of the gay world is to expose himself to howls of wrath and betrayal" (246). Yet a process of critique, of a "deterritorialization" of social order, characterizes Rechy's vision of an outlaw world. The narrative thus offers insight into what one

critical construction of a marginal masculine identity may look
like.

Gilles Deleuze and Félix Guattari discuss deterritorialization
and reterritorialization as connected processes of group consciousness. To "territorialize" is to stratify, organize, signify, attribute—to fix identity. Against this, "deterritorializations" signify
those points that traverse a fixed identity. This can only be met
with a move toward reterritorialization, the configuration of a
new order. The critical work of these French critics suggests an
endless interrelation between liberating and oppressive movements. Even if identity is questioned and social stratification dis-
solved, "there is still a danger that you will re-encounter organizations that restratify everything, formations that restore power to
a signifier, attributions that reconstitute a subject."[5] *The Sexual
Outlaw* thus serves to document how the deterritorializing activity
of public homosexuality ruptures society's territorializations of
sexual identity, of criminality, of sin. Even within this experience
of rupture, however, movements toward new stratifications
emerge: the opposition of homosexuality to racial and ethnic identity, the primary valuation of beauty and youth, the retreat into
the closet from which a safe and pragmatic homosexuality can
be practiced.

The revolutionary impulse of the sexual outlaw leads toward a
"reterritorialization" of identity: stratified, ossified, segmented.
Rechy's work explores the tension between the revolutionary impulse of its male subject and the internal and external forces that
seek to contain any sense of rupture. The erotic sections are episodic and repetitious, presented as "lines of flight" away from the
strictures of correctness articulated by the social discourse of the
novel. Simultaneously, an irreducible tension emerges between
the sense of flight and liberation suggested by the erotic discourse
and the isolation and stratification its form implies: only sexuality
informs these erotic sections and every other object—food and
clothes and all physical movement—becomes subordinated to its
drive.

The erotic discourse deterritorializes the well-defined moral
and legal segments invoked in the social discourses of the novel.

This discourse also reterritorializes the significance of eroticism—sexual outlawry is and must *always* be disruptive. The narrative offers no image of the "perverse" in the sense Barthes (1985) speaks of perversion as "the search for a pleasure that is not made profitable by a social end, a benefit to the species. . . . It's on the order of bliss that exerts itself for nothing. The theme of expenditure" (232). Jim's eroticism is all-consuming, charging his clothes, food, and gesture with an eroticism itself equivalent with social rupture—a revolutionary and liberating benefit "to the species." Rechy's text thus foregrounds the theme of (capital) exchange rather than (perverse) expenditure.

The erotic discourse, in consuming and so assigning significance, silences all that is not of use to the aleatory movement of sexual outlawry. Thus Jim's ethnic background becomes subordinated to his homosexual identity:

Jim—he calls himself that sometimes, sometimes Jerry, sometimes John—removes the bikini, lies boldly naked on the sand. Because of a mixture of Anglo and Latin bloods, his skin quickly converts the sun's rays into a tan; the tan turns his eyes bluer; long-lashed eyes which almost compromise the rugged good looks of his face, framed by dark hair. The sun licks the sweat from his body. (23)

The erotic narrative subordinates any sense of ethnic or racial identity to the erotic, the physical, the homosexual. Rechy, a Chicano, writes a narrative that makes hidden any connection to a nonsexual self. Indeed, the long lashes of his eyes "almost compromise" the protagonist's good looks. As constructed by the narrative, the racial self even threatens the sexual self.[6] In addition, the protagonist's own name—sometimes Jim, sometimes Jerry, sometimes John—has no significatory power against the segmented and wholly consuming identity of homosexual hunter.

Yet, for all this, the narrative evokes various strata of homosexual identity. Homosexual groups in the narrative function as sects with their own secret rites and rituals. In this vein, homosexuality is still tied to "the values and systems of interaction of the dominant sexuality. Its dependence upon heterosexual norms can be seen in its policy of secrecy, of concealment—due partly to the repression and partly to the sense of shame which still prevails in the 'respectable' circles."[7] The landscape Jim traverses in his journey is dotted with the glitter bars, the leather bars, the costume bars representing enclosed domains of concealed rituals of contact. Jim himself usually remains at the periphery of these bars, moving through the alleyways or parking lots outside. He attempts to be truly marginal, an outlaw/existentialist/romantic hero walking on the fringe of the already socially marginal. When Jim does enter these bars, he feels himself surrounded by churning bodies and bare torsos, a charade of ramrod poses that cause him to leave for the ostensibly liberating streets, beach fronts, and hiking trails—the open and more dangerous world of an indifferent rural/urban landscape.[8]

The social narrative examines a group who contest the grip of heterosocial power on their lives. They represent a militant homosexuality that demands its right to exist as a valid sexual, social, and moral entity. As a result, a sense of group identification begins to emerge through the text. The narrator speaks about the Hollywood Gay Parade: "There was plenty of dignity, and, embarrassing to admit—man—I felt the itchy sentiment that signals real pride. Here you are, and here they are, and here we are. I remember Ma Joad's proud speech of the Okies' eventual triumph in 'defeat.' We keep coming, she said, because we're the people" (179). This passage reveals the easy sentimentality and reliance upon cliché "hip" diction that often plague Rechy's writing. This passage compounds these problems by referring to the sentimental movie version of Steinbeck's already sentimental "proletarian" novel *The Grapes of Wrath*. Nevertheless, the passage reveals a strain of resistance manifesting itself as minority group identity. The homosexual forms a margin of opposition challenging the authority of heterosexual power. A movement away from gays having to explain themselves to the heterosexual world propels such resistance and becomes, according to Guattari, "a matter of heterosexuality's having to explain itself; the problem is displaced, the phallocratic power in general comes into question."[9] A resistant homosexual identity inverts a traditional relationship to heterosocial power. It ceases to explain its own existence and instead questions and critiques the centrality of the other's position.

Rechy's narrative, however, does not fully achieve the critical (and some might say facile) point of inversion Guattari's analysis champions. *The Sexual Outlaw* explores a homosexuality that is both reliant upon and resistant to the values and systems of the dominant society. It engages with a notion of the marginal quite distinct from the sense of pure otherness posited by Guattari. The narrative suggests that a reliance upon heterosocial norms leads to a false and destructive sense of identity while also indicating that a powerful belief in the fully resistant and militant quality of homosexual revolt can lead to a code that reterritorializes identity:

> Increasingly easy on campuses and within other enclosed groups to announce openly that one is gay. The shock is gone. . . . It is equally easy to say "gayisbeautiful—gayisproud." Almost one word, meaning obscured. But are homosexuals discovering their particular *and varied* beauty? From that of the transvestite to that of the bodybuilder? The young to the old? The effeminate to the masculine? The athletic to the intellectual? Gay must be allowed variations. It is gay fascism to decree that one *must* perform this sex act, and *must* allow that one, in order to be gay; it is gay fascism to deny *genuine* bisexuality, or to suspect all heterosexuals. (243)

The narrative calls for (but does not necessarily privilege) a genuine multiplicity of identity and sexuality. It thus explores the complicated and compromised position of a resistant homosexual minority, yet it leaves intact the sense of irresolvable contradiction it finds there. Ultimately, Rechy's text is useful less as a meditation on what homosexual "being" means than as an anticipation of how homosexual "becoming" can move beyond the binaries of heterosocial order.

III. Becoming Queer

Heterosocial order defines masculinity through a manifestation of physical and social strength. Physical prowess and politico-economic power are the marks of heterosexual machismo. In his outward appearance, the homosexual can represent an exaggerated image of male heterosocial power. Bulging muscles, cowboy boots, leather jackets, worn blue jeans as cultural icons evoke images of masculine heterosexual power. The male hustler assumes the physical role traditionally assigned to that faction most empowered by society and that most insists upon separating itself from homosexual behavior: the macho heterosexual male. One manifestation of becoming queer involves the ironic appropriation of those signs belonging to the powerful, turning those signs "queer" and resisting their circulation within heterosocial systems of exchange.[10] This appropriation does not imply the simple inversion of signifying systems, however. As Rechy's text all too clearly reveals, inversion only recreates a mirror image of asymmetrical power relations.

The Sexual Outlaw signals the inevitable repression when becoming queer is fixed (reterritorialized) as a form of homosexual being. The narrative problematizes the process of discursive appropriation as the protagonist assumes modes of being that fix trajectories of empowerment and disempowerment. In order to attain a degree of agency and control, Jim feels he must affirm his subjectivity by always being a passive object of desire as an assertion of his masculine allure. He moves through a point where, incorporating contradictory heterosocial sexual roles, those passive modes of behavior socially sanctioned for women cross with the dominant modes of behavior appropriate for men. Jim's identity incorporates the binaries of socially sanctified sexual identity, reveals their contradictions, but does not move beyond them. Homosexual being in the narrative is fixed, stuck, unable to reach out beyond the series of irreducible conflicts Jim employs to define himself. Bound by a code circumscribed by heterosocial norms, the homosexual in *The Sexual Outlaw* becomes a critical locus at which the contradictory trajectories of his dominant society converge. The novel thus posits a rebellious hero but offers us something less. In so doing, it presents an image of a compromised critique that the narrative seeks all to easily to resolve.

The narrative expresses an impossible desire for resolution and transcendence that only serves to re-entrench the contradictory position of the hustling outlaw. As the narrator explains, the "warring attempts to fuse heterosexual expectations with homosexual needs and realities create the contradictions in the gay world" (242). The homosexual world, Rechy's text implies, would be free of contradictions if freed of restraints. Or as the authorial voice articulates:

Release the heterosexual pressures on our world—convert the rage—and you release a creative energy to enrich two worlds. Pressurize the homosexual world further, and it may yet set your straight world on fire.

And when the sexual revolution is won—*if it is ever won*—what of the fighters of that war? Doesn't a won revolution end the life of the revolutionary? What of the sexual outlaw?

One will mourn his passing. (301)

The narrative points toward an apocalyptic completion of the outlaw function—toward the resolution of contradictions—as it looks forward to a social order liberated from the restraints imposed upon sexual behavior and, emblematically, upon all creative human endeavors. Such a resolution of mutual destruction posits a transcendent image of the revolutionary that the entire narrative has to this point found impossible.

Moreover, Rechy's narrative evokes a portrait of the male hustler premised on culturally inscribed discourses of rebellion, resistance, and revolution. This resistance can be viewed from a historical perspective as part of a larger movement of civil disobedience integrally related to the conditions of American civil rights activism in the 1950s and 1960s. From a cultural perspective, the resistance also evokes a romantic tradition traceable in American letters from Cooper and Emerson to (yes) Hemingway and Mailer. The artist stands as the creator of order within a disordered world, an agent of resistance to oppression and persecution. So too does the sexual outlaw.

As the narrative projects this image of the hustler, it becomes clear that the social order forming the "outside" also informs the psychosexual "inside." The novel thus describes sadomasochistic practices in the gay community as a dark imitation of heterosocial repression. In his journey through a maze of bathhouse orgies, paid sexual contact, and random encounters, Jim feels the appeal of sadomasochism as a play for power and dominance. He surrenders "to the part of him he hates," the master of "reeling scenes, spat words, rushing sensations, clashing emotions" (251). Similarly, the narrative surrenders to the strutting power of the ultramacho hustler and the garish femininity of the amazonian drag queens. Both are interiorized versions of sexual roles found in the straight world, roles against and also out of which the homosexual defines himself. The narrative thus proves ambiguous when indicating which sociosexual identities allow for a critical appropriation and which create a repressive interiorization. Rechy's novel fails to articulate adequately where critical inversion ends and slavish imitation begins.

As a repeated thematic and structural motif, the tensions and contradictions between opposites—repression and freedom, hegemony and alterity, masculinity and femininity, passivity and activity—create a picture of a fully traversed, schizophrenic world.[11] The heterosocial arena scrutinized in *The Sexual Outlaw* attempts to create a black-and-white vision in which the actions it views as wholly good seek to repress those it perceives as wholly evil. Rechy's novel reveals this to be wholly inadequate and instead disrupts the neat acts of heterosocial definition and circumscription. In so doing, however, the narrative indicates that a movement beyond binary opposition is desirable while at the same time failing to effect such a movement. The narrative seeks an answer to problems of identity through what is essentially a strategy of appropriation and inversion. In appropriating discourses of oppression, the novel oscillates between exposing and hiding, attacking and bolstering, destroying and reconstructing repressive discursive acts. Finally, the desire for a world of absolutes—the sexual outlaw as absolute other, heterosocial order as absolute evil—mirrors the repressive practices against which this desire ostensibly speaks.

Though failing to articulate a truly revolutionary function for the sexual outlaw, the novel does not represent failure. Although it calls for synthesis and transcendence, the novel cannot accomplish either. Instead, it replicates, doubles, refutes, and challenges those signs of repression and discord that map the delimiting and silencing geography through and against which the male sexual outlaw acts. Clearly the novel reveals an ideological enslavement to the binaries of heterosocial sexual identification. In its exposure of this enslavement, in its attempt to reveal that which it has in 1977 not yet the vocabulary to articulate, *The Sexual Outlaw* not only reinscribes the binary of heterosocial order. It accepts it and rejects it and reveals an impossible topology from which future constructions of sexual identity may move.

Notes

1. Eve Sedgwick (1985) employs the term *homosocial* to name the social order of heterosexual society that is a form of displaced homosexual desire. Throughout this chapter the term *heterosocial* is meant to signify the repressive sexual/social order that employs heterosexuality in order to maintain social order. I use this to distinguish from the ostensibly revolutionary and liberating "homosocial" order Rechy's sexual outlaws are meant to prefigure. This division between "heterosocial" and "homosocial" is in keeping with the basic binary constructions upon which Rechy's text rests.

2. Gayatri Spivak (1991) writes about the role of "margins" as privileged sites of questioning, those places that "haunt what we start and get done, as curious guardians" (158).

3. For a complete discussion of Bakhtin's (1981) position, see the chapter "Discourse in the Novel."

4. See Rechy (1984, 57). While the book was originally published in 1977, all further page references cited in the text refer to the 1984 edition.

5. Deleuze and Guattari discuss territorialization and reterritorialization throughout their work. This quote is from *A Thousand Plateaus* (1987, 9).

6. Though Rechy is one of the most prolific of Chicano novelists, his name is not often associated with Chicano literature. There seems to be a double silencing occurring where the Chicano community of letters by and large has refused to talk about Rechy, and Rechy, until recently, has not emphasized his Chicano identity.

7. Félix Guattari (1984) outlines some of the characteristics of "minority" group identification. See p. 233 passim.

8. The rural scenes in the novel are all enclosed by the urban world of Los Angeles. Griffith Park and the beach at Santa Monica, ostensibly oases of isolated "nature," stand surrounded by city. The "central" urban space and the "marginal" rural space form interpenetrating worlds where danger—from police or gay-bashers—is everpresent. Even the geographic within the novel underscores the dissolution of center and margin.

9. Guattari (1984) goes on to note: "In theory there is at this point a possibility of feminist and homosexual action merging" (233). Both groups question the construction of gender and sexuality in the service of social power.

10. The word *queer* here signals the radical revision of homosexual identity undertaken by such political activists as Queer Nation and the recent considerations of Queer Theory. The reappropriation of the

once pejorative term *queer* represents a discursive assertion of self-identification not available to Rechy in 1977.

11. The term *schizophrenic world* is meant to evoke a number of critical discussions surrounding postmodernity as a schizophrenic condition in which, as Fredric Jameson (1984) notes, "syntactical time breaks down, leaving behind a succession of empty signifiers, absolute moments of a perpetual present" (200). Rechy's narrative evokes a compromised world in which repressive and liberating forces problematically interpenetrate each other.

Works Cited

Bakhtin, M. M. *The Dialogic Imagination: Four Essays.* Trans. Caryl Emerson and Michael Holquist; Michael Holquist, ed. Austin: University of Texas Press, 1981.

Barthes, Roland. *The Grain of the Voice: Interviews 1962–1980.* Trans. Linda Coverdale. New York: Hill and Wang, 1985.

Deleuze, Gilles, and Félix Guattari. *A Thousand Plateaus: Capitalism and Schizophrenia.* Trans. Brian Massumi. Minneapolis: University of Minnesota Press, 1987.

Guattari, Félix. *Molecular Revolution: Psychiatry and Politics.* Trans. Rosemary Sheed. London: Penguin Books, 1984.

Jameson, Fredric. "Periodizing the 60s." In *The 60s without Apology,* ed. Sohnya Sayres, Anders Stephanson, Stanley Aronowitz, Fredric Jameson. Minneapolis: University of Minnesota Press, 1984.

Rechy, John. *The Sexual Outlaw: A Documentary.* 2nd ed. New York: Grove Press, 1984.

Sedgwick, Eve Kosofsky. *Between Men: English Literature and Male Homosocial Desire.* New York: Columbia University Press, 1985.

Spivak, Gayatri. "Theory in the Margin." In *Consequences of Theory,* ed. Jonathan Arac and Barbara Johnson, 154–80. Baltimore: Johns Hopkins Press, 1991.

10

The Lack of Gender in Frank O'Hara's Love Poems to Vincent Warren

Jim Elledge

Between August 1959 and July 1961, Frank O'Hara wrote a number of love poems chronicling his relationship with the Canadian dancer Vincent Warren, from its nervous but exuberant birth to its quietly despairing demise.[1] Despite the fact that the poems are about, on one level, one man's love for another man, readers unaware of O'Hara's homosexuality and of his relationship with Warren will not readily perceive the poems' gay concept or themes. O'Hara never identified the gender of the speaker in any of the poems in the sequence or, except in one instance—"Those Who Are Dreaming, A Play about St. Paul"—the gender of the individual to whom the poems are addressed.[2] Instead, O'Hara's speaker, an "I," offers a "you" observations about love and its high *and* low points.

Because in his poetry O'Hara typically presented his experiences as they had occurred without tampering, the reader of the Warren sequence cannot help but question why O'Hara disguised, obscured, ignored, or lied about the genders of the poems' lovers. Privately, O'Hara appears to have been relaxed about his homosexuality, because both his heterosexual and homosexual friends and acquaintances knew about it. In some cases, his sexual exploits have been recorded in the memoirs of those who knew him and published, for example, in the section of the journal

226

Panjandrum devoted to O'Hara and in the festschrift *Homage to Frank O'Hara.*[3] Publicly, not only in his poetry but also in his prose, he was not so open. We can ascertain at least four reasons why.

Readers must remind themselves that the atmosphere surrounding a vast majority of gays in pre-Stonewall America was one of rampant homophobia.[4] The era in which O'Hara wrote and published did not recognize homosexuality as an alternative lifestyle but deemed it either, from one extreme point of view, a crime against God, nature, and state or, from the other extreme, as quaint aberration. Martin Duberman, for example, has recalled this phenomenon in his "Gay in the Fifties," one of a number of gay memoirs currently available in print.[5] Few male or female homosexuals of those days, much less a publishing poet and a public figure who was gay and whose career had begun to thrive, willingly became victim to a heterosexual, patriarchal society eager for sacrifices. O'Hara recognized the threat. He wrote "Homosexuality," his only poem to reveal openly his view of gay life, in 1954, six years before his and Warren's relationship began, but the poem did not appear in print until May 1970, in *Poetry*, four years after his death (531). That O'Hara did not publish "Homosexuality" during his life shows his caution, because to acknowledge openly in print during the 1950s and 1960s a homosexual life-style was, for gays and lesbians, to walk to the volcano's rim and leap.

O'Hara's oeuvre, now available to the O'Hara devotee in three collections,[6] reveals that he seems to have been disinterested in using homosexuality per se as a topic for his poetry and disinterested in making his career a vehicle for political statement. O'Hara could have written any number of overtly gay poems, had he had the interest, need, or desire, and left them unpublished had he been wary only of reactions to them by a homophobic readership. He didn't. Of the hundreds of poems published posthumously in O'Hara's *Collected Poems*, only "Homosexuality" openly addresses gay life in the 1950s. O'Hara also must have realized that for him to focus overtly in any of his poems on homosexuality as subject or to acknowledge openly in his poetry his homosexual life-style or even a single sexual liaison with another man certainly would have been construed as a political statement, whether or not he meant or wanted it to be. Allen Ginsberg, O'Hara's friend, serves as an example of a poet who wrote openly homosexual poems viewed by society as political statement. Indeed, Andrew Ross has claimed that O'Hara's "blithe disregard for politics" in general was "well-known, a disregard, for example, that caused a stir when, in 1966, a minor quarrel broke out among certain literati over his refusal to sign a petition condemning U.S. involvement in Vietnam."[7] Even a quick reading of O'Hara's life's work indicates that, despite the many major, sometimes near-catastrophic sociopolitical events that occurred at the same time in which he wrote some of his best, most often anthologized work, O'Hara's poems don't reveal a political consciousness per se.

For example, "Poem [Khrushchev is coming on the right day!]," written during the cold war, opens with a reference to the leader of the Soviet Union, but ignores the importance of the Premier's visit to the United States. The poem mentions the Soviet chief only in passing and focuses, instead, in true O'Hara fashion, on the narrator's, not Khrushchev's, experiences of that particular day, on what many readers might consider unimportant minutiae of one New Yorker's everyday life: the weather, a statement remembered from a conversation of the night before, reading François Villon's poetry, and so forth. Similarly in "Personal Poem" (335–36), O'Hara frames a report of a racially motivated attack on jazz trumpeter Miles Davis with chitchat—a passage of gossip and self-absorption preceding the lines concerning Davis; one displaying black humor following them. The framing by seemingly inane lines serves to intensify the horror of the Davis incident. The framing also suggests that O'Hara viewed all experiences as equal, equally important, or equally unimportant.

We would be hard put to deny that the fear of reprisal by a homophobic society, a disinterest in homosexuality as theme or content in poetry, and a disregard for politics in general may have played a role in O'Hara's practice of omitting gender in the Warren poems. To deny them their influence on O'Hara would be foolish. However, speculation concerning the lack of gender based simply on one or any combination of the three reasons seems just as foolish and even unfair to O'Hara, who died on July 24, 1966—

three years before the birth of Gay Liberation and before activists chanted "Proud to Be Gay" and other slogans in large metropolises across the United States, especially New York and San Francisco. Both events made it "OK," at least in theory and at least among very small enclaves of artsy types and intellectuals, to be gay. Yet if we investigate the poems themselves, we learn a great deal, not only about the Warren sequence but also about O'Hara's view of gender and love in poetry.

A number of the Warren love poems "tend to be less factual, more emotional, direct, Romantic"[8] than the " 'I do this I do that' poems" (341), which readers most often associate with O'Hara. Indeed, O'Hara himself labeled them "delicate and caressing poems" in "Avenue A" (356). Although a number of the Warren poems are, for the most part, far more accessible than one often considers O'Hara's poetry to be, the sequence does contain, in typical O'Hara fashion, several poems with obscure allusions, skewed syntax, and personal references that threaten their accessibility. Readers must contend, here and there, with allusions that only O'Hara could have interpreted, such as "the clouds are imitating Diana Adams" (339), or, as in "Ballad," with unpunctuated, run-on lines and sentences that create confusing syntax. Because he often employs in his poems the names of his friends, the poems also sometimes bog down in obscurity. In "Poem [Now the violets are all gone, the rhinoceroses, the cymbals]," for example, O'Hara mentions several individuals—Janice, Kenneth, Ned—but doesn't offer their significance to the poem, if it exists.

O'Hara's practice of omitting gender identification in most of the Warren poems balances such obstacles to reader accessibility, allowing them to be understood, appreciated, and enjoyed by any reader, not by male homosexuals exclusively. For example, O'Hara's narrator addresses a "you" with quiet desire in "Now That I Am in Madrid and Can Think" and with exuberant abandon in "Steps." By ignoring the gender of "you," O'Hara frees the reader to identify "you" as anyone of any sex, any age, any race, and not simply as "Vincent Warren." He thus creates a universal "you." Simultaneously, by ignoring the gender of "I," O'Hara also creates a universal speaker, one not necessarily "Frank O'Hara" or any specific individual at all, but perhaps even the reader.

Although O'Hara obscured the identities of his lovers, a universal couple, he deftly painted their personalities, especially his speaker's. For example, O'Hara's "I," so much in love that self-restraint is impossible, virtually gushes, "oh god it's wonderful" to "love . . . so much" (371).

Because O'Hara omits gender identification from most of the Warren poems, he focuses readers' attention on matters that transcend gender, a factor that restricts the poet, the reader, and the poem. Specifically, O'Hara investigates the nature of love, its intricacies, ironies, and paradoxes—not male-male love, not male-female love, not female-female love, but individual-individual love: "I"-"you" and "you"-"I" love.

At the beginning of the sequence, the narrator of "Joe's Jacket" (329–30) contemplates the beginnings of a new love relationship. The poem concludes on Monday morning as the speaker, now at home, prepares to leave for work, borrowing "Joe's seersucker jacket," a symbol: "It is all enormity and life it has protected me and kept me here on / many occasions . . . / a precaution I loathe." Joe's jacket protects because of the friendship, that is, the platonic love, the "I" and Joe share, but the speaker both wants and does not want protection. The pun on "kept me" reveals the dilemma the "I" faces. On one hand, the jacket keeps the narrator safe by preserving and protecting; on the other, it restricts, keeping the narrator from life's successes as well as its failures. By extension, the speaker feels just as ambivalent over the new, erotic love with the poem's "you." The narrator accepts the fact that, after all, love comprises an integral part of the first day of the new week and that love has its very desirable and its less than desirable sides. The narrator, secure in the thought that, because of love, one can "face almost everything that will come up," allows the jacket simply to be "just what it is" and the future, with its potential for a lasting love, "just what happens."

In the poems that follow, O'Hara now describes the love that earlier had belonged to a "questionable moment" (330) with more emotional security and in a more favorable light. In "You Are Gorgeous and I'm Coming," for example, the narrator portrays love, and its accompanying passion, as a speeding Paris Métro train. In "Personal Poem," the speaker realizes love makes all of us happy because at least one person may be thinking of us, and love reminds the narrator in "Variations on Pasternak's 'Mein Liebchen, Was Willst Du Noch Mehr?'" (339) that, because it exists, beauty is possible. The narrator's recognition of love does even more. It offsets life's mundane moments and even the fact of our ultimate mortality. It offers the narrator warmth in "Les Luths," and in "Poem 'A la recherche d'Gertrude Stein,'" O'Hara recognizes that love strengthens life. Love makes existence as perfect as possible in an imperfect world, as the speaker in "Poem [Light clarity avocado salad in the morning]" realizes, and it affords one the possibility of understanding the darker side of life and human nature, as the narrator admits in "Poem [So many echoes in my head]." In "Now That I Am in Madrid and Can Think," love ironically lends human beings a near-divine stance in the world, and in "Cornkind," O'Hara shows it invests life and itself with meaning.

However, bliss does not characterize love in all of the Warren poems. A number of them reveal love's negative side, about which the narrator had worried in the beginning of the sequence. In "Sudden Show" (354–55), for example, the speaker, melancholy and afraid that love may be transitory, decides that "love is like the path in snow we are making / though no one else can follow, leading us only / to the ocean's sure embrace of summer." Doubt again intrudes into an otherwise happy moment in "Song" (361): "in a world where you are possible / my love / nothing can go wrong for us, tell me." The poem's last phrase, "tell me," concisely expresses the speaker's urgent need to be assured that all is well with the couple's love, while the phrase suggests the speaker's doubts. In "Those Who Are Dreaming, A Play about St. Paul" (373–75), the narrator admits to not having "known / a loveless night for so long, each night has been filled / with love" then quickly adds, afraid of jinxing the relationship, "And it might mean bad luck, to imagine / such a thing." O'Hara's speaker decides in "An Airplane Whistle (After Heine)" that too much of a good thing may be destructive to it. The concluding section of "Trying to Figure Out What You Feel" makes it apparent that the lovers are getting on one another's nerves and that the speaker has become resentful. Ultimately, O'Hara's narrator realizes love's transitory nature. Left alone in "[The light comes on by itself]" (388) to fill up time with life's mundane details, the narrator repeats five times, in urgent refrain, *I am waiting for you to love me"* after each stanza. Almost in summary, then, O'Hara asserts in "St. Paul and All That" (406–7) that love leaves one "full of anxious pleasures and pleasurable anxiety."

Although in a majority of the Warren poems O'Hara never identifies the gender of "you," he nevertheless mentions Vincent Warren by name in nearly a third of them. Yet, at the same time that he alludes to Warren, O'Hara hides the role Warren plays in the poems—and in O'Hara's line. For example, O'Hara uses Warren's first name in the opening line of "Joe's Jacket," but we are unable to ascertain from the poem anything more about "Vincent" and the poem's speaker than they, and "Jap," are traveling together. Later in the same poem, O'Hara again mentions "Vincent," but simply as a companion. The poem's "you"—the beloved of its "I"—is never linked to Warren. Instead, O'Hara employs "Vincent" simply as a part of the landscape the speaker inhabits.

In fact, even when O'Hara overtly links a poem's "you" to Warren (as happens in "The Anthology of Lonely Days," "Vincent and I Inaugurate a Movie Theater," "Vincent," "Vincent, [2]," "At Kamin's Dance Bookshop," and "St. Paul and All That"), O'Hara never discloses the romantic relationship the "I" and "you" share. We can ascertain their relationship *only* if we apply to the poems the biographical tidbits O'Hara's friends and critics have published about him.

However, O'Hara occasionally covertly refers to Warren in the poems, and for the most part, these link Warren romantically with the speaker. For example, the first letter of each line of "You Are Gorgeous and I Am Coming," an acrostic, spells *Vincent Warren,* identifying the poem's "you." Nevertheless, very few readers would think to read the poem, or any of O'Hara's work, as an acrostic. Similarly, in "Poem [That's not a cross look it's a sign of life]" (353–54), the speaker, thinking about "our elephantine history," a combination of personal and public events, repeats the name *Warren* three times, twice in "Warren G. Harding" and one in "Horace S. Warren," coyly playing with the identity of "you." Yet once again, only readers aware of O'Hara's homosexuality and his love for Vincent Warren before they approach the poem will pinpoint such obscure references and understand them.

In the Warren love poems, O'Hara presents the concept of gender as secondary to that of love. O'Hara could have used *she* to refer to the speaker's beloved, but to do so would be to lie about his relationship—and about his life. O'Hara could have used *he*, but by doing so, he would have associated love only with male-male relationships, which would have been to deny love's accessibility to, and existence in, the lives of those different than he—lesbians and heterosexuals. Indeed, to do so would be tantamount to the practice of our patriarchal, homophobic society that would have readers believe, "not by declaration but by implication,"[9] that love exists only in the realm of heterosexuality, the only territory in which it is legitimate.

Readers eager to destroy the restrictions society has placed upon the literary canon and to uphold those works historically excluded from it—a noble, laudable venture—often allow their zeal to blind them to the very work they champion and, in essence, to restrict that work exactly as those they challenge have done in the past. Readers informed about O'Hara's homosexuality may too quickly assume the lovers of the Warren poems must be male, whereas those unaware of his being gay may see no expression of homosexuality at all. By asserting their agendas upon O'Hara's work, rather than reading his poetry on its own terms, both camps reveal not only their prejudices but also their ignorance of human sexuality and human sexual practices and of the complexity of O'Hara's work. The last stanza of "Cornkind" (387), with its sexually charged concluding line, illustrates the point.

On the one hand, the stanza, "you are of me, that's what / and that's the meaning of fertility / hard and moist and moaning," will indeed suggest to some readers who are aware of O'Hara's sexual orientation that the poem is a statement of male-male love and sex. To them, the first line of the stanza will infer that the "you" and the "I" are the same sex, and those readers will continue to analyze what follows in the stanza within the perimeters that their knowledge of his homosexuality constructs around it. Indeed to them, the word *hard*, when used within the context of sexual relations, will imply a gay interpretation because, in our culture, the word is so often associated with an erect penis. On the other hand, those who read the stanza only within the perimeters of male-female sexual intercourse will see no gay possibility in "you are of me" at all. Instead, the phrase will suggest to them that the lovers share some spiritual or intellectual attribute that unites them in a manner that transcends the physical, a concept as old as, perhaps older than, the Bible. To those readers, *hard* will also suggest a male, but *moist* will connote a female, specifically vaginal fluid during intercourse. To support their interpretation, they may argue that *fertility* cannot be applied to male-male sex, because reproduction is a possibility only in male-female intercourse.

To read the stanza exclusively from the point of view of homosexuality or of heterosexuality is to deny a third possible interpretation, that the stanza actually addresses love and sexual intercourse between human beings of any sexual orientation—gay, straight, or lesbian. We can see this possibility most readily in the concluding line. Of course, *hard* may refer to an erect penis, but it may also refer to a clitoris and/or to nipples during sexual excitement. (*Hard* may also connote the type of sex in which the couple engages, some version of bondage and discipline or of sadomasochism. Such an interpretation could be supported by the last word of the stanza, *moaning*, which suggest pleasure and/or pain.) Of course, *moist* may infer vaginal fluids, but it may also refer to lubricants gays use during anal intercourse and/or to perspiration of either gender during sexual excitement. Because we can read "hard and moist" in an all-encompassing manner, *fertility* can also be interpreted not only as the heterosexual ability to reproduce oneself physically, but also, and simply, the ability of anyone to create, or give life to, anything whether physical or not: love, a poem, a child, and so forth. Similarly, "you are of me" may be interpreted as a gender reference, but we must also admit that it may refer to male-male, male-female, and female-female union of a nonphysical sort. For any reader to limit the interpretation of this stanza, or any poem in the Warren sequence, to the point of view of any one sexual orientation is to deny the stanza its obvious complexity and to be as exclusive as those who held patriarchy and heterosexuality as guiding principles when compiling the literary canon.

O'Hara's sequence of poems to Vincent Warren emphasizes the availability of love to any and all, at turns as exhilarating and depressing to one individual as to any, regardless of the sexual preferences of those who love. In short, O'Hara accepted and wrote about the experience of love as an integral part of the *human*—not the male or the female, not the heterosexual or the homosexual—condition. In his love poems to Warren, O'Hara suggests love influences life so vastly that its particulars, specifically gender, pale in comparison.

One cannot deny that fear of the repercussions from homophobia, disinterest in homosexuality as a topic of poetry, and disregard for politics may have played in varying degrees a role in O'Hara's practice of omitting gender identification. Although the omission of gender in love poetry by anyone would give meaning to the poems (as does its assertion), we cannot simply assume that O'Hara's practice of ignoring words that indicate gender only reveals a fearful, disinterested, and negligent poet. Instead, to understand most fully not only the poems but O'Hara's stance vis-à-vis the sequence and his environment, we must realize that the poet is very conscious of, and conscientious about, the effect simply common words such as *he* or *she* or *him* or *her* may have on readers. O'Hara realized that, in love poetry, omitting words that refer to gender liberates. By denying gender, O'Hara obliterated the limitations his society placed on individuals—those written about, those writing, and those reading—as well as the restrictions society placed on poems and on texts in general. Indeed, he liberated his art, and himself, by removing the obstacle to their appreciation by a homophobic society and, as important, by focussing attention on the poems' theme—love—rather than on his life. Simultaneously, by not narrowing the poems to a readership comprised solely of gays or their supporters, O'Hara gave his poems a broader possible readership. O'Hara did not want to run the risk of denying love in any of its possibilities and, consequently, chose to keep his work free of the restraints sexist language would impose upon it. While not *political* in the way that

Andrew Ross uses the word, O'Hara nevertheless made a very clear and powerful political statement by disregarding gender in his love poems for Vincent Warren. In essence, O'Hara consciously preserved, perhaps even sanctified, the universality of love by writing his love poems to Vincent Warren without regard to gender-identifying words. In fact, we may view him as having championed against the use of sexist language long before it became a cause of general concern in our society.

Notes

1. In Marjorie Perloff, *Frank O'Hara: Poet Among Painters* (New York: George Braziller, 1977), 156–63; and in Alan Feldman, *Frank O'Hara* (Boston: Twayne, 1979) 126–33 and 163, n. 7.

   Although Perloff and Feldman agree that at least some of the poems O'Hara wrote between August 1959 and July 1961 should be considered the Warren sequence, they disagree over which. They concur that the following poems belong to the sequence: "You Are Gorgeous and I'm Coming," "Saint," "To You," "Poem [Now the violets are all gone]," "Poem V(F)W," "Poem 'A la recherche d' Gertrude Stein,'" "Variations on the 'Tree of Heaven,'" "Poem [Light clarity avocado salad in the morning]," "Hôtel Transylvanie," "Poem [So many echoes in my head]," "Present," "Poem [That's not a cross look it's a sign of life]," "Sudden Snow," "Avenue A," "Now That I Am in Madrid and Can Think," "Having a Coke with You," "Song [I am stuck in traffic in a taxicab]," "An Airplane Whistle (After Heine)," "Trying to Figure Out How You Feel," "Poem [Some days I feel that I exude a fine dust]," "Cohasset," "Song [Did you see me walking by the Buick repairs?]," "Ballad," "Flag Day," "Those Who Are Dreaming, A Play about St. Paul," "Variations on Saturday," "What Appears to Be Yours," "You at the Pump," "Cornkind," "To Canada," "Vincent," "Vincent, [2]," "Poem [Twin spheres full of fur and noise]," and "St. Paul and All That."

   Perloff also includes in the sequence a number of poems Feldman ignores: "September 14, 1959 (Moon)," "Poem [Now it is the 27th]," "Poem [Wouldn't it be funny]," "Poem [O sole mio, hot diggety, nix 'I wather think I can']," "How to Get There," "Liebeslied," and "Poem [It was snowing and now}." Feldman lists several titles that Perloff excludes: "Joe's Jacket," "Personal Poem," "Variations on Pasternak's 'Mein Liebchen, Was Willst Du Noch Mehr?,'" "Les Luths," "Leafing Through Florida," "Steps," "A Warm Day for December," "[The light comes on by itself]'" "The Anthology of Lonely Days," "Vincent and I

Inaugurate a Movie Theater," "At Kamin's Dance Bookshop," and "A Chardin in Need of Cleaning."

Other poems from O'Hara's *Collected Poems* should be added to their list(s) because of the dates of the poems' composition, their concern with love, and their covert reference to Warren: "Poem [The fluorescent tubing burns like a bobby-soxer's ankles]," " 'L'Amour avait passé par là,' " "Poem [I don't know as I get what D. H. Lawrence is driving at]," "Naphtha," "Getting Up Ahead of Someone," "In Favor of One's Time," "Dances Before the Wall," "Ode to Tanaquil Leclercq," "American," "On a Birthday of Kenneth's," "Pistachio Tree at Chateau Noir," "On Rachmaninoff's Birthday #158," and "Causerie de A. F."

O'Hara's *Poems Retrieved* (See note 6), published after Perloff's and Feldman's studied, offers other poems also belonging to the Warren sequence: "Dear Vincent," "Congratulations in the Snow of Christmas Eve 1961," "Poem [You do not always seem able to decide]," "Young Girl in Pursuit of Lorca," "Poem during Poulenc's *Gloria*," "Shooting the Shit Again," "[I will always remember]," and "Poem [lost, lost]."

2. Frank O'Hara, "Those Who are Dreaming, A Play about St. Paul," in *Collected Poems*, ed. Donald Allen (New York: Alfred A. Knopf, 1979), 373–75. All poems mentioned and quoted appear in O'Hara's *Collected Poems*. The pagination for each quoted poem is documented parenthetically within the text.

3. *Panjandrum: A Journal of Contemporary Poetry*, nos. 2–3 (1973); n. p., and *Homage to Frank O'Hara*, ed. Bill Berkson and Joe LeSueur (Berkeley, CA: Creative Arts, 1980).

4. Stonewall, a gay bar, was the site of a riot by gays in 1969, an event historically used to mark the birth of Gay Liberation.

5. In *Men's Lives*, ed. Michael S. Kimmel and Michael A. Messner (New York: Macmillan, 1989), 321–44.

6. *Early Writing*, ed. Donald Allen (Bolinas, CA: Grey Fox, 1977), and *Poems Retrieved*, ed. Donald Allen (Bolinas, CA: Grey Fox, 1977), supplement O'Hara's *Collected Poems*.

7. Andrew Ross, "The Death of Lady Day," in *Frank O'Hara: To Be True to a City*, ed. Jim Elledge (Ann Arbor: University of Michigan Press, 1990), 383.

8. Perloff, *Frank O'Hara*, 117.

9. Robert K. Martin, "Introduction," in *The Homosexual Tradition in American Poetry* (Austin: University of Texas Press, 1979), xv.

IV

Crossing Cultures, Crossing Sexualities

11

Engendering the Imperial Subject: The (De)construction of (Western) Masculinity in David Henry Hwang's *M. Butterfly* and Graham Greene's *The Quiet American*

Suzanne Kehde

> By the time of his death this month at the age of eighty-six, Greene had become a kind of Grand Old Man of the left, and *The Quiet American* stood as his anti-imperialist masterpiece.
> —Richard West, "Graham Greene and *The Quiet American*"

Richard West's summary judgment[1] described a text so different from the one I remembered that it sent me back to reread Greene's novel set in Vietnam at the moment when, unnoticed by the American public, the U. S. military was about to replace the French forces being driven out by the Vietminh. Written by a member of the governing classes,[2] who during the Second World War had engaged in espionage in Africa for the British government, the novel is narrated by a character who never scrutinizes his own subject position. Here Greene's imperial attitudes, embedded in a web of colonial and gender discourses, are considerably more problematic than West's formulation suggests.

A more powerful critique of imperialism is David Henry Hwang's *M. Butterfly*, which lays bare the processes of Western male engenderment supporting the structures of imperial power.

As a Chinese-American and heir to a double culture that straddles Western-Oriental alterity, Hwang is admirably situated to undertake such a critique. The play offers a useful paradigm of imperialism by exposing and elaborating the premises on which it is based.

In the *New York Times* report of a French diplomat accused of spying, who had lived for twenty years with a Chinese lover without noticing she was a man, Hwang saw an emblem of the imbrication of gender and colonial discourses. In *M. Butterfly* he lays bare the connection between Western ideas of masculinity and the rationale for imperialism by situating his critique in a rewriting of Puccini's opera. Hwang initiates his deconstruction by a gender reversal, casting his female lead with a male actor from the Beijing opera. This man, Song Liling, acts as other for René Gallimard, who projects on his lover a fantasy of femininity reflecting his own self-image—an image of the man he thinks appropriate for his class, race, and nationality. Song Liling identifies the roles in Gallimard's "favorite fantasy" as "the submissive Oriental woman and the cruel white man."[3] Gallimard, says Hwang in the Afterword, "fantasizes that he is Pinkerton and his lover is Butterfly. By the end of the piece, he realizes that he had been Butterfly, in that the Frenchman has been duped by love; the Chinese spy, who exploited that love, is therefore the real Pinkerton" (95–96). The role identified as feminine and "Oriental" in Puccini can be played by a white Frenchman; the "dominant man" can be played by a Chinese. Further, although the structure of the play does not emphasize this reversal of gender expectations to the same degree, women can also play the dominant role, sexually, as does Isabelle, Gallimard's first lay; intellectually, as does Renée, the Danish schoolgirl who interrogates Gallimard on the rationalization for male power systems; and politically, as does Comrade Chin, Song Liling's spymaster. By describing the play as his "deconstructivist *Madame Butterfly*" (95), Hwang explicitly aligns it with theoretical preoccupations, thus, in Judith Mayne's words, "submitting theory to the test of narrative."[4]

Gallimard's fascination with the scenario of Madame Butterfly centers on the masculine power manifested by Pinkerton. Conflating Chinese and Japanese under the sign of Western alterity, he observes that "Oriental girls want to be treated bad" and congratulates himself that when he leaves Beijing, "she'll know what it's like to be loved by a real man" (6), who, the play proceeds to make clear, must be white.

For Gallimard, masculinity has always been primarily associated with sexual dominance. As a boy of twelve he had become excited by his uncle's girlie magazines—not so much by lust, as he now recognizes, but by the power he imagined himself to exert over the exposed women. When he meets Song Liling, desire and power become inextricably imbricated. The position that allows him "to abuse [her] cruelly" (36) soon comes to seem "natural," to be built into the structure of the universe. He says, "God who creates Eve to serve Adam, who blesses Solomon with his harem but ties Jezebel to a burning bed—that God is a man" (38). Thus he essentializes the engenderment that has been constructed by the contingencies of power.

But the abusive relationship he thinks to enjoy with Song Liling depends on other factors besides the expectations of Western male-female sexual relationships. Gallimard would never dare treat his wife or his girlfriend in such abusive ways—perhaps because he knows he could never make them suffer as he imagines Song Liling suffers. It is her Oriental nature, he believes, to submit to his domination. Edward Said, noting that the Orient is one of the West's most persistent images of the other, has demonstrated the historical growth of the discourse of Orientalism, which he sees as "a Western style for dominating, restructuring, and having authority over the Orient."[5] Further, he maintains that "European culture gained in strength and identity by setting itself off against the Orient as a sort of surrogate and even underground self" (20). The long tradition of Orientalism that the French and British in particular have enjoyed allows Gallimard, unchallenged, to make pronouncements like "Orientals will always submit to a greater force" (46). This dominance is not accorded to him as an individual but as a function of group entitlement. He specifically denies his personal qualifications: "We, who are not handsome, nor brave, nor powerful, yet somehow believe, like Pinkerton, that we deserve a Butterfly" (10). His sense of entitlement to a submissive Oriental Butterfly comes from his membership in the governing class of a Western imperial power.

The metaphor of man as the West, woman as the Orient that hovers in the margins of the text is not constant, vehicle and tenor being subject to reversal and recirculation. During the course of the play, the relationship between man and woman enacted between Gallimard and Song Liling comes to represent the relations between the decolonized and the imperial nations. Colonization thus entails feminization of the colonized, enforced by the masculine imperialist. This mechanism is underscored by Gallimard's feminization of Song Liling. Western imperialism has "feminized" the Third World the better to exploit it. Song Liling voices this analysis: "The West thinks of itself as masculine—big guns, big industry, big money—so the East is feminine—weak, delicate, poor" (83). The Western will to power over Asian nations parallels Gallimard's masculine bullying of the submissive Oriental "woman." Vietnam in 1961, when the French had retreated and the United States had not yet openly committed troops to Indo-China, serves as the model for Asian colonial ventures in general. Gallimard expects the United States to take over Vietnam without opposition after the French leave because, he says, "Orientals simply want to be associated with whoever shows the most strength and power" (45). As Charlotte Bunch, among others, has pointed out, what starts out as colonization of women ends up as colonization of the world.[6]

The relationship between Gallimard and Song Liling thus exhibits the stereotypical signs of both male/female and imperialist/colonized relationships. As Homi Bhabha suggests, stereotyping, a fixed form of difference, exists for the production of the colonized as a fixed reality that is at once other and yet entirely knowable.[7] Thus Gallimard's stereotyping comes from his intense need to establish difference between himself and Song Liling. Conscious that he is modeling his lover on Madame Butterfly, he nonetheless seems oblivious that he is inventing a character for Song. As Bhabha says, the closer the resemblance between the colonizer and colonized, the more closely the colonizer subjects the colonized to surveillance in order to discover difference (164). By fixing his gaze on Song—by keeping him under surveillance—Gallimard can avoid scrutinizing his own subject position.

Gallimard's understanding of his relations with Song is determined by his notions of the colonial situation in a classic case of the triumph of hope over experience. As Bhabha theorizes,

the construction of the colonial subject in discourse, and the exercise of colonial power through discourse demands an articulation of forms of difference—racial and sexual. Such an articulation becomes crucial if it is held that the body is always simultaneously inscribed in both the economy of pleasure and desire and the economy of discourse, domination and power. (150)

However, in *M. Butterfly* the "racial and sexual" are conflated; the economy of "pleasure and desire" is imbricated with the economy of "discourse, domination, and power."

The operant tool of this imbrication is the penis/phallus—the conflation of which, although resisted by some Lacanian theorists, is demonstrable in Lacan's work and, in any case, is manifest in Hwang's play. Gallimard has to read Song as woman, who signifies phallic lack. By concealing his penis Song can carry Gallimard's discourse. Throughout the play, various characters draw attention to the penis in both valorized and unvalorized states, from the anonymous Frenchman's suggestion of "misidentified equipment," to Gallimard's "How's it hangin'?" A young Danish woman meditates on "this little . . . flap of flesh." She continues:

No one knows . . . who has the bigger . . . weenie. So, if I'm a guy with a small one, I'm going to build a really big building or take over a really big piece of land or write a really long book so the other men won't know, right? But see, it never really works, that's the problem. I mean, you conquer the country, or whatever, but you're still wearing clothes, so there's no way to prove absolutely whose is bigger or smaller. And that's what we call civilized society. The whole world run by men with pricks the size of pins. (55)

Gallimard refuses to listen to a "schoolgirl who would question the role of the penis in modern society" (58). One might perhaps conclude that his downfall stems from precisely his failure to theorize the penis—ironically, to give the function of the phallus in the symbolic register too little attention.

The trajectory of Gallimard's narrative shows the construction of (Western) male subjectivity on the establishment of sameness as well as difference. Gallimard's relationship to other men is based on what Eve Kosofsky Sedgwick calls homosociality, the order of "male homosocial desire," of the "potentially erotic" (1) which marks "the structure of men's relations with other men" (2). She pointedly refuses to essentialize, however, historicizing the particular formulation of homosociality by concentrating chiefly on "the emerging pattern [in English culture of the eighteenth and nineteenth centuries] of male friendship, mentorship, rivalry [which] was in an intimate and shifting relationship to class [and no element of which] can be understood outside of its relation to women and the gender system as a whole."[8] Although her study *Between Men* mainly confines its examples to the British novel of the mid-eighteenth to mid-nineteenth centuries, her perceptions are generally applicable to the power structures Hwang posits as the factors engendering Gallimard, who appears to have been raised in a middle-class professional French family and trained to the civil service in much the same way as his historical counterpart in Britain. Gallimard's retrospective interrogation of his sexuality is marked by a strong homosocial component. During a replay of a scene from his student years, a friend invites him to a swim party with this description: "There's no moon out, their boobs are flapping, right? You close your eyes, reach out—it's grab bag, get it? Doesn't matter whose ass is between whose legs, whose teeth are sinking into who" (8). The language of pressure to engage in aggressive, anonymous group sex suggests that the most important feature is the participation of other men.

Marc, the boyhood friend at whose father's condo this group sex took place, appears as a voice "everywhere now" (32), reinforcing throughout Gallimard's imprisonment the unacknowledged premises that have constructed Gallimard's relations to other men and to women, premises that in short have engendered him. These, the premises of homosociality, are constructed on (major) sameness as well as on (minor) difference, on the acquisition and maintenance of power on "our" side as an extension of self. The exchange of women, Sedgwick points out, is one of the major ways in which relations between men are secured (179). Just such an exchange has taken place: The image of Marc demands a return on his gift of Isabelle, whom he persuaded to initiate Gallimard into sex. Gallimard, however, pinned in the dirt under her, thought only, "So this is it?" The power relations implicit in his inferior position as much as the physical discomfort of having his buttocks pounded into the ground seem to have severely restricted his enjoyment.

The acquisition of Song Liling, the ostensibly lovesick lotus blossom he delights in humiliating and neglecting, advances Gallimard in the French colonial service. The ambassador to China, impressed by Gallimard's sexual swaggering, transfers the vice-consul and promotes Gallimard. Retrospectively Gallimard understands how the ambassador's reaction reveals the operations of the homosocial order: "Toulon . . . approves! I was learning the benefits of being a man. We form our own clubs, sit behind thick doors, smoke—and celebrate the fact that we're still boys" (46). As suggested by Lacan's dictum that the phallus is veiled, echoed here by the schoolgirl's meditation on the "weenie," any given homosocial order is felt to be in flux; the hierarchy of sameness, unlike the hierarchy of difference, can never be presumed permanently fixed.

The discourses of gender and colonialism whose operations Hwang sought to expose are omnipresent in Greene's *The Quiet American* with no critique of gender stereotypes and little of imperialist assumptions, certainly without any acknowledgment that there might be some connection between them. Like Gallimard, Fowler reads his Vietnamese lover as doubly other in her gender and nationality but, unlike him, for Fowler that fixed difference is not the focus of his most earnest scrutiny. The major strand in Fowler's engenderment—the one that occupies him most consistently, driving him at last to complicity in murder—is the homosocial, which in the colonial setting is maintained by both gender and colonial discourses. The construction of Fowler's subjectivity depends primarily on his surveillance of signs of sameness in Pyle; he needs to scrutinize all suggestion of similarity in order to focus on difference. The overt emphasis on the homosocial order throughout Greene's public school and Oxford education must have made its primacy seem natural, much in the way, satirized by Hwang, that Gallimard comes to see man's domination of woman as mandated by the universe itself.

Sedgwick's study of homosociality notes René Girard's work on "the relation of rivalry between the two active members of an erotic triangle. . . . The bond that links the two rivals is as intense and potent as the bond that links either of the rivals to the beloved." Girard's analysis focuses on the "male-centered novelistic tradition of high European culture" (Sedgwick, *Between Men*, 21), a tradition to which *The Quiet American* clearly belongs. The rivalry that forms between Fowler and Pyle runs conspicuously along the opposed axes of sameness and difference. Seen alongside the constant surveillance this rivalry demands, the construction of Phuong as doubly other is static—always-already present, it is sited in a latent nostalgia. In Bhabha's terms, Phuong is a stereotype of the exotic. Fowler mounts a satiric critique against Pyle that sweeps from his conduct as a U.S. economic adviser to his understanding of Phuong's character, intellect, and values—matters on which Fowler feels eminently qualified to pontificate. He sneers at Pyle's reasons for the ostensibly humanitarian American presence in French Indo-China, pressing for a scrutiny of the concept of democracy, which, assuming that government depends on the consent of the governed, has been a reasonably stable component of modern concepts of liberty. He mocks the simplistic evocation of the ideal by noting the express wish of Phuong, his mistress and eventually Pyle's fiancée, to see the Statue of Liberty. He attempts to call into question the idea of liberty promulgated by Pyle. Holed up in a watchtower waiting for the Viet Cong to attack, he calls across to the two Vietnamese guards, "*La liberté— qu'est ce que c'est la liberté?*", eliciting a remonstrance from Pyle: "You stand for the importance of the individual as much as I do."[9] Fowler, however, objects to Pyle not only as an individual but also as a representative of the United States, whose citizens he resents as a class: "I was tired of the whole pack of them with their private stores of Coca-Cola and their portable hospitals and their too wide cars and their not quite latest guns" (31). In short, he falls back on the unexamined assumptions of privilege due nationals of a European imperial power.

In the "natural" way one understands the hidden hierarchies

of one's own culture, Fowler knows how to negotiate the power structures of the multicultural homosocial order of Saigon. Lying in his bed smoking opium, he refuses to arise to greet the (Vietnamese) police officer who summons him to the Sureté. He is "fond of" and dependent upon Dominguez, his (male) Indian assistant who, like a well-trained American secretary (female) mediates the local culture for him. He recognizes the legal power of Vigot at the Sureté, who investigates Pyle's death but treats Fowler reciprocally as a comrade, just as Fowler treats Trouin, the pilot who takes him on a bombing raid, or the French officers he gambles with on trips up-country.

Such an amicable relationship between the two major Orientalist powers is a comparatively recent historical development. Said describes their intense late nineteenth-century competition for imperial acquisition, pointing out that the Sykes-Picot agreement of 1916 to carve up Arabia between them—which, ultimately determining national boundaries in the Middle East, led to the present unrest—was a deliberate attempt to control this rivalry. *The Quiet American* suggests that it disappeared with the collapse of both empires and, perhaps equally important, the appearance of the United States on the imperial scene. This appearance, constituting an assault on powerful members of an existing homosocial order, minimizes the focus on difference and fosters perceptions of sameness between the French and British.

Fowler mounts a verbal attack on American involvement in Vietnam in an attempt to maintain his own position in the homosocial order. Privately and publicly Fowler denies involvement, defining himself as a reporter rather than a correspondent: "I wrote what I saw. I took no action—even an opinion is a kind of action" (28). Denying that he himself has any "mental concepts" (94), he lays claim to an impossible objectivity, the hypothetical "view from nowhere." Under Pyle's questioning, he admits his sympathy toward old-style imperial colonialism: "I'd rather be an exploiter who fights for what he exploits, and dies with it" (96). In the narrative economy, he figures the British attitude toward the European colonial presence, the disengagement that Captain Trouin attributes to the whole nation: "We are fighting all of your wars, but you leave us the guilt" (151). There is historical support for Trouin's position: the British encouraged the reconquest of Vietnam in 1945, providing arms to the French soldiers interned by the Japanese during World War II. In spite of his pretence of disengagement, Fowler claims membership in the club of "the old colonial peoples" (157).

The impulse to typify, which Bhabha perceives as a ubiquitous tool in the colonial's kit, plays a large role in Fowler's management of his world. Early in the novel, Phuong's function as a symbol of Vietnam is specified; she is *"[le] pays qui te ressemble"* (14). Successful with the labels *woman* and *Oriental*, he tries to use the same technique with *American* although, as his constant scrutiny suggests, he feels less secure in his attempt to constitute a white man as a "fixed difference." He positions Pyle as "the quiet American" of the title, the man full of ironies but without ambiguities, who belongs to "a psychological world of great simplicity, where you talked of Democracy and Honor without the *u* as it's spelt on old tombstones, and you mean what your father meant by the same words" (90). Falling back on a trait associated with America from the time of Columbus, Fowler repeatedly comments on Pyle's innocence. His implication that there is an American character historically consistent and impervious to contingency essentializes Pyle.

This savage stereotyping comes from Fowler's intense need to repress his knowledge of sameness and establish difference between himself and Pyle. Invested as he is in the position of (ex)colonial disengagé, he must at all cost avoid noticing the resemblances between their situations. By fixing his gaze on Pyle—by keeping him under surveillance in his role of reporter—he can avoid self-scrutiny. However, Fowler is quite aware of the similarity in their colonial empowerment: the Vietnamese "don't want our white skins around telling them what they want" (94). In a racist conflation of the peasants and their animals, he tells Pyle that "in five hundred years ... small boys will be sitting on the buffaloes. I like the buffaloes, they don't like our smell, the smell of Europeans. And remember—from a buffalo's point of view you are European too" (95). In order to prove Pyle wrong, Fowler insists on both their common imperial status and the continuity of Western imperialism.

    In spite of Fowler's frenzied attempts to establish and maintain
difference, the similarities between Fowler and Pyle are brought
into focus by their common attraction to Phuong. Until Pyle declares his interest in her, Fowler regards him as "a prize pupil"
(24). In a classic demonstration of the structure of the homosocial,
Fowler's posture toward Pyle is paternal, with the familiarity an
older man from an older culture feels free to use toward a younger
one. He interrogates Pyle and berates him about the simplistic
nature of his mental operations, his dependence on romantic abstractions (though Fowler's cynicism itself is merely an inversion
of romanticism). When the dialogue goes in unexpected directions,
Fowler blames these turns on Pyle. He complains that "my conversations with Pyle seemed to take grotesque directions. . . . Was
it because of his sincerity that they so ran off the customary rails?
His conversation never took the corners" (104); that is, it never
follows the direction laid down by the paternal speaker, the acknowledged superior in the homosocial order. Their relationship
is well established by the time Pyle becomes a rival for Phuong—
a development as much a product of that relationship as a response to her. Their contest for Phuong echoes the contest between
European and American imperialism: it is a question of who has
the biggest resources at his disposal (Hwang's Danish schoolgirl
could provide a Lacanian insight here). Pyle can offer her "security and respect" (78). Because he possesses "the infinite riches of
respectability," he can marry her, whereas Fowler, whose wife
refuses to divorce him, offers only a temporary home. Fowler
becomes so obsessed with Pyle that he reflects, "It was as if I had
been betrayed, but one is not betrayed by an enemy" (140). This
perception gestures toward the structure of his relationship with
Pyle but does not acknowledge it. Only with Pyle's death—in
which Fowler tells himself he must connive because Pyle's endorsement of terrorist activities endangers the civilian population—and the consequent disappearance of Pyle's threat to
Fowler's domestic peace can Fowler acknowledge his affection for
Pyle. Pyle's death forces Fowler to ponder the similarities from
which he has averted his gaze: "Was I so different from Pyle? . . .
Must I too have my foot thrust in the mess of life before I saw the
pain?" (186).

The Oedipal nature of the homosocial relationship [10] with its antifilial outcome is underlined by Fowler's observation that "the sight of Oedipus emerging with his bleeding eyeballs from the palace at Thebes would surely give a better training for life today" (182)—better than the American movie articulating Pyle's fantasy, in which the hero rescues a girl, kills his enemy, and leads a charmed life. In Fowler's reinscription of the Oedipus myth, the father triumphs in the ritual *agon*.

Quite capable of understanding that he is "inventing a character" (133) for Phuong (as he has for Pyle without acknowledgment), Fowler is nonetheless oblivious to his part in her expropriation. Abjuring "mental concepts" and thus construing his environment in material terms, he thinks of Phuong much as the drunken Granger does, as "a piece of tail" (36). He muses "she was the hiss of steam, the clink of the cup, she was a certain hour of the night and the promise of rest" (12), but his characteristic thought of her is of "the soft hairless skin" when he goes off to sleep with his hand between her legs—in which position, not so incidentally, he formulates his last idea about Pyle, which is inextricably imbricated with his idea of himself: "Am I the only one who really cared for Pyle?" (22). His irritated response to Pyle's concern for Phuong's best interest shows his perception of Phuong: " 'If it's only her interests you care about, for God's sake leave Phuong alone. Like any other woman she'd rather have . . .' the crash of a mortar saved Boston ears from the Anglo-Saxon word" (59). In short, in Fowler's psychological economy, Phuong is only a cunt to be had for the asking without any obligation on his part to arouse or fulfill desire.

Fowler does not scrutinize any aspect of male engenderment beyond the parameters of homosocial rivalry; he does interrogate the sign *man*, but only as regards American usage. He pretends not to understand what Granger means by "a man's man" (66) or by the compliment "Anyway you're a man" (36) to an acquaintance who accompanies Granger on a quest for girls. Fowler, himself no stranger to brothels, once again averts his gaze from self-scrutiny in order to persist in his perpetual monitoring of difference in similarity.

Articulating no regrets for the British empire itself, Fowler needs only the homosocial colonial situation. Gallimard, stripped of all support for his engenderment, forced to recognize that he is object in Song Liling's narrative as well as subject of his own, has at last no site from which to position his subjectivity. Fowler, however, can continue to exist as long as he is supported by the colonial situation, a white man still comfortably engendered in a homosocial order empowering white men bent on careers of privilege and exploitation.

But the ideology of privilege is veiled from its beneficiaries. Fowler must remain oblivious to the deep structures of gender differentiation upon which imperialism, as Hwang so eloquently shows, ultimately rests. Thus the features of imperial rule rooted in the female imaginary, which are critiqued in *M. Butterfly*, appear as "nature" in *The Quiet American*. Although Greene does suggest that the rivalry of imperial nations, specifically that of Britain and the United States, can be read through the lens of the family romance, there is no hint that he recognizes the way in which imperialism subsumes the colonized into already existent structures of gender relations. Although the defining characteristics of the imperial subject fingered by Hwang are evident in Greene, the destructiveness of the model seems merely contingent, an accident. In no way does Greene address the gender assumptions underlying the justification of imperial power. Indeed, Fowler's cynicism barely covers the traces of Greene's nostalgia for the power configurations of nation and gender prevalent before the Second World War. Benedict Anderson speaks to this situation: "It is always the ruling classes . . . that long mourn the empires, and their grief always has a stagey quality to it."[11] This observation nicely conveys the tone of *The Quiet American*, which throbs with an urgent desire to seize the day when the sun is already sinking fast.

Notes

1. Richard West, "Graham Greene and *The Quiet American*," *New York Review of Books* 24 (May 1991): 49.
2. Greene, born into an upper-middle-class professional family, was a

member of the governing classes. His father was headmaster of Berk-hampsted School, where Greene himself was educated before he went up to Oxford. At both, but particularly at school, the attitudes and values appropriate to a citizen of the empire would have been incul-cated: "The public schools . . . were geared to the empire's needs. Many of the ideals they aimed at, the qualities they worked to instill in their wards—notions of service, feelings of superiority, habits of authority—were derived from, and consequently dependent upon, the existence of an empire: of colonial subjects to serve, feel superior to, and exert authority over"; from Brian Porter, *The Lion's Share: A Short History of British Imperialism, 1850–1970* (London: Longman, 1975), 103.

3. David Henry Hwang, *M. Butterfly* (New York: Plume, 1989), 17. Sub-sequent references will be in parentheses in the text.
4. Judith Mayne, "Walking the *Tightrope* of Feminism and Male Desire," in *Men in Feminism*, ed. Alice Jardine and Paul Smith (New York: Methuen, 1987), 70.
5. Edward W. Said, *Orientalism* (New York: Vintage, 1979), 20.
6. Cited in Arthur Brittan, *Masculinity and Power* (Oxford: Blackwell, 1989), 83.
7. Homi K. Bhabha, "The Other Question: Difference, Discrimination and the Discourse of Colonialism," in *Literature, Politics and Theory* (New York: Methuen, 1986), 164.
8. Eve Kosofsky Sedgwick, *Between Men: English Literature and Male Homosocial Desire* (New York: Columbia Univ. Press, 1985) 1–2.
9. Graham Greene, *The Quiet American* (1955; reprint, New York: Pen-guin 1962), 97.
10. Sedgwick, *Between Men*, 22.
11. Benedict Anderson, *Imagined Communities* (London: Verso, 1983; re-print, 1991), 111.

12

J. R. Ackerley and the Ideal Friend

David Bergman

Perhaps only the lesbian transvestites is a more assiduous student of male heterosexual behavior than the homosexual man, but homosexual men—because they are males and can socialize with straight males in all-male contexts—have a privileged place from which to examine the subject. Homosexual men and lesbian transvestites are keen observers of straight masculinity for a variety of reasons, but no doubt key among them is the desire "to pass" in order to be accepted as a heterosexual male. But passing as a straight man is more than trying to take on the protective coloring that helps homosexuals and lesbian transvestites survive in an intensely homophobic society; for both groups the role has a particular allure of power and freedom, not to mention eroticism. And it is also a source of deep resentment and conflict. Straight masculinity—and let it be clear from the outset that for me the phrase is not redundant—straight masculinity is never a neutral subject of inquiry.

But homosexual men are not merely students of heterosexual masculinity; in some sense they are its creators. A number of scholars (David W. Halperin and Eve Kosofsky Sedgwick among them) have argued that both in English and German the term *homosexuality* predates the invention of the word *heterosexuality*. Indeed, heterosexual seems to have been invented to give semantic symmetry to the taxonomic label of homosexual. Who first used these terms and what was meant by them remain in doubt and perhaps never will be resolved, but whether the terms were first created by Karl Heinrich Ulrichs, Karl Maria Kertbeny, or John Addington Symonds, the fact remains that the words were coined by homosexual men.[1] Moreover, many of the most powerful images of heterosexual masculinity have been homosexual men— from Ivor Novello to Rock Hudson and James Dean; thus gay or homosexual men have been among the most enduring models of heterosexual masculinity.

Whether it is useful to think of homosexuality as giving rise to heterosexuality, or as in Sedgwick's case as poles on a spectrum of homosociality, it is important to note that their differences do not keep them far apart. They are separated not by cultural mountains and oceans, but at most by picket fences and railroad tracks. They are nodes in a highly complex interactive communications systems. They are nextdoor neighbors, with abutting property lines.

Strict constructionists of sexuality, of course, will argue that drawing a line *is* the problem, and that such categories as heterosexual and homosexual are merely imposed on the great polymorphous perversity of the population, a mere invention that has regimented itself. I do not mean to take issue with such an analysis of how sexuality should be conceptualized. Perhaps the concepts that the anthropologist Gilbert Herdt has developed can make clear the mapping of cultural boundaries I have in mind. Herdt argues for the existence of a *gay* culture, as opposed to a *homosexual* culture, in which there is a "distinctive system of rules, norms, attitudes, and, yes, beliefs from which the culture of gay men is made, a culture that sustains the social relations of same-sex desire."[2] Herdt's gay cultural space is epitomized by the gay ghetto, but is not limited to it. And just as the gay ghetto exists within the straight city, sharing many of its properties, such as fuzzy, ever-shifting borders, so to the cultural space of gay writing exists within but is ambiguously sectioned off from the straight literary practice. In homosexual culture, even more than in gay culture, boundaries were tightly sealed because of the need to keep sexuality a secret, albeit at times, an open secret.

Homosexual and gay writers have spent a great deal of energy surveying this boundary, although in the last twenty years the figure of the straight man has had a diminishing presence in gay literature, at least as an erotic object. In an as-yet-unpublished essay "Straight Women, Gay Men," Edmund White notes:

When I was a kid back in the fifties . . . gay men hated each other so much they longed to seduce heterosexual men, "real men." . . . After the 1960s all that began to change. . . . No longer was their fondest hope (a hope by definition always frustrated) to sleep with straight men. Now those gay men who prized rough-and-ready masculinity began to embody it. In droves gay men went to the gym, sprouted mustaches, took up such professions as truck driving, heavy construction and farming. . . . Masculinity seemed more like a costume than an eternal and natural privilege.[3]

For Edmund White, the homosexual fascination with straight masculinity was structured by three interrelated myths about sexuality and gender. The first was that masculinity and sexuality were inseparable categories that were "eternal and natural." Second, that these "eternal and natural" properties gave the individual superiority, "privilege," glamour. Finally, because of his innate and abiding inferiority, the homosexual will always lack these qualities and have access to them vicariously only by loving the heterosexual male. Gay liberation, by unpacking the notion of the "eternal and natural privilege" of heterosexuality and espousing the value of same sex desire, has converted "masculinity" into a costume that can be worn by all without any particular distinction. In the debate over allowing acknowledged homosexuals into the armed forces, one of the most curious arguments surrounds the shower room where homophobes fear the lustful homosexual gaze will corrupt the sanctity of the heterosexual male body. A different fear seems to be behind this argument: the straight man's narcissistic loss of the adoring but covert gaze of homosexual men. For if the straight soldier loses his privileged licensed gaze—and what guy hasn't "clocked out his buddies"?—he will no longer be able to bask in the furtive, adoring one.

Gay writers, freed to look at gay men approvingly, have gazed less and less at their straight cohorts. Consequently the heterosexual male plays a stronger role in pre-Stonewall homosexual writing than in post-Stonewall gay writing, and perhaps no one has more assiduously charted the force fields between the homosexual and the heterosexual than J. R. Ackerley, whose entire oeuvre seems concerned with it. I turn to his work and to examine it in historical relief as a point from which contemporary gay writers have moved.

J. R. Ackerley is a difficult person to place in literary history— a little too young for Bloomsbury and a little too old for the Auden gang, he nevertheless was a close friend of E. M. Forster and a generous supporter of the young Auden. From 1935 to 1959 he was the literary editor of *The Listener.* Anthony Howard has called him "the greatest Literary Editor of his time—perhaps of all time," and *The Times* in its obituary called him an "incomparable" editor. A playwright and novelist, his strongest work as a writer was his nonfiction: a memoir of India, *Hindoo Holiday* (1932); a study of canine affection, *My Dog Tulip* (1956, rev. 1966); and an exploration of his relationship to his father, *My Father and Myself,* (1968) finished the last year of his life and published posthumously. Although Charles Monteith has called him "one of the best writers of prose of this century," his limited output and his employment of rather oddly mixed genres have kept his work from being fully appreciated.[4]

Yet as varied as these books appear to be, all of Ackerley's work deals with the same obsessive theme: losing the Ideal Friend. The Ideal Friend, like all ideals, is by definition never found, although his sighting is always rumored: in Ackerley's emotional calculus, the Ideal Friend is a sum that is approached and then fades into an approximate distance. In his masterpiece *My Father and Myself* he presents his definition of the Ideal Friend:

I think I can put him together in a partly negative way by listing some of his main disqualifications. He should not be effeminate, indeed perfectly normal; I did not exclude education but did not want it, I could supply all that myself. . . . He should admit me but no one else; he should be physically attractive to me and younger than myself—the younger the better, as close to innocence; finally he should be on the small side, lusty, circumcised, physically healthy and clean.[5]

It is useful from the outset to see the contradictions that run through this definition. Ackerley was himself aware that his desire to find the Ideal Friend may seem a rather dubious enterprise on moral and practical grounds: "It may be thought that I had set myself a task so difficult of accomplishment as almost to put success purposely beyond my reach; it may be thought too that the reason why this search was taking me out of my own class into the working class . . . was guilt" (126). But one contradiction may escape immediate notice: English working-class males are rarely circumcised. Ackerley set himself an almost impossible task when he set out to find a man both from the working classes and circumcised. Again, Ackerley appears to favor men of a robust constitution, nevertheless he prefers' those who are smaller. The Ideal Friend must be smart but not too smart, strong but not too strong, heterosexual but not too heterosexual.

The definition is quite obviously filled with internalized homophobia, of which Ackerley was also well aware. The ostensibly heterosexual Ideal Friend—what I will simply call the I.F. (the great *IF* of Ackerley's romantic desire)—maintains the elevated position of normality, while the homosexual is lowered to the abnormal, the sick, the perverse. Of the young sailor who came closest to fulfilling the requirements of I.F., Ackerley wrote:

I did not want him to think me 'queer' and himself a part of homosexuality, a term I disliked since it included prostitutes, pansies, pouffs and queens. Though he met some of my homosexual friends, I was always on edge in case they talked in front of him the loose homosexual chatter we talked among ourselves. My sailor was a sacred cow and must be protected against all contaminations. (127)

Ackerley condescends to his I.F., whom he prefers to be poorer, smaller, as well as less educated, but despite this condescension—perhaps because of it—he wishes to protect both himself from the humiliation of being thought "queer" and the Ideal Friend from the contagion of being around homosexuals. Ackerley regards homosexuality as a contagion that might spread and that demands eternal vigilance to control. A word at the wrong time or the wrong place is all that is needed to corrupt the Ideal Friend who must remain innocent. In deference to the vulnerability of the Ideal Friend, whose innocence can never be immunized against the queer, Ackerley must adopt the manner of the heterosexual no matter how alien to himself or frustrating to the formation of genuine friendship.

But we can exaggerate the degree of condescension. The metaphor of the I.F. as a "sacred cow" sounds like a put-down, but it's not. Animals have a particularly elevated status in Ackerley's work; no one is treated with more respect than his beloved dog Queenie, who is the heroine of his novel *We Think the World of You* and *My Dog Tulip*. Queenie's special role is anticipated in Ackerley's travel book *Hindoo Holiday*, which recounts his short stay in India, where he encountered the sacredness of beasts with Sharma, the maharaja's "lover boy." "I gazed in wonder and admiration," Ackerley records,

at the huge white marble form and calm majestic face. How peaceful were the long drooping ears! How beautiful the line of the heavy dewlap and gentle jowls. . . . The large dark glowing eyes set far apart were finely marked with black. . . . The great white face [bore] a grave wisdom and benignity of expression. . . . No wonder, I thought, these beasts are generated and the females thought to be the seat of Generation. I glanced at Sharma. . . . 'Ah, my fine young bullocks!' I thought.[6]

To be a sacred cow is to be something quite extraordinary! Powerful, peace, and privileged, the sacred cow represents a divine androgyny whose sensitivity and nurturance is never compromised by weakness or nerves.

Nor should Ackerley's desire for "innocence" be viewed as condescending because he saw himself, despite his rather large number of sex partners, as essentially innocent. For Ackerley the sure sign of innocence is a belief in romantic love between equals. In *My Father and Myself*, Ackerley recalls a Persian whom he knew from his Cambridge days when Ackerley mooned over him from afar. Ten years later they meet again. The Persian, who is gay, invites Ackerley back to his flat where, according to Ackerley, "my apparently artless ideas of love had no place in his highly sophisticated repertoire . . . and the attentions and even acrobatics he required to stimulate his jaded sex were not merely disagreeable to me but actually uncomfortable. . . . He said scathingly at last, 'The trouble with you is you're innocent' " (120). The I.F. must be innocent so that he can be Ackerley's equal. Sex that does not derive from love is tainted by the power relations of age and class. Jadedness—the sin of lower-class heterosexuals—is almost as repellent to Ackerley as the sophistication of upper-class homosexuals, because it makes him feel inferior. What Ackerley really wants is to create a space outside of either homo- or heterosexuality where he and the I.F. can live in childlike innocence, freed from the labelling that elevates one at the expense of the other.

We can, I think, regard this hypothesized space as an escape to some prelapsarian world, and frequently it is such a space. But it also can be, as Thomas Yingling has argued "a privileged site outside cultural convention from which it is possible to critique the patriarchal structures of bourgeois desire," a place that is "marginalized and potentially revolutionary."[7] Ackerley describes his place on the sexual map as beyond labels; nevertheless, he "stood among the men, not among the women. Girls I despised; vain, silly creatures. . . . Their place was the harem, from which they should never have been released; true love, equal and understanding love, occurred only between men. I saw myself therefore in the tradition of the Classic Greeks surrounded and supported by all the famous homosexuals of history" (118).

I do not want to excuse Ackerley's misogyny or his gynophobia undisguised in this and other passages. But I do not want his misogyny to obscure the revolutionary potential of the equality he wishes to achieve with other men—the "equal and understanding love" that he feels occurs "only between men." Such mutuality of affection *is* a radical departure for an Englishman of his generation. Significantly, Ackerley locates that equality within "the Greek view of life," an ideology he inherited from Goldsworthy Lowes Dickinson, the teacher of E. M. Forster and his closest friend and mentor, and from Edward Carpenter, himself an apostle of Whitmanian adherence.

The impulse among British homosexuals to seek sexual partners from a different class is one of the more problematic elements in the structure of their desires. It is all too simple to see this tendency as exploitation of the poor. No doubt exploitation was involved. As Jeffrey Weeks points out, Roger Casement was in the habit of recording not only the size of his pick-ups' penises, but their price.[8] Yet for Edward Carpenter, "The blending of Social Strata in masculine love seems . . . one of its pronounced, and social hopeful features,"[9] and Carpenter's life-long relationship to George Merrill appears to have been unmarred by economic exploitation. Ackerley's relationship with working-class men was neither as exploitive as Casement's nor as idealistic as Carpenter's. W. H. Auden, I believe, shrewdly sees both the appeal and the necessity of Ackerley's arrangement:

All sexual desire presupposes that the loved one is in some way "other" than the lover: the eternal and, probably, insolvable problem for the homosexual is finding a substitute for the natural differences, anatomical and psychic, between a man and a woman. . . . A homosexual who is like Mr. Ackerley, an intellectual and reasonably well-off is very apt to become romantically enchanted by the working class, whose lives, experiences, and interests are so different from their own, and to whom, because they are poorer, the money and comforts he is able to provide can be a cause for affectionate gratitude.[10]

For Auden, Ackerley's involvement with the working class is explained by mutual give and take. Ackerley could share with his working-class lovers the pleasure of exchanging different sorts of experience, and for the material benefits Ackerley could provide they could return the pleasure of having truly helped. Auden is impatient with anyone who might question the morality of such an arrangement. "A great deal of nonsense has been spoken and written about the sinfulness of giving and receiving money for sexual favors," and Auden wants none of it.[11]

But Weeks suggests another strain to the cross-class tendencies of English homosexuals. He finds these liaisons "suggestive of the guilt-ridden fear of relationships within their own class."[12] Ackerley's anxiety about what his friends might say or do in the presence of the I.F. suggests his discomfort with his own class status. Ackerley's hold on upper-middle-class status was extremely loose. His parents were from the lower classes, and through hard work and good luck, Roger Ackerley made a fortune in the fruit importing business by finding successful ways of promoting bananas. (One of his more amusing stunts was running a contest awarding £1000 to the first person to discover a "perfectly straight banana.")[13] When Roger died, he left his family in straightened conditions, and J. R. Ackerley struggled all his life to earn enough to maintain his mother, aunt, and neurotic sister.

As Ackerley views it, the "equal and understanding love" of the I.F. is threatened on three flanks: on the right by silly, manipulative girls; on his left by competitive capitalism and materialism, which breaks down the compassion necessary for real equality and emotional mutuality, and from his rear by heartless pouffs and queens. Only homosexuals, like himself, who honored " 'the manly respectability' of our relationship" are capable of achieving equality, mutuality, and understanding (127). Indeed, one might trace Ackerley's misogyny to the competition between heterosexual women and homosexual men over the pool of I.F.s. As he wrote in *My Father and Myself:* "The girlfriend was a situation all too liable to be found in the lives of normal boys, and . . . they had to be admitted; I never suffered much from jealousy and the Ideal Friend could have a girl or wife if he wished, so long as she did not interfere with me. No wife ever failed to interfere with me" (137). For Ackerley, female homophobia results from female possessiveness. Under the conditions of late capitalism, women "traffick in men," as exchange quantities that establish their value.

No doubt, here both Ackerley and I risk strenuous opposition. Michael Pollak has argued that "of all the different types of masculine sexual behavior, homosexuality is undoubtedly the one whose functioning is most strongly suggestive of the market."[14] Traditionally both in Europe and Asia, homosexual behavior has had no other institutional structure but the house of prostitution. But just as homosexuals have entered into the sexual market, they have also complained most vehemently against it. What I think needs to be explored is not merely the way men treat others as objects, but how they objectify themselves.

It is odd, to say the least, that feminist theory—which has developed a subtle, elaborate, and accurate analysis of how men objectify women—has failed to see in its equally subtle, elaborate, and accurate analysis of heterosexual male ego structure the very same objectification. If, as Nancy Chodorow has argued, masculinity is defined through greater ego independence and firmness of ego boundaries that block both emotional expression and empathetic understanding, then masculinity is by far the more objectlike gender role.[15] If men don't complain about such objectification, it is because objectification rather than chaffing against a man's sense of his masculinity, confirms and extols it. This desire for objectification becomes the greatest obstacle in becoming the Ideal Friend.

I want to look at two instances in Ackerley's work where the drive *for* objectification becomes the obstacle to ideal friendship. The first occurs in his play *Prisoners of War*, his first published work. The action takes place during the Great War in a hotel in the Alps where the Germans have interned captured British officers. In many ways this magic mountain ought to be the marginal site where ideal friendship should be able to blossom, but it's not. The play follows two pairs of homoerotic relations between Tetford and Rickman, and between Conrad and Grayle. Tetford and Conrad are older, socially higher, and homosexual; Rickman and Grayle are younger, of a lower class, and assertively heterosexual. Tetford's relations with Rickman work out by the end of the play because their relationship has been squarely placed within the objectifying context of a business partnership. In Act III, they decide to go to Canada—Rickman's country—to work together. Tetford's suggestion is carefully monitored to erase any strong emotions: "I thought we might start something [in Canada] on our own. We'd pull along all right together, I guess—and you need me to keep hold on you." Rickman agrees, but with one caveat, "Well, you ain't what one's call extra tough; and you need to be tough out there." Tetford replies "scornfully," "I bet I'm as tough as you—at the moment." They shake on their "partnership" and according to stage directions *"Something passes between them."*[16] The preconditions of toughness and business—both objectifying conditions—are necessary before any contact can be made.

Conrad's relationship to Grayle—his "holy grail," so to speak— is less successful. Suffering from depression, Conrad asks Grayle while stroking "the curly head affectionately," if he'll "stick by" him. Grayle, who suffers this affection because—again according to the stage directions—he had "been educated at a good public school," breaks away as soon as others appear. Grayle cannot deal with Conrad's increasing demands to empathize with his subjective experience. When Conrad suffers a psychotic break, Grayle is unwilling to be left alone in the room with him, and it is Tetford who upbraids Conrad for his lack of sympathy, "Can't you be decent to him even now?" Grayle's need for objectification— his fear of subjectivity—is exemplified by his affair with Madame Louis, the Jewish widow, who in the antisemitism of the day is quite transparently a fortune hunter. Grayle can manage his relationship with Mme Louis because it is a mercantile exchange that requires no intersubjectivity. In some of the more famous lines of the play, Mme Louis asks Conrad whether it is true that he "does not like much the fair sex." "The fair sex?" Conrad asks her in reply, "Which sex is that?" (119) As a Jew, she is neither "fair" in coloring nor in her business deals. She exemplifies the commodification of sex that Ackerley associates with heterosexuality.

The second incident takes place in India—again a locale that Ackerley hopes might take him outside of capitalist relations. But colonialization and patriarchy once more have warped the concept of masculinity despite the rhetoric extolling friendship. Ackerley is told that during *Holi,* a festival in honor of Krishna, "all men are equal and may be treated so in the name of Friendship" (201), but the reality falls far short. Narayan and Sharma are best friends, who, although married, sleep together, but without sex. Once Sharma, who is the maharaja's paramour, kissed Narayan who pretended to sleep. Sharma tells Narayan that if Narayan dies, he could not continue living. Ackerley sees in this relationship the asymmetry that ruins all his own friendships. Narayan's feelings for Sharma are not as honest and simple as Sharma's feelings. Ackerley comments that Narayan's affection "is based chiefly on possession; he is proud of the influence he has over this wild handsome creature, Sharma's unquestioning, unswerving devotion and respect. . . . Narayan is not unkind to him, but he is . . . contemptuous of the childish mind, and treats him usually as if he were a slave or a hopelessly backward student"(244). Heterosexual males, then, fall into two categories: They either objectify others and themselves, contemptuously treating the innocence that is necessary for true love and intersubjective understanding; or they are vulnerably innocent, subject to exploitation or corruption. Only under the protection of a noneffeminate homosexual can the heterosexual be protected, and his egalitarian feelings cultivated.

And yet, even Ackerley cannot protect himself or his potential Ideal Friends from the corruption and competition of heterosexuality and capitalism. He finds himself using a ploy "akin to my

father's technique of bribery in advance for special . . . service"
(*My Father*, 136). But finally the I.F. is a highly conflicted figure,
always already lost, because he is the screen for Ackerley's incestuous desires for his father. *My Father and Myself* is not merely an
account of Ackerley's search for the real man beneath the successful Edwardian exterior, but also a love letter to revive and consummate his desires for his father. If the only copulative Ackerley
can engage in is the one in the title, it is a sign that he has
sublimated his incestuous wishes and belated his desires. For although Ackerley doesn't spell it out, it is his father who is best
described by his formula for the Ideal Friend; his father was generous, clean, seemingly innocent, less educated, and bisexual. Ackerley's discovery that his father headed an entirely different family in the same neighborhood and had probably worked as a
homosexual prostitute allows him to fantasize the imaginary
home he might have had with his own father, the illicit and egalitarian love he never found.

Although Ackerley traveled in Japan, India, Italy, and England,
he found no place where friendship can flourish between equals;
nor could he find the male free from the forces of objectification
and competition. All men would sooner or later betray the love he
would give them, as he himself betrayed his own feelings in the
silence and the distance he put between everyone. Ironically, although no human could occupy the space of the Ideal Friend, his
beloved Queenie, the German shepherd to whom he dedicated *My
Father and Myself* and about whom he wrote so lovingly in *My Dog
Tulip*, came as close as he was ever to find.

Notes

1. For a lengthy treatment of this issue see David M. Halperin, *One
   Hundred Years of Homosexuality* (New York: Routledge, 1990), 155, n.
   1; 158, n. 17; Eve Kosofsky Sedgwick, *Epistemology of the Closet*
   (Berkeley: University of California Press, 1990), 2.
2. Gilbert Herdt, "Introduction," in *Gay Culture in America: Essays from
   the Field*, ed. Gilbert Herdt (Boston: Beacon, 1992), 5.
3. "Straight Women, Gay Men," unpublished manuscript in my personal possession.

4. All these critical comments may be found in Peter Parker, *Ackerley: The Life of J. R. Ackerley* (New York: Farrar Straus, 1989), 1–2.

5. J. R. Ackerley, *My Father and Myself* (New York: Harcourt Brace Jovanovich, 1968), 125. Subsequent references will be in parentheses in the text.

6. J. R. Ackerley, *Hindoo Holiday: An Indian Journal* (New York: Poseidon Press, 1960), 253. Subsequent references to this work will be in parentheses in the text.

7. Yingling, Thomas E., *Hart Crane and the Homosexual Text: New Thresholds, New Anatomies* (Chicago: University of Chicago Press, 1990), 30.

8. Weeks, Jeffrey. *Coming Out: Homosexual Politics in Britain, from the Nineteenth Century to the Present.* (London: Quartet, 1977), 40.

9. Quoted in Weeks, *Coming Out*, 41.

10. W. H. Auden, "Papa Was a Wise Old Sly-Boots," in *Forwards and Afterwards* (New York: Vintage, 1974), 451.

11. Auden, *Papa*, 451.

12. Weeks, *Coming Out*, 41.

13. Parker, *Ackerley*, 43.

14. Michael Pollak, "Male Homosexuality; or Happiness in the Ghetto," in *Western Sexuality: Practices and Precept in Past and Present Times*, ed. Phillippe Arias and Andre Bejin (Oxford: Oxford University Press, 1985), 44.

15. Nancy Chodorow, *The Reproduction of Mothering: Psychoanalysis and the Sociology of Gender* (Berkeley: University of California Press, 1976), 167–69.

16. J. R. Ackerley, *The Prisoners of War*, in *Gay Plays*, ed. Michael Wilcox, vol. 3 (London: Methuen, 1925), 128–29. Subsequent references will be in parentheses in the text.

13

E. M. Forster at the End

Richard Dellamora

In the 1890s in England there occurred both a renaissance of cultural production by male homosexuals and a major onslaught against them that took as its focus Oscar Wilde, the cynosure of upper-class masculine difference. The successful prosecution of Wilde on charges of "gross indecency" in 1895 brought this renewal to an end with a crash that has continued to be heard across several generations of middle-class men, sexually and emotionally attracted to other men. The effect on the generation born around 1880 was particularly severe as instances the case of E. M. Forster, who was 16 years of age at the time of Wilde's debacle. Young men like John Gray, Aubrey Beardsley, and Alfred Douglas, who were in their late teens or early to mid-twenties between 1890 and 1894, experienced moral and practical support when they questioned hegemonic values. Forster also found friendship and encouragement among homosexuals such as Oscar Browning, G. Lowes Dickinson, and others; and he became romantically entangled with H. O. Meredith while an undergraduate at King's College, Cambridge. But Meredith was at least nominally straight, and sexual fulfillment eluded Forster for many years. Not until he fell in love with a young man named Mohammed el Adl while in Alexandria during World War I did he become sexually experienced.

In the meantime, Forster enjoyed friendships with homosexual men and supportive women while also undergoing a series of intense, sexually frustrated relationships with heterosexual or bisexual men. Whereas no definitive answer is available as to why Forster's homosexuality was for so long blocked at the site of the genitals, the end of relatively open homosexual self-expression posed major difficulties in his personal life and in the career that unfolded for him during the first decade of the new century—as an ironic observer of the tragicomedy of English upper-middle-class life and manners.

"Albergo Empedocle" (1903), Forster's first published short story, was suitable for publication in one of the homosexual magazines that had appeared at Oxford and London early in the decade. After 1895 these were gone or else under changed editorial policies. Wilde had made writing for a double audience the height of chic, but the glamour disappeared after male homosexuality had been negated in the most public fashion. Male heterosexual writers too lost the opportunity critically to assess gender norms.[1] The relatively public opportunities for socializing and collaborative work that male homosexuals had briefly enjoyed ceased to exist. As a young homosexual writer with a keen eye for the details of bourgeois domestic life, Forster found himself without a suitable social or publishing context. That he overcame these limits in a string of successful novels, climaxing in the publication of *Howards End* in 1910, was a triumph that could not be sustained indefinitely. Forster expresses the situation as early as a diary entry of June 16, 1911. Shortly after the success of *Howards End* and at a time when he was in his early thirties, he writes: "Weariness of the only subject that I both can and may treat—the love of men for women & vice versa."[2]

Even when Forster in his fiction resolutely focuses on male-female relations, they have as a limiting term the dangers posed by excessive investments between men. The threat of what Victorian sexologists defined as sexual inversion actively shapes the representation of conventional sexuality in Forster's writing, and this fact is already true in "Albergo Empedocle." In referring to this novel situation, which pertains not only to Forster's difficulties but to his social milieu, I use the term the *heterosexual contract*, by which I mean the prescribed investment of young men in relations with women whose main significance is their relation to social (re)production.³ This contract, which defines both male-female relations and the male relations that frame them, marks a significant change from the male homosocial construction of sexuality prevalent in the mid-Victorian period. The contract demands a "forgetting" of desire between men that Forster figures at the literal level through the use of amnesia. As for young women, in their roles as fiancées or wives, they must sacrifice the slightest suggestion of a female difference that might exist outside the limits of the phallogocentric order.⁴

The new context has implications for the structure of Forster's fiction, in particular for the function of irony with respect to the reader as an excluded third term who is, nonetheless, implicated in the text by the way in which desire is structured between a narrator and narratee.⁵ In a recent study, Ross Chambers has argued that oppositional writing depends primarily upon irony, a trope that can be put into operation only in the presence of a reader, who provides a necessary third term in addition to the first two. Chambers distinguishes two such operations: an irony of negation, which negates values of the dominant culture to whose members the text is in the first instance addressed; and an irony of appropriation, whereby the text suggests different desires to a reader or group of readers in opposition, wittingly or unwittingly, to the values of the dominant group.⁶ Remaining for the most part within the limits of reader-response theory, Chambers does not exploit the possibility that structural irony affords for calling into existence as yet indeterminate social groupings. "Albergo Empedocle," while addressed to conventional readers of *Temple Bar*, the journal in which it first appeared, appeals to a second set of readers who share Forster's need both to express and to dissemble a special interest in male intimacy.

This latter group are in an oppositional relation to the heterosexual contract along with its affiliations of class, rank, and nationality—even if, like Harold, the protagonist of the story, they aren't quite aware of the fact. In "Albergo Empedocle," male-male desire places one at the margin of the heterosexual contract but not altogether outside it.⁷ This positioning at the margin is necessary if the processes of group formation are to occur but also opens possibilities of self-deception and of failure in personal relations that neither Harold nor Tommy, the framing narrator of the story, escapes.

The significance of the setting of Forster's story amid Greek ruins on Sicily brings to mind the end during the 1890s of the discussion, dating from the late Enlightenment, of the significance of intimacy between males in the institution of pederasty as it had existed in different forms at ancient Athens and Sparta. While Forster as a boy was recoiling from the philistine atmosphere of Tonbridge School, Victorian philology entered a final phase as Walter Pater and Wilde, between 1890 and 1892, continued ironically to undercut the uses to which Greek models were conventionally put in elite education. Even when Greek studies were used to serve the political, social, and economic purposes of male elites, philology performed a useful function in foregrounding the connection between male intimacy and cultural and social production. As part of conventional education, such ties were subjected to critique by writers like Pater and Wilde; on the other hand, the debates compelled homosexual polemicists to theorize connections between masculine desire and positive outcomes in cultural and social relations. In slightly different terms, male homosexual discourses were necessarily preoccupied with the utilities of male intimacy. The forced abandonment of this project for young people of Forster's generation was to have negative consequences for the process of transforming Great Britain into a fully democratic state.[8]

In "Albergo Empedocle" Forster responds to both of these endings by drawing on tropes of metempsychosis and amnesia. On a visit with his bride-to-be and her parents to Sicily, Harold dreams that he has lived before as a Greek at Girgenti, the site of the former city of Acragas, a major commercial and cultural center during the Age of Pericles. The experience seems to suggest that whereas it may no longer be possible to *think Greek*, it is possible to *become Greek*. This rapture, however, can be achieved only at the cost of disconnection from normal existence; in other words, only at a moment when it has become impossible to envisage a hermeneutics of Greek love does the protagonist overleap the work of intellection by assuming for himself a metaphoric identification with the Other. This projection is precipitated by the refusal of

Mildred, Harold's fiancée, and her family to comprehend the possibility of being different. Harold is pushed into a breakdown and has to be repatriated by force to that other island, Great Britain, the counter to Sicily in the story. There he becomes the permanent ward of a mental hospital: "Long before Harold reached the asylum his speech had become absolutely unintelligible: indeed by the time he arrived at it, he hardly ever uttered a sound of any kind" (62).

Under the pressure of rejection by others, metempsychosis becomes an identification that captures the subject within a virtually complete solipsism. The recovery of a prior existence is incompatible with modern life because "we" (that is, we late Victorians) are amnesiacs. "We" have forgotten what it means to think Greek—even though as few years ago as the early 1890s writers were showing us how to do so.[9] Accordingly, although philology retains the grammar and syntax of ancient Greek, in Forster's rhetoric it has lost—as have modern subjects generally—the capacity of enunciation. Only Tommy, whose avowals of "love" for Harold equivocally frame the story, shares his friend's belief: "I firmly believe that he has been a Greek—nay, that he is a Greek, drawn by recollection back into his previous life. He cannot understand our speech because we have lost his pronunciation" (62). Tommy, however, does not speak Harold's language either or, rather, he can speak it only with the language of the body, the most equivocal of utterances, in the kiss that he receives from Harold at the end of the story. The role that Tommy plays needs to be regarded warily because his witness leaves Harold fixed in place as the subject of an existence almost totally estranged from "ours" and onto which, in view of Harold's muteness, Tommy is free to project what he will. Yet his fidelity to a love that cannot be voiced in return is the one space that Forster finds for expressing desire between men.

The extremity of Harold's situation suggests yet one more ending, this time generic, implied in Forster's short story; that is, the end of realist narrative, particularly in the novel, as a story in which two male rivals struggle for possession of a woman.[10] When Forster uses male-homosocial triangulation, he uses it differently so as to show that, at least in his fiction, the mediation of desire between men in a female object has ceased to constitute the terms of normal sexuality. Writing from a tacit homosexual subject-position, Forster frames relations between men and women with an eye to desire between men. This framing poses the possibility of another narrative trajectory to some readers while presenting male-female relations not so much as normal but as representative of the institution of heterosexuality. In this context, Forster describes the implications for female subjectivity of the position of women as "wife" or "woman" within this order. This representation, particularly in Mildred, contributes to the critique of marriage but operates as well so as to limit Forster's awareness of the ways in which female subjectivities can exist in resistance to the formation of gender. Forster demonstrates the cost to women of their positioning within heterosexuality but at the expense of failing to respond to their capacity to differ from their prescribed roles.

In "Albergo Empedocle," the triangle of Harold, Mildred, and Tommy focuses on Harold. Despite the fact that Tommy and Harold's mutual if asymmetrical desires for each other set the interpretive horizons of the story, after Harold's experience Mildred reveals another, more forceful triangle at work: that of herself, her future husband, and her father, Sir Edwin. Mildred takes the following view of Harold's experience: "Worn out," Harold "had fallen asleep, and, . . . had indulged in a fit of imagination on awaking. She had fallen in with it, and they had encouraged each other to fresh deeds of folly. All was clear. And how was she to hide it from her father?" (55) As the family expedition indicates, Harold is marrying not just Mildred but also her family. In return, the contract guarantees Mildred a fixed place in the scheme of things.

As Eve Kosofsky Sedgwick has shown in her discussion of Charles Dickens's *Our Mutual Friend* (1864–65), woman's work in the triangle, as it functions in mid-Victorian fiction, is to save the male from his own indecisive and unrecognized desires. Harold conforms to this script when he insists that Mildred validate his dream by kissing him with passion, something previously absent in their relations. His demand for her knowing acceptance belongs yet more properly to a moment late in male homosocial existence when, as Sedgwick shows, this time by way of her reading of James's "The Beast in the Jungle," woman as "friend" serves the function of cherishing the secret of John Marcher, a man so deeply closeted that he forgets that he has told her his "secret."[11]

Like a number of late Victorian wives who married men attracted to other men,[12] Mildred's ambivalent relation to her status as woman makes her initially prepared to undertake this exacting role but only on condition that she too can become Greek—that is, that within her role as wife she can occupy the place of an imaginary Other to Harold and thereby become more nearly his equal. When she decides that supporting Harold will, to the contrary, require self-sacrifice on her part while reinforcing her subordination as woman and her exclusion from "Greek" culture, she turns on him with remarkable vehemence. As for Harold, he is innocent of what his secret might be or why it needs to be a secret at all. His incomprehension signals that the male-homosocial role of woman as the friend or wife who keeps a man's secret does not in this story provide an effective bound to errant desires. Harold's Greek experience has begun to move him outside the terms of the contract. What he needs are interlocutors who can share his memories.

I. A Roman Ending

"Albergo Empedocle" begins with a letter that seems to set in place the sort of male homosocial triangulation that is a familiar aspect of realist narrative in Victorian fiction. As described by Harold, however, the situation sounds not quite right:

We've just come from Pompeii. On the whole it's decidedly no go and very tiring. What with the smells and the beggars and the mosquitoes we're rather off Naples altogether, and we've changed our plans and are going to Sicily. The guidebooks say you can run through it in no time; only four places you have to go to, and very little in them. That suits us to a T. Pompeii and the awful Museum here have fairly killed us—except of course Mildred, and perhaps Sir Edwin.

Now why don't you come too? I know you're keen on Sicily, and we all would like it. You would be able to spread yourself no end with your archaeology. For once in my life I should have to listen while you jaw.

You'd enjoy discussing temples, gods, etc., with Mildred. She's taught me a lot, but of course it's no fun for her, talking to us. Send a wire; I'll stand the cost. Start at once and we'll wait for you. The Peaslakes say the same, especially Mildred.

My not sleeping at night, and my headaches are all right now, thanks very much. As for the blues, I haven't had any since I've been engaged, and don't intend to. So don't worry any more.

Yours,
Harold (36)

In fairly evident transcoding, Harold's dissatisfaction with traveling expresses an underlying awareness that the engagement mentioned at the end of the letter is a mistake. The prenuptial tour is, in reality, a series of detours that "go" nowhere and whose predetermined stops on the way have "very little" in them, except, that is, for threatening Harold with annihilation. "Pompeii" and its "awful museum" are associated in his mind with marriage, the family, philistine culture, and the burdens of imperium: in other words, with the responsibilities upon which he is about to enter. For his part, Harold would rather be on another trip, one that would "suit" him "to a T"—that is, to a T/*Tommy*.

In this light, it is not surprising to find Harold resisting his fiancée in her role of *cicerone*. As Tommy writes, submaliciously, a bit later: "Mildred . . . was the fount of information. It was she who generally held the Baedeker and explained it. She had been expecting her continental scramble for several years, and had read a fair amount of books for it, which a good memory often enabled her to reproduce" (37). The key word here is memory, figured in the Baedeker, which connotes repetition. Memory in this sense only appears to "scramble" because it knows where it's headed, having learned its object by rote before meeting it. In contrast to this work of memory is recollection or metempsychosis or the belief, held by Empedocles who once lived at Acragas, in "the transmigration of souls" (41). This latter condition, implicitly recalling efforts within nineteenth-century philology to recover Greek consciousness, enables one to be constituted as wholly other.

Early on in the story, Mildred defends Harold's capacity for imagination against her father, who doubts that Harold has any. As well, it is Mildred who sets matters in motion by telling Harold en route to Girgenti that "today you must imagine you are a Greek" (42). Yet Mildred's capacity for sympathy is put cruelly to the test when Harold experiences his prior existence at Acragas. His continuing psychic stability depends on her sharing this belief with him; with no sense of exaggeration, he says to her: "I might have died if you hadn't believed me" (50). And Mildred does try. "Oh, Harold," she says, "I too may remember. . . . Oh, Harold! I am remembering! . . . . In the wonderful youth of Greece did I speak to you and know you and love you. We walked through the marble streets, we led solemn sacrifices, I armed you for the battle, I welcomed you from the victory. The centuries have parted us, but not for ever. Harold, I too have lived at Acragas!" (53) Without a guidebook to con, however, Mildred fails. She can become Greek only by translating Greece and Greek love into the parodic form of suburban bliss. One imagines her waving Harold from the door as he carries his briefcase into the urban fray. Her difference, which accommodates no difference, is fake, as she says later: "pure imagination, the result of sentimental excitement" (54). Harold's sleep, however, has converted him into a truth-sayer. In response to her claim to have lived at Acragas, he quietly responds: " 'No, Mildred darling, you have not' " (53).

The reader shortly learns that, contrary to his report to Tommy, headaches and insomnia do continue to trouble Harold. Mildred shows no awareness of these symptoms of bodily and spiritual disease. To her as to her father, Harold might just as well be a piece of classical statuary. His external deportment conforms to the observation of an educator like Benjamin Jowett that:

You may look at a Greek statue and be struck with the flexure of the limbs, the majestic folds of the drapery, the simplicity, the strength. And yet scarcely any topics arise in the mind of the uncritical [viewer]. . . . The highest art is colorless like water, it has been said; it is a surface without prominences or irregularities over which the eye wanders impressed by the beauty of the whole with nothing to detain it at a particular point. . . . It is a smooth surface over which the hand may pass without interruption, but the curious work lies beneath the surface: the effect only is seen from without. The finer the workmanship the more completely is the art concealed.[13]

This remark is, if not colored, then shadowed by the preterition that draws attention to while denying the fact that Greek "limbs" may draw "the eye" (and "the hand") to a "particular point," a point that redirects attention from a surface without openings to "the curious work" accessible only from the inside. Precisely Harold's presentation of "a surface without prominences or irregularities" makes him a suitable candidate as son-in-law, almost too suitable.

In Sicily, however, Harold betrays a disturbing propensity to imagine that he is "someone else," a "dodge" (39) he confesses that he occasionally resorts to when he has trouble falling asleep, or when he has "the blues" (40). When Sir Edwin discovers this capacity, he is shocked: "It is never safe to play tricks with the brain," he admonishes. "I must say I'm astonished: you of all people!" (40) It's even worse after Harold's dream when Sir Edwin demands that unless the young man acknowledges that he has been deluded, the marriage will not take place. What is troubling ("queer" in Sir Edwin's usage) is Harold's ability to change when he encounters something or someone different.

As the mention of Sir Edwin in Harold's letter indicates, Harold's contract is only incidentally with Mildred even as it is only incidental that she has something to say about the Greek temples at Girgenti: she can repeat what she has read. Similarly, in the role of wife and mother, she will repeat the genealogy of the Peaslakes. The corporate character of the engagement is implicitly extended in the brief reference at opening to another ending, the destruction of Herculaneum and Pompeii as a result of an eruption of Vesuvius in 79 A.D. "Pompeii" signifies English as an analogue of Roman culture both in the static density of existence as recovered from the ashes in archaeological digs and in the characteristic twinning of Roman with British imperium in nineteenth-century English thought.[14] The sense of closure impressed on Harold during his visit to "the awful Museum" helps set the stage for the crisis at Girgenti.

On the train from Palermo, Harold's view of Sicily comments ironically on England's economic and political position at the end of the century: "They had hardly crossed the watershed of the island. It was the country of the mines, barren and immense, absolutely destitute of grass or trees, producing nothing but cakes of sallow sulphur, which were stacked on the platform of every wayside station. Human beings were scanty, and they were stunted and dry, mere withered vestiges of men. And far below at the bottom of the yellow waste was the moving living sea, which embraced Sicily when she was green and delicate and young, and embraces her now, when she is brown and withered and dying" (42). This vision suggests both the actual as opposed to the putative effects of Empire because Sicily's denudation is a result of centuries of foreign invasion and domination. Tommy/Forster's outburst contrasts, however, to the commentary of the tenth edition of *The Encyclopaedia Britannica* (1902), which blandly remarks on the systematic transfer of capital from Sicily to the north after the unification of Italy:

Like all southern Italy, Sicily in 1860 was poor, notwithstanding the possession of notable reserves of monetary capital. On the completion of Italian unity part of this pecuniary capital was absorbed by the sudden increase of taxation, and a much greater part was employed by private individuals in the purchase of lands formerly belonging to the suppressed religious corporations. . . . Both the revenues acquired by taxation and the proceeds of the land sales were almost entirely spent by the State in northern Italy, where the new Government, for administrative and military reasons, had been obliged to establish its principal organizations, and consequently its great centers of economic consumption. (vol. 9, 618)

The Peaslakes identify with Sicily's conquerors. After the small upset that occurs when Sir Edwin learns about Harold's "dodge," Mildred restores quiet by returning to the guidebook: she "passed on to the terrible sack of Acragas by the Romans. Whereat their faces relaxed, and they regained their accustomed spirits" (41).[15]

Tommy's "keen" interest in Sicilian archaeology, however, associates him with the world, both pastoral and civic, of *Greek* Sicily, which appears to offer in Acragas a far different model of colonization from Italian, Roman, or English. Harold's letter betokens the wish to recover this existence in company with Tommy (even if the wish can only be uttered in negation and displaced onto Mildred). In the absence of Tommy, the possibility of recovery is open to Harold only in something like the form of his experience at Girgenti, where he falls asleep in the afternoon sun between the legs of a toppled colossal statue of Atlas and wakes convinced that, in an earlier life, he has lived as a citizen of Acragas.

[There] were two fallen columns, lying close together, and the space that separated them had been silted up and was covered with flowers. On it, as on a bed, lay Harold, fast asleep, his cheek pressed against the hot stone of one of the columns, and his breath swaying a little blue iris that had rooted in one of its cracks. . . .

Sleep has little in common with death, to which men have compared it. Harold's limbs lay in utter relaxation, but he was tingling with life, glorying in the bounty of the earth and the warmth of the sun, and the little blue flower bent and fluttered like a tree in a gale. The light beat upon his eyelids and the grass leaves tickled his hair, but he slept on, and the lines faded out of his face as he grasped the greatest gift that the animal life can offer. (47–48)

Mildred frames the scene as a tourist should: "He looked so picturesque, and she herself, sitting on the stone watching him, must look picturesque too. She knew that there was no one to look at her, but from her mind the idea of a spectator was never absent for a moment. It was the price she had paid for becoming cultivated" (47).

By 1903, high culture, including Greek culture, had been thoroughly commodified for the consumption and adornment of members of Mildred's class. Exotic locales provided the props for situating members of this group in preformulated ways. Mildred responds to such a scene as a masculist observer would. Her gaze is from the position of one who is already an object within such a scene. This framing excludes the possibility that instead of responding in a "cultivated" way Mildred might be changed by contact with "animal life" or by a pastoral existence that combines both spontaneous and cultivated responses. Hence the metonymic function of the travel book, whose mapping determines before one leaves home what knowledge will or will not be ascertained while abroad.[16]

For a middle- or upper-class male homosexual, Greek culture could be commodified in another way in the form of sexual tourism—whether the object of desire remained fantasmatic as it did for Forster on his Italian and Greek tours of 1902 and 1903 or whether it was acquired in more practicable ways. When Baron von Gloeden, for instance, photographs young Sicilian peasants in the ungarb of ancient youth, the discrepancy between sign and signifier indicates the inability of representation to suture the difference between material and imaginary reality. Nonetheless, these images, with the blessing of local Sicilians, drew homosexuals to the villa at Taormina from which von Gloeden sold his postcards.[17] Forster pitches the attraction in another register. In "Albergo Empedocle," Greek culture provides the opportunity of imagining a "better love," as presumably it does for Tommy, whose interest in Sicily is described as that of an archaeologist, not of a tourist. Yet even when resolutely scientific or high-minded, trips like Forster's 1902 visit to Girgenti exist within a structure of erotic fantasy that is marked by class and ethnic snobbery. Forster/Harold/Tommy's aspiration to a better love is distinguishable but not dissociable from the other meanings of fin-de-siècle tourism. For these men, absorption in Greek culture, though oppositional in Chambers's use of the word, signifies economic and national distinction.

Against these significations, Forster buttresses the oppositional meaning of Harold's experience through intertextual reference to polemical texts of the homosexual renaissance of a few years before. Mildred's gaze at Harold recalls that of the Prior at the sleeping figure of Apollo/Apollyon in Pater's "Apollo in Picardy," an imaginary portrait of 1893.[18] In the story, Pater uses the setting of a monastic community in order to analyze the psychological effects of homophobia on a male homosocial subject. The blue iris recalls the hyacinths that blossom after the murder, probably at the hands of the Prior, of his young companion, Hyacinth. Harold's habit of looking out the window of the asylum recalls the Prior's similar practice after he is judged to be insane and placed under house arrest. "Gazing . . . daily for many hours, he would mistake mere blue distance, when that was visible, for blue flowers, for hyacinths, and wept at the sight."[19] In Forster's less ironic text, we simply don't know what Harold sees. The references to Pater, however, provide textual means of overcoming the limiting terms of the "spectator" envisaged by Mildred.

II. Sweet Nothings

At the end of "Albergo Empedocle," the narrator observes:

Most certainly he is not unhappy. His own thoughts are sweet to him, and he looks out of the window hour after hour and sees things in the sky and sea that we have forgotten. But of his fellow men he seems utterly unconscious. He never speaks to us, nor hears us when we speak. He does not know that we exist.
    So at least I thought till my last visit. I am the only one who still goes to see him; the others have given it up. Last time, when I entered the room, he got up and kissed me on the cheek. I think he knows that I understand him and love him: at all events it comforts me to think so. (63)

Just as the story begins with a missive from Harold to Tommy, it ends with another, with Harold's chaste kiss. In a story in which the reader has learned something of the semiotics of kissing, this kiss is a bodily sign of Greek love in contrast both to the proffered kiss of conscious desire that Mildred rejects at Girgenti and to the "decorous peck" (50) that had earlier sealed her engagement. In a world that has become amnesiac by resolutely turning away from *thinking Greek*—and Tommy includes himself among the "we" who have forgotten—Tommy can at best be only nearly sure what the language of the body means when, in the final words of the story, he says: "I think he knows that I understand and love him: at all events it comforts me to think so" (63). Tommy needs comfort because, though his absence from Sicily was necessary, it meant that he was not at hand at Harold's moment of truth. Accordingly, Tommy has missed, perhaps for good, his own chance to reenter Greek subjectivity.

    In adhering to the Christian counsel to visit the sick, Tommy does on the other hand give witness to his love for Harold. Indeed, in Tommy's telling, his love frames the story even though at the start that love appears to have been baffled and remains so throughout. Harold, Tommy confides, is "the man I love most in the world" (37). Yet the role of witness and the confidence with which Tommy uses the verb are odd in view of the ignorances that usually attend love within the story. In addition, by proffering this knowledge to the reader as though it were fairly straightforward, Tommy posits a line of shared cognition between Harold, himself, and the reader despite the fact that the story is structured in such a way as to leave such a possibility in suspension. At no time do Harold and Tommy clearly understand love in the same way. Instead, the assumption of intelligibility on Tommy's part depends on a reading-effect. In the experience of readers of the story, there may exist relations that will complete Tommy and Harold's untold, unconsummated "love." Tommy makes a utopian appeal to a reader who has recovered the ability to *think Greek*, who understands touch, and who has enough imagination to project a world in which it would make sense to say as Harold does: "I was better, I saw better, heard better, thought better. . . . I loved very differently. . . . Yes, I loved better too" (51, 52). By this appeal, Tommy calls into being a reader of the future who may be described as the subject of a gay erotics. Moving beyond the frame of the heterosexual contract, the text implies the potential existence of cultural and social spaces in which men will be able to voice and to enact their mutual sexual and emotional bonds.

At this point, the ends that accompany Forster's hesitant beginnings as a writer help explain discrepancy between hope and contingencies. Forster, who was born on New Years Day 1879, was sixteen years old during the Wilde trials of 1895. As "a little cissy" aware of the distances—including distances of desire—between himself and others his age, Forster was both appalled and instructed by the punishment meted out to Wilde, the only homosexual of his class who seemed able simultaneously to appeal to newly emergent groups, including male homosexual and lesbian ones; sharply to satirize the powers that be; yet to continue to enjoy entry and success in the worlds both of middlebrow and highbrow culture.[20] Two years later, when Forster left Tonbridge School to enter King's College, he found a place at which the conditions for a life of Greek harmony still seemed to exist:

Body and spirit, reason and emotion, work and play, architecture and scenery, laughter and seriousness, life and art—these pairs which are elsewhere contrasted were there fused into one. People and books reinforced one another, intelligence joined hands with affection, speculation became a passion, and discussion was made profound by love.[21]

Forster achieved this sense of wholeness especially as a result of being selected for membership in the Apostles, the Cambridge undergraduate society of which Alfred Tennyson and Arthur Henry Hallam had been early members and that achieved new distinction at the turn of the century through the membership of men like Bertrand Russell, Alfred North Whitehead, Lytton Strachey, Leonard Woolf, and John Maynard Keynes.[22] Moreover, the line into this group was affective: Forster was sponsored for membership by H. O. ("Hom") Meredith, a handsome, bright, athletic, sexually confused young man, with whom Forster fell in love.[23] Although arguments in defense of male homosexuality were put forward at the weekly meetings, members kept quiet about their sexual involvements; and Forster and Meredith's intimacies were confined to "kisses and embraces."[24]

In a biography of Forster that is marked by homophobia, Francis King comments that "Meredith, a basically heterosexual man, probably took the physical lead, either out of kindness or out of curiosity, but Forster was the one who was in love."[25] Yet there is evidence that Meredith signed the heterosexual contract with difficulty. Shortly after he and Forster became friends, Meredith became engaged to Caroline Graveson, then "had a nervous breakdown."[26] In 1906, Meredith wrote to Keynes from Manchester: "I think I am dead really now. . . . Or perhaps I should say I realize now what was plain to others two years ago. I come to life temporarily when I meet Forster." Furbank remarks: "Forster, as was his habit in friendship, made vigorous efforts to rouse Meredith out of his apathy. They would go for long walks, endlessly discussing Meredith's problems, or sometimes walking in total silence while he brooded."[27] In this relationship, Forster appears to have played the role of "Tommy."

Homosexual members of the Apostles or, later, Bloomsbury lived in a country in which their exchanges could subject them to ignominy, blackmail, and legal prosecution. Under the relatively new terms of the Labouchère amendment, the prohibition of "gross indecency" brought a far wider range of acts between men, including kissing, within the net of the Law. Indeed, even those Saturday night deliberations about the nobility of male love were potentially liable to prosecution. Within these circumstances, Forster, referring to himself as a homosexual, uses the term *"minority."* Returning from a trip to Greece in 1904, he describes himself as though he were part of a barren Mediterranean landscape:

I'd better eat my soul for I certainly shan't have it. I'm going to be a minority if not a solitary, and I'd best make copy out of my position. There is nothing contemptible or cynical in this. I too have sweet waters though I shall never drink them. So I can understand the drought of others, though they will not understand my abstinence.[28]

For Forster being a minority at that time meant living privately and celibately. Faced with this sort of isolation, it is not surprising that the insulation of groups like the Apostles increased or that homosexual involvements came to appear to outsiders to be a part of a "cult."[29]

Forster's decision not to reprint "Albergo Empedocle" during his lifetime is in keeping with the extreme sense of apartness expressed in the preceding quotation. Yet it is a part of the continuing interest of this story that it calls into existence the members of a minority *group*. This structure depends in turn upon contingencies: on the existence of a homosexual radical culture before 1895, on its subsequent suppression, and on the continuing effects of the work of gender in Victorian Greek studies. Even when it was no longer possible to contest the meaning of masculinity within philological inquiry, the efforts of writers like Pater, Wilde, and others continued to lend fortitude to men like Forster.

Forster is often thought of as a man with a double career: the first climaxed with the publication of *A Passage to India* in 1924, after which he ceased to publish new fiction. The second career is a posthumous one as the writer of gay short stories and the novel *Maurice*, which were published after his death in 1970. The two parts of Forster's career, however, and the frustration of his work as a novelist after 1924 are conditioned by the institution of heterosexuality, which both impels the novels that deal with conventional sexuality and ensures that, in various ways as in "Albergo Empedocle," they work out a complex relationship to a specifically homosexual desire. In this sense, there are not two careers but one marked by continual compromise and resistance.

III. Another Difference

And, finally, Mildred, archetype of what Noel Annan refers to as "the self-satisfied, uneducated, conventional Edwardian girl, whom Forster knew so well, corseted by the conventions of her class and determined, come what may, to impose her will."[30] Her representation in "Albergo Empedocle" demonstrates the production of "woman"—in marriage or a picturesque setting—as a heterosexual institution. Viewed in this light, the sympathetic woman of the James short story is a logical impossibility. In a story that refers in many ways to the love that dare not speak its name, Mildred vindictively insists on naming Harold a "charlatan and cad" (56). She does so, moreover, in defense of herself as a woman, convinced that in turning back her wish to participate in his other life, Harold means to subordinate her:

How patiently he had heard her rapturous speech, in order that he might prove her silly to the core! How diabolically worded was his retort—"No, Mildred darling, you have not lived at Acragas." It implied: "I will be kind to you and treat you well when you are my wife, but recollect that you are silly, emotional, hypocritical; that your pretensions to superiority are gone for ever; that I have proved you inferior to me, even as all women are inferior to all men. Dear Mildred, you are a fool!" (55–56)

Mildred's reaction shows that, in her scrutiny of Baedeker, she has been in search of cultural capital for herself, something she needs to offset the assured superiority of her better educated male co-evals. This capital prominently includes the Greek studies that put a premium on male relations—so that the translation of Harold into Greek experience must either be recoded by Mildred or else be felt by her to be utterly demeaning.

Mildred responds in terms of her position as a future wife: what is implicitly in contest is her rivalry over Harold with Tommy, which she translates into archaeological terms. Mildred perceives her failure to be one of "archaeology" (55), the field of Tommy's expertise. The knowledge possessed by male subjects of elite education excludes her. She won't bear it. She lashes out. In a barely concealed metaphor, she kills Harold. Or, at least, Tommy thinks so: "I . . . believe that if things had happened otherwise he might be living that greater life among us, instead of among friends of two thousand years ago, whose names we never heard. That is why I shall never forgive Mildred Peaslake as long as I live" (63).

As enforcer of the contract and an outmoded novelistic realism, Mildred merits Tommy's anger. Yet the word *cad* suggests some of the ambiguities in gender and sexual relations in these years. Forster himself would use the term at Alexandria a number of years later at a moment when anxieties of class, gender, and race combined to prompt him to lose confidence in his first lover, Mohammed el Adl. In a letter of April 4, 1918, to Florence Barger, the wife of a former Cambridge classmate and a lifelong friend and confidante, Forster writes: "I thought he had meant to insult me, and left in a fury. He was puzzled and distressed, but very dignified. All through it is *I* who have endangered the thing. . . . I have found it so hard to believe he was neither a traitor or [*sic*] cad."[31] Poised on the fine line that separated friend from traitor, lover from cad, Forster was in a position to understand the volatile insecurity that a young upper-class woman might feel shortly before her marriage.

The writer of "Albergo Empedocle" was younger, less experienced, and less reflective than the Forster of 1918. He represents Mildred through the medium of Tommy's animosity, an effect reinforced by the way in which other characters likewise see her. Mildred's father, for instance, is confident that, despite occasional flights of fancy, "she could be trusted to behave in a thoroughly conventional manner" (45). This comment in indirect discourse, written by Tommy/Forster, is as reliable but only as reliable as is the narrator. Tommy assures the reader: "I am well acquainted with all who went then, and have had circumstantial information of all that happened, I think that my account of the affair will be as intelligible as anyone's" (36). Well, yes. . . .

The containment of Mildred's subjectivity within her function as "woman" prompts questions about the capacities of the narrator to envisage feminine difference. As for Forster, in contrast to his ability to register masculine differences, he gives no clue that Mildred might have a capacity to be different from the roles that she has been called upon to play. Yet the nonnegotiability of Mildred in the role of a May Bartram or a Florence Barger does indicate the high price that women who invested in such a compromise had to be willing to pay. Her refusal to pay this price is a noteworthy revolt and could be admirable though unfortunately, in Forster's ironic presentation, she revolts not in the direction of dis-identification with "woman" but in the direction of an accentuated identification with her place in the heterosexual contract. The expression of feminine differences would have to wait for writers such as Radclyffe Hall, who, in "Miss Ogilvy Finds Herself" (1926), writes her own story of a subject of same-sex desire who is rapt into another world. But in Hall's story, the protagonist is *Miss* Ogilvy.

Notes

1. The scandal attending publication of *Jude the Obscure* later in 1895 indicates the negative impact for male heterosexual writers of the Wilde scandal. See Richard Dellamora, *Masculine Desire: The Sexual Politics of Victorian Aestheticism* (Chapel Hill, NC: University of North Carolina Press, 1990), 212–17.
2. Quoted in Oliver Stallybrass, "Introduction," in E. M. Forster, *The Life to Come and Other Stories* (Harmondsworth: Penguin, 1975), 16. Citations from "Albergo Empedocle" refer to this edition and appear in parentheses in text. Unless otherwise cited, biographical information is from Claude Summers, *E. M. Forster* (New York: Frederick Ungar, 1983), chap. 1.
3. I adapt the phrase from Teresa de Lauretis, "The Female Body and Heterosexual Presumption," *Semiotica* 67, no. 3/4 (1987): esp. pp. 260, 277 n. 1; and from Monique Wittig, *The Straight Mind and Other Essays*, trans. Louise Turcotte (Boston: Beacon Press, 1992), 24–25. See also Teresa De Lauretis, "Eccentric Subjects: Feminist Theory and Historical Consciousness," *Feminist Studies* 16 (Spring 1990): 128–29. I supplement her work by suggesting that the contract is implemented with special aggressivity in the years immediately following Wilde's imprisonment.
4. My suggested dates for the installation of this shift in the construction of conventional sexuality parallel the development, in Continental psychoanalysis, of Freud's model of female sexual difference, a model that Mary Jacobus argues instates "the phallus" as "an arbitrary and divisive mark around which sexuality is constructed" (*Reading Woman: Essays in Feminist Criticism* [New York: Columbia University Press, 1986], 122). For a discussion of the problematic of

"woman" in male modernity, see Alice Jardine, *Gynesis: Configurations of Woman and Modernity* (Ithaca, NY: Cornell University Press, 1985), chap. 4.

5. See Ross Chambers, *Room for Maneuver: Reading (the) Oppositional (in) Narrative* (Chicago: University of Chicago Press, 1991), 24, 32.

6. Chambers, *Room for Maneuver*, 237–41.

7. Chambers, *Room for Maneuver*, 217.

8. I follow Alan Sinfield's argument in *Literature, Politics, and Culture in Postwar Britain* (Berkeley: University of California Press, 1989), esp. chap. 5.

9. I mean showing us how in the sense described by David Halperin in a discussion of heroic male friendship in the *Iliad* and other early texts. Halperin argues that interpretations of "homosexuality" in these works tell us more about the understanding of sexuality in the culture of the interpreter than in the cultures in which the works themselves were first performed or written (*One Hundred Years of Homosexuality and Other Essays on Greek Love* [New York: Routledge, 1990], 87).

10. See Eve Kosofsky Sedgwick, *Between Men: English Literature and Male Homosocial Desire* (New York: Columbia University Press, 1985), especially chapter 9. Subsequent page references to this book are included in the text.

11. Eve Kosofsky Sedgwick, *Epistemology of the Closet* (Berkeley: University of California Press, 1990), 210.

12. For the wives of Oscar Wilde and Edmund Gosse, see, respectively, Anne Clark Amor, *Mrs. Oscar Wilde: A Woman of Some Importance* (London: Sidgwick and Jackson, 1983) and Ann Thwaite, *Edmund Gosse: A Literary Landscape: 1849–1928* (Chicago: University of Chicago Press, 1984). See also Francis King, *E. M. Forster* (London: Thames and Hudson, 1988), 22–23.

13. Quoted in Lesley Higgins, "Essaying 'W. H. Pater Esq.': New Perspectives on the Tutor/Student Relationship between Pater and Hopkins," in *Pater in the 1990s*, ed. Laurel Brake and Ian Small (Greensboro, NC: ELT Press, 1991), 90.

14. Linda Dowling, "Roman Decadence and Victorian Historiography," *VS* 28 (Summer 1985): 579–607. Similarly, in "Ansell," another early story, the narrator's upper-class father is distressed when his son loses interest in the history of Rome after he makes friends with a garden boy: "My father did not like my entire separation from rational companions and pursuits. I had suddenly stopped reading and no longer cared to discuss with him the fortunes of the Punic War or the course of Aeneas from Troy" (Forster, *The Life to Come*, 28).

15. Acragas is the Greek name of Girgenti, known to the Romans as Agrigentum and, since 1927, as Agrigento, a change of name conso-

nant with the fascist program of invoking an earlier empire. Forster visited the town in April 1902.

16. See John Frow, "Tourism and the Semiotics of Nostalgia," *October* 57 (Summer 1991): 123–51.

17. Tom Waugh, "Photography, Passion and Power," *The Body Politic* (March 1984): 30. Additional information provided by Tom Waugh in a phone conversation on August 11, 1992.

18. For a discussion of "Apollo in Picardy," see Dellamora, *Masculine Desire*, chap. 9. For the connections between Pater and Forster, see Robert Martin, "The Paterian Mode in Forster's Fiction: *The Longest Journey* to *Pharos and Pharillon*," in *E. M. Forster: Centenary Revaluations*, ed. Judith Scherer Herz and Robert K. Martin (Toronto: University of Toronto Press, 1982), 99–112.

19. Walter Pater, *Miscellaneous Studies* (London: 1910. Reprint. New York: Johnson Reprint Co., 1967), 170.

20. Quoted in King, *E. M. Forster*, 17. One of the features of the last fifteen years of the century, as discussed in George Gissing's *New Grub Street* (1891) and in such recent studies as Jonathan Freedman's *Professions of Taste: Henry James, British Aestheticism, and Commodity Culture* (Stanford, CA: Stanford University Press, 1990), is the emergence of what is now referred to as "middlebrow" taste. Middlebrow taste, which might be described as the revenge of Philistinism on Matthew Arnold, was—and is—averse to *thinking Greek.*

21. Quoted in King, *E. M. Forster*, 19.

22. For a discussion of the sexual politics of the Apostles in the 1830s, see Dellamora, *Masculine Desire*, chap. 1.

23. P. N. Furbank, *E. M. Forster: A Life* (London: Secker and Warburg, 1977), vol. 1, 78.

24. Furbank, *Forster*, vol. 1, 98.

25. King, *E. M. Forster*, 34.

26. Furbank, *Forster*, vol. 1, 140.

27. Furbank, *Forster*, vol. 1, 141.

28. Furbank, *Forster*, vol. 1, 111.

29. See Noel Gilroy Annan, *Our Age: English Intellectuals Between the World Wars—A Group Portrait* (New York: Random House, 1990), chaps. 7, 8.

30. Annan, *Our Age*, 111.

31. Quoted in Philis Gardner, "The Evolution of E. M. Forster's *Maurice*," in *E. M. Forster: Centenary Revaluations*, ed. Judith Scherer Herz and Robert K. Martin (Toronto: University of Toronto Press, 1982), 218. The letter is not included in E. M. Forster, *Selected Letters: Volume 1, 1879–1920*, ed. Mary Lago and P. N. Furbank (Cambridge: Harvard University Press, 1983).

14

Richard Rodriguez's Poetics of Manhood

Martin A. Danahay

"I became a man by becoming a public man."
—Richard Rodriguez
Hunger of Memory:
The Education of Richard Rodriguez

In his ethnographic study of a Cretan village, *The Poetics of Manhood*, Michael Herzfeld has emphasized the way in which masculinity is enacted in the process of narrating a story. Herzfeld analyzes the ways in which Cretan men construct their masculinity in telling stories; when relating their tales of sheep stealing Cretan men are dramatizing their masculine status. Herzfeld describes the self-dramatization of Cretan men as a "poetics," a "performance of selfhood" that "depends upon an ability to identify the self with larger codes of identity."[1] Herzfeld's ethnography is concerned with "the poetics of being a true Glendiot man" (46), and analyzes the various ways in which Glendiot males perform their masculinity in public, particularly in sheep-stealing narratives in which the speaker's performance demonstrates that one is "good *at being* a man" (46, 209). Herzfeld provides a particularly fruitful theoretical model for the analysis of narratives in terms of their staging of masculinity as a public performance.[2] Taking my cue from his book, in the following pages I will analyze Richard Rodriguez's *Hunger of Memory: The Education of Richard Rodriguez* as a "poetics of manhood" that dramatizes his status as a man, especially as a "public" man engaged in writing an autobiography.[3]

Richard Rodriguez's *Hunger of Memory: The Education of Richard Rodriguez* has been analyzed, even by myself, as primarily a text about ethnicity and the problems of growing up as the child of Hispanic immigrants in Anglo America.[4] However, I wish to give a different reading of the book here, and suggest that it be viewed as a meditation on being *masculine* in America. In other words, the book dramatizes the condition of being masculine and plays out a dialectic between ways of being masculine and being feminine in contemporary America. *Hunger of Memory* therefore represents a fascinating complementary text to contemporary autobiographies written by women, such as Maxine Hong Kingston's *The Woman Warrior* and Maya Angelou's *I Know Why the Caged Bird Sings.*

Rodriguez claims, like Maxine Hong Kingston in *The Woman Warrior,* to be breaking an injunction to silence in writing his autobiography. Rodriguez claims that he is "writing about the very things my mother asked me not to reveal" (175) in publishing *Hunger of Memory,* just as Kingston in *Woman Warrior* represents herself as breaking her mother's injunction "Don't tell."[5] However, where Kingston's *Woman Warrior* focuses almost entirely upon her mother as a symbol of her relationship to the Chinese community, Rodriguez's text enacts a complex set of identifications with both his mother and father. In particular, Rodriguez identifies his father with silence, and opposes him to his mother's acquisition of English and success as a secretary to the governor of California.

As the title of his book indicates, Rodriguez's story is about the effects of American socialization on him as a male from a Hispanic background. The word that sums up the effect of this education as Rodriguez sees it is "separation." Summarizing his educational career, Rodriguez says: "What I am about to say has taken me more than twenty years to admit: *A primary reason for my success in the classroom was that I couldn't forget that schooling was changing me and separating me from the life I enjoyed before becoming a student*" (45).

Rodriguez equates his successful career as a student with his increasing alienation from his family, and apparently accepts this as the inevitable cost of his "success."[6] Rather than record with ambivalence his separation from his family and his community, Rodriguez celebrates his learning of English as a sign of his gaining autonomy and a public identity. Rodriguez's text is not written in opposition to the cultural hegemony of education as a process that deracinates its subjects. For Rodriguez, his education was fundamentally a benign exercise of turning him into a citizen of the United States. Education gave him a voice. This education was also explicitly a matter of class, as he uses "American" and "middle-class" as synonyms. He calls his narrative "an American story" (5) and a "middle class pastoral." (6) When Rodriguez says that "I had grown culturally separated from my parents," (72) he is describing what he sees as a natural and all-American process of turning the lower-class immigrant kid into a middle-class American citizen.

Rodriguez's attitude to his socialization can be accounted for in terms of gender. *Hunger of Memory*, like such narratives as *The Autobiography of Malcolm X* by Alex Haley, is a masculine success story. Malcolm X's story records the way in which he escaped the ghetto, his drug habit, and jail and is told as a conversion narrative in which he finds Allah and is saved. Rodriguez's is an educational success story in which he receives a Ph.D. as the ultimate reward. Rodriguez therefore interprets his increasing estrangement from his family as an ambiguous development; on the one hand he is losing contact with his parents, especially his father, but on the other he is enjoying increased success in his academic work.

Hunger of Memory is thus a form of bildungsroman; it describes the career of a middle-class male from his successes as a "scholarship boy" to his studies as a graduate student at Berkeley. Rodriguez is clearly ambivalent about this success, but it is this success story that gives his narrative coherence. The narrative dramatizes how Rodriguez becomes a "public man," and dramatizes his masculine status in the process. Although Rodriguez questions racial categories, his narrative rests on a fundamental dichotomy in terms of gender that reinscribes the gendered division of labor in American society.

Rodriguez's public work, writing, involves a denial of the feminine, private part of his life embodied in his Mexican family. Much of Rodriguez's book concerns the disappointments he experienced in his chosen work, and his consequent romanticization of family life. Andrew Tolson explains this aspect of masculinity as an inevitable result of the gendered division of labor: "In capitalist societies, with their highly developed divisions of labour, and the widening split between 'work' and 'home,' masculine expectations can only be maintained at the price of psychological unity. At work, a man's gender identity is no longer complete—it is slowly split apart."[7]

Rodriguez registers this split in American masculine gender identity in his insistence on the separation of male and female aspects of his narrative. *Hunger of Memory* is a eulogy for those aspects of his identity that he feels he must reject, such as intimacy and the domestic life of the Spanish-speaking family, but also romanticizes. This process has been described by Jonathan Rutherford in *Men's Silences* in the following terms:

Masculinity is defined in dividing off the elements it must disavow and projecting them into the subordinate term of femininity, filling it with the antithesis of its own identity. The female body in its very alienness is both idealised and loathed by men. . . . To maintain the fiction of its own identity, the masculine must maintain the binary distinction. Splitting and projection illustrate how psychic processes are mobilised in defence of frontiers.[8]

In order to create a unified self in the face of the split between masculine and feminine, Rodriguez valorizes the masculine "public man" over the private and feminine. Equating speaking Spanish with the domestic and feminine, he comes to the conclusion that to be a man he must separate himself from his family. This is the source of Rodriguez's ambivalence toward his socialization; he sees his separation from his family as natural, but he also projects values such as intimacy into the feminine domestic sphere that he rejects. Rodriguez therefore views separation from his family in positive terms as an assertion of autonomy, and subscribes to an interpretation of his life history as one of increasing distance from his family and from Hispanic culture. *Hunger of Memory* would not be a very interesting or complicated book, however, if Rodriguez's attitude was monovocal and unified in its appreciation of the effects of his socialization upon him. In the latter stages of the book he describes visiting home after being away at college, and feeling like an intruder in the house: "Living with my parents for the summer, I remained an academic—a kind of anthropologist in the family kitchen, searching for evidence of our 'cultural ties' as we ate dinner together" (160).

Hunger of Memory becomes a eulogy for a lost intimacy embodied in his Spanish-speaking childhood, an Eden lost for Rodriguez in becoming an "academic." The most striking aspect of this quotation is the way that "academic" and "anthropologist" are used as the antithesis of "family." Rodriguez sees his professional, public persona as inimical to the intimacy he equates with family. Rodriguez feels that "I had shattered the intimate bond that had once held the family close" (30) by learning English, and the "hunger" in *Hunger of Memory* is for this lost intimacy. However, "intimacy" in the book is seen as inimical to a number of other of Rodriguez's "public" identities, especially his masculinity and his profession.

Rodriguez's subject position as "male academic" turns him into an "anthropologist" in his own family kitchen. Like many men, Rodriguez both celebrates and marginalizes intimacy, making it into a value that is fundamentally at odds with the public performance of masculinity. He simultaneously praises intimacy and makes it into a "lost" ideal that he once possessed but reluctantly has had to forego in order to become a public man. His sentiments here corroborate Tolson's description in *The Limits of Masculinity* of the radical separation of work and home, and the psychic cost for men. Rodriguez experiences masculine and feminine and work and home as diametric opposites that are mutually exclusive. Constructing a masculine identity involves denying the incompatible aspects of his personality.

Rodriguez's success story is complicated, however, by the way in which he identifies with Anglo culture in gendered terms, and his view of his chosen profession as a "feminine" form of work. A set of counteridentifications works against the simple equation of public as masculine and private as feminine. He identifies his own success in school with his mother's accomplishments in learning

English and finding herself a job. He sees the negative effects of his education in terms of his father's inability to get ahead in his new environment and his difficulty with the English language. The book ends with a sudden realization of his father's silence during a family gathering. His father asks him a question and Rodriguez realizes that is "the only thing he has said to me all evening" (95); the story of his own success, therefore, is implicitly contrasted with his father's increasing silence. His book ends with an image of his father's silence that, like the silence of other marginalized figures, "remains to oppress them" (185). His father through his silence is associated with figures like *los pobres*, poor Mexican immigrants who are unable to adopt the "public" voice of spoken English and thus become victims of exploitation and oppression.

Describing his parents' reaction to their children's increased use of English at home, Rodriguez says that his mother spoke more, his father less:

My mother and father, for their part, responded differently as their children spoke to them less. She grew restless, seemed troubled and anxious at the scarcity of words exchanged in the house. It was she who would question me about my day when I came home from school. . . . By contrast my father seemed reconciled to the new quiet. Though his English improved somewhat, he retired into silence. (24)

As a result, it was his mother who "became the public voice of the family" and would talk to Anglo officials and strangers (24). In the public/private dichotomy that underlies Rodriguez's story, it is his mother, not his father, who is identified with the "public" world of spoken English. Rodriguez comes to associate the two languages, through his parents, with different ways of being masculine and feminine. Reacting against the description of his father as "shy," Rodriguez points out that when speaking Spanish his father's behavior changed:

But my father was not shy, I realized, when I'd watch him speaking Spanish with relatives. Using Spanish he was quickly effusive. Especially when talking with other men, his voice would spark, flicker, flare alive with sounds. In Spanish, he expressed ideas and feelings he rarely revealed in English. With firm Spanish sounds, he conveyed confidence and authority English would never allow him. (25)

The "firm" and masculine sounds of his father's Spanish voice contrast with his increasing silence in English. For Rodriguez silence becomes synonymous with victimization and exclusion from the public, Anglo world, so that his father is a figure who symbolizes the silence that Rodriguez himself both valorizes and rejects. His father as a symbol of masculinity becomes a symbol of Rodriguez's ambivalence about his education and his profession.

Rodriguez's ambivalent attitude to his father is made into the overt theme of *Days of Obligation*, the subtitle of which is *An Argument with My Mexican Father*. This subtitle is misleading. Rodriguez's father does indeed appear in this autobiographical essay, but the subtitle makes little sense if one understands it to mean that the text is a literal argument with an individual identifiable as his father. The "father" in the title is not an individual but a symbol, standing for Rodriguez's Mexican family and his ambivalent attitude to its Mexican past. The book opens with Rodriguez travelling through Mexico with a foreign T.V. camera crew searching for the archetypal Mexican village that will stand for his parents' origins. The text moves on from this opening to dramatize Rodriguez's own opposed tendencies, one to search for and venerate his family's Mexican past and the other to embrace the forgetfulness and rejection of the past by Puritan American culture. His journey in search of the sites of ruined Catholic missions in Protestant California is another version of this meditation on the relationship between his past and present, as is his movement back and forth over several weeks between Tijuana and San Diego. His father comes to represent the past for Rodriguez, his mother someone who has succeeded in entering Anglo America.

Days of Obligation, like *Hunger of Memory*, is organized around gendered dichotomies. This is startling because the text has many astute and sometimes hilarious observations about the condition of being a mestizo, which in Mexican Spanish means "mixed, confused."[9] The book explores the many contradictions in Rodriguez's identity as an American mestizo returning to Mexico, and the many contradictions and dichotomies within his relationship to American and Mexican culture. The book is grounded, however, in starkly drawn gendered opposites, as is *Hunger of Memory*. Whereas Rodriguez explores with great sensitivity the blurred boundaries between racial categories, he uses "masculine" and "feminine" as unproblematic polar opposites. In *Days of Obligation* Mexico is female, whereas America as Uncle Sam is male: "you betray Uncle Sam by favoring private over public life" (in other words, by favoring feminine over masculine), whereas "Mama Mexico" is private and intimate and feminine (62–63). In religion, Protestantism is male, Catholicism is voluptuous and female (181). Rodriguez reads the movement of young Mexican males from Mexico to the United States as a version of his own autobiography in which they leave behind "Mama Mexico" and become a man: "*You are a boy from a Mexican village. You have come into the country on your knees with your head down. You are a man*" (78).

The gender dichotomies in *Days of Obligation* are much more strongly delineated than in *Hunger of Memory*, largely because Rodriguez's mother is largely absent from this "argument" between father and son. In *Hunger of Memory* Rodriguez's mother is a focal point for his anxieties about the gendered associations of teaching and literary criticism. Teaching in America is viewed as a "feminine" occupation, especially at the primary and high school levels where the majority of teachers are women. As a man who has, at least initially, chosen a career in education, Rodriguez wrestles with the gender-based assumptions about teaching as work. This identification of his occupation in gender-based terms is heightened by his having chosen *literature* as his area of expertise within academic specializations, because this subject is traditionally associated with "feelings" and "emotions," all of which for Rodriguez connote femininity. Rodriguez worries at one point that "education was making me effeminate" (127), a worry that leads him to consider his education within the context of *machismo*: "I knew that I had violated the ideal of the *macho* by becoming such a dedicated student of language and literature. *Machismo* was a word never exactly defined by the persons who used it. (It was best described by the 'proper' behavior of men.)" (128).

This is a succinct statement of one of the cultural dichotomies underlying Rodriguez's autobiography; in order to be a successful Anglo professional he has to become a student of language, thereby "violating" the tenets of *machismo*. A "real" man "never verbally revealed his emotions" (128–29), although "it was permitted a woman to be gossipy and chatty" (128). In obeying his teachers' injunctions to speak in class, Rodriguez implicitly aligns himself with a "chatty" feminine way of behaving, and distances himself from his father's more reserved, or in Spanish *formal*, way of behaving. As Rodriguez's remarks make clear, at stake here is a gender-based way of *behaving*, that is, of performing one's masculinity in public. The more "successful" Rodriguez is in school or in work, the less "masculine" he is in the terms of *machismo*. He finds himself caught between two culturally defined ways of behaving that are in conflict with one another. If he were to follow his father's behavior he would be *macho*, and identify himself with reserve, silence, and the repression of emotion. He finds himself, however, drawn to a Protestant, Anglo model of behavior that aligns him with the feminine. This gendered dichotomy leads him to identify more and more closely with his mother:

I often was proud of my way with words. Though, on other occasions, for example, when I would hear my mother busily speaking to women, it would occur to me that my attachment to words made me like her. Her son. Not *formal* like my father. At such times I even suspected that my nostalgia for sounds—the noisy, intimate Spanish sounds of my past— was nothing more than effeminate yearning. (129)

At this point the nexus of gendered identifications at work in *Hunger of Memory* becomes clear; intimacy, literature, and speaking English become associated with the "feminine" aspects of Rodriguez's personality, whereas silence, sexuality, and power become associated with his father and the "masculine" aspects of his personality. In order to resist his effeminization, Rodriguez must reject his "effeminate yearning" for the intimate sounds of Spanish. The Spanish sounds of his past become the locus of an intense nostalgia for a set of associations embodied in his mother. Rodriguez's father is a problematic symbol of masculinity in *Hunger of Memory* because of his increasing silence. Rodriguez values a *formal* way of behaving, but associates it with silence and victimization in Anglo America. This simultaneous appreciation and rejection of silence as a marker of masculinity is made most obvious in Rodriguez's attitude to *los braceros*, the working-class manual laborers who come to symbolize "real" men's work in the text, as opposed to the "effeminate" labor of the intellectual. Rodriguez calls *los braceros* "powerful, powerless men" (114); they are "powerful" because their muscles represent for Rodriguez a muscular, *macho*, silent form of masculinity; and "powerless" because their very silence marks them for him as oppressed victims of Anglo cultural dominance. These men become for Rodriguez objects of simultaneous fear and desire:

I continued to see the *braceros*, those men I resembled in one way and, in another way, didn't resemble at all. On the watery horizon of a Valley, I'd see them. And though I feared looking like them, it was with silent envy that I regarded them still. I envied them their physical lives, their freedom to violate the taboo of the sun. Closer to home I would notice the shirtless construction workers, the roofers, the sweating men tarring the street in front of the house. I was unwilling to admit the attraction of their lives. I tried to deny it by looking away. But what was denied became strongly desired. (126)

The *braceros* come to represent for Rodriguez those aspects of his masculinity that he would deny in himself, namely his body and the darkness of his skin. They also become symbols of a repressed sexual desire; the "attraction" of these men is partly erotic. Rodriguez to an extent internalizes the racist categories of Anglo culture that associate "white" with good and "dark" with the evil and dangerous. This is also, however, a typical reaction by an intellectual, especially a male academic, to images of working-class, muscular labor. Rodriguez idealizes working-class manual labor because American intellectual labor devalues the physical in favor of the mental, seeing the two as in some way opposed. Rodriguez began to associate with a self-consciously intellectual group of students who would refer to fellow students playing baseball or football as "animals" (126). As Rodriguez explains, "the sensations that first had excited in me a sense of my maleness, I denied" (126). The *braceros* come to symbolize the denied and repressed masculinity embodied in *machismo*, and thus function as both objects of fear (because they represent the repressed body) and desire (because they represent a sexuality he denies in himself).

Rodriguez turns to literature and intellectual pursuits as compensation, a deliberate turn to the "feminine," that excludes the repressed masculine body and masculine desire. Rodriguez turns to literature to recapture in a vicarious and mediated form the "intimacy" he associates with his mother and early family life. While literature cannot be "intimate," it approximates what he is looking for in terms of the "personal." Literature comes to represent the lost community of Spanish culture, albeit in attenuated form. Listening to a nun reading aloud in his school, Rodriguez glimpses the possibilities of written communication as a form of "fellowship": "I sat there and sensed for the very first time some possibility of fellowship between a reader and a writer, a communication never *intimate* like that I heard spoken words convey, but one nonetheless *personal*" (60).

Reading for the young Rodriguez from this moment comes to represent a compensation for the estrangement from his family. It restores a lost intimacy in the imaginary relationship between a writer and a reader. The urgent autobiographical confessions of his books in this context become imaginary compensations for the domestic intimacy he has lost in becoming a "public" man. He says that lyric poetry especially came to function as a reminder of the kind of intimacy he felt he had lost when he grew apart from his family: "As public artifact, the poem can never duplicate intimate sound. But by imitating such sound, the poem helps me recall the intimate times of my life. I read in my room—alone—and grow conscious of being alone, sounding my voice, in search of another" (38).

The poem serves as a "memory device," reminding Rodriguez of lost intimacy, but as he makes clear, it can never replace intimacy. In some ways it makes him even more acutely aware of his isolation, and thus precipitates an even more desperate search for more intimacy. Rodriguez writes that "I vacuumed books for epigrams, scraps of information, ideas, themes—anything to fill the hollow within me and make me feel educated." (64) As the metaphors of "vacuum" and "hollow" make clear here, Rodriguez imagines that he has lost something essential that reading English literature can only partially compensate for.

Like his ambivalent attitude toward his body, Rodriguez's ambivalent attitude toward education is inflected by gender contrasts. Rodriguez strongly identifies with a description of "the scholarship boy" as a figure who "does not straddle, cannot reconcile, the two great opposing cultures of his life" (66). This is in some ways an accurate description of the way his mind works, in that he continually poses dichotomies, like public/private or masculine/feminine, and then finds himself unable to reconcile them. The larger pattern of *Hunger of Memory* is the creation of such dichotomies, then the despairing rejection of one side of the dichotomy in favor of the other. However, the term boy in "scholarship boy" also underlines the extent to which Rodriguez experiences American education as a diminishment of his masculinity. Education is for boys, not men. As in his idealization of the *braceros*, Rodriguez represents education, his chosen field of work, as inimical to masculinity.

Although reading books holds out the promise of an attenuated intimacy, it also connotes for Rodriguez isolation and withdrawal. When describing the experience of reading poetry in the quotation Rodriguez emphasizes that he reads poetry *alone* in his room. As Rodriguez progresses in his career he comes to feel increasingly isolated, so that he begins to wonder, "Was my dissertation much more than an act of social withdrawal?" (70). Through his studies Rodriguez gains a sense of vicarious community of scholars "united by a common respect for the written word and for scholarship," but this was a "union" in which "we remained distant for one another." (70) Rodriguez's academic research and writing thus come, like his reading when younger, to both assuage a need for intimacy, and to further exacerbate his feelings of isolation and estrangement from any community.

Rodriguez continually compares his current position as a male academic in disparaging terms with other forms of social identity. Calling himself "a citizen of the secular city" (107), Rodriguez reads his autobiography as part of a wider social movement away from the "communal Catholicism" of his youth. Once again, Rodriguez reads this aspect of his life in terms of both his loss of intimacy with his family and the development of his masculine identity. When it occurs to him to ask himself if God is dead, he answers the question with an affirmation of his faith: "I would cry into the void. . . . If I should lose my faith in God, I would have no place to go where I could feel myself a man. The Catholic Church of my youth mediated with special grace between the public and private realms of my life, such was the extent of its faith in itself" (108–9).

Rodriguez dramatizes here his self-conflict between his past as Catholic boy, and his adult persona, which he labels "individualist Protestant." He claims that "I have become like a Protestant Christian" and become a member of a sect whose experience of community is as "a community of those who share with each other only the experience of standing alone before God" (110). Rodriguez's religious experience here comes to sound exactly like his experience of becoming a professional academic; he loses his sense of belonging to a community and finds it replaced by an individualistic gathering of people with only a weak sense of connection to one another.

We should not accept this master narrative at face value, however. As the previous quotation shows, Rodriguez's sense of religion, like his professional identity, is bound up with his image of himself as masculine; only in church, he says, can "I feel myself a man." However, he is only aware of this aspect of himself because he has already withdrawn from his community, and separated from his family. This awareness is predicated upon an act of withdrawal from the start. This apparently paradoxical combination of "social withdrawal" and desire for community is expressed with particular force in his attitude toward silence in the closing pages of *Hunger of Memory*. As the story nears closure, Rodriguez describes the process of writing the book itself. The "poetics of manhood" that lie behind the tale become apparent when in a parenthetical aside Rodriguez says: "(In writing this autobiography, I am actually describing the man I have become—the man in the present.)" (176).

At this moment Rodriguez names *Hunger of Memory* as about the process of "becoming a man," and of staging that masculinity in the narrative. In writing about this process Rodriguez confronts some of his central self-contradictions, especially in his radically opposite valuations of silence and writing. In order to complete the manuscript, Rodriguez shuts himself in his apartment "to closet myself in the silence I both need and fear" (176). Like the figures of the *braceros*, silence is a source of both desire and danger. The desire finds its source in the *macho* image of men as essentially silent about matters of emotion; the fear comes from Rodriguez not wanting to be identified with *los pobres*, poor Mexican immigrants who, unlike him, have not found a public voice.

Rodriguez claims that in writing *Hunger of Memory* he has overcome the dichotomies that underlie the book, especially that between public and private:

The loneliness I have felt many mornings, however, has not made me forget that I am engaged in a highly public activity. I sit here in silence writing this small volume of words and it seems to me the most public thing I ever have done. My mother's letter has served to remind me; I am making my personal life public. (176)

Such a description implies that he has in some way transcended the dichotomies that inform the text. This is not the case, as his final image of his almost silent father makes clear. Rodriguez has opted in publishing *Hunger of Memory* to become a "public man." He has chosen, as his mother recognizes, to establish an identity that in his terms separates him from the "private" life of his family. Publishing *Hunger of Memory* is a declaration of independence on his part.

Perhaps the most courageous aspect of *Hunger of Memory* is Rodriguez's unflinching insistence on the cost that lies behind the statement that "I became a man by becoming a public man." Given the gendered dichotomies within which he works, becoming a "public man" means renouncing the "private," feminine-identified aspects of his identity, including his profession as an effeminate form of work. Rodriguez summarizes the damaging effects of conventional American masculinity; to be masculine men must be "public," they must be professional, they must be "silent" on emotional matters. The American ideal is close to the definition of *macho* Rodriguez gives in *Days of Obligation* when he says "there is sobriety in the male, and silence, too—a severe limit on emotional range. The male isn't weak. The male wins a Purple Heart or he turns wife beater. The male doesn't cry" (57). While the easy transition from not being "weak" to wife beating is disturbing, this collection of phrases summarizes many of the stereotypes of American masculinity.[10]

As the intense nostalgia for intimacy and community in *Hunger of Memory* shows, this idea entails repressing and denying one's family and any real sense of community. Such a definition of masculinity leads to intense feelings of isolation that such vicarious communities as literature and scholarship can only partially assuage. *Hunger of Memory*, therefore, makes dramatic statements about being masculine in contemporary America. Rodriguez's attitude toward masculinity is given particular ethnic inflections by his attitudes to the ideal of *machismo*, but overall the book has far more to say about being an American middle-class man than any other subject. The autobiography is a "middle-class pastoral" (6) that tells the story of how he became "the man that I have become" (176). *Hunger of Memory* captures extremely well the dichotomies underlying masculine self-fashioning in America.

Rodriguez's texts are problematic when one tries to account for their positions on race and gender. His attitude toward race is so radical that it subverts conventional popular political categories; *Hunger of Memory* can be cited both as a justification for and a refutation of bilingual education, and thus serves both left- and right-wing arguments. Overall, especially in *Days of Obligation*, Rodriguez deconstructs with breathtaking insight the racial categories operating in American English. He is particularly insightful and ironic on the uses of the term *Indian*. His position on gender roles, however, is more troubling. I am left wondering after reading his books whether it makes any sense whatsoever to characterize Protestantism as "male," literature as "feminine," or Mexico as "female." The essentializing and stereotyping in such moves makes the gender-based categories upon which he is relying seem like blunt instruments that do violence to their subject. However, Rodriguez in the final analysis is a courageous writer. He tackles in personal terms the issues that are dealt with more obliquely by academic writers. Peter Middleton's recent theoretical analysis of masculine conventions is an interesting example of the way in which the issues addressed through autobiography by Rodriguez are transmuted into academic discourse by professional critics. Middleton begins his book by describing the ways in which he first tried to write about masculinity: "My first attempts were poems. My first discursive writing about masculinity was intended to be a prose fiction about the violence of writing. . . . Whenever I tried to write, the ball-point would dig deeper and deeper into the paper, incising the words and then tearing through" (1).

Middleton's description of writing is striking in its emphasis upon violence. His analysis in *The Inward Gaze* of myths such as Superman documents the cost to its subjects of contemporary versions of masculinity. He does so, however, within the measured vocabulary of academic theory; the violence of the poems and fiction with which he started writing is muted by the conventions of academic discourse in his literary analysis.[11] Rodriguez deals with a similar subject, but more overtly. The self-inflicted violence implicit in becoming a "public man" is registered overtly in *Hunger of Memory*. Rodriguez gains his masculinity by rejecting aspects of himself associated with the "feminine": Mexico, intimacy, and Catholicism. Turning vice into virtue, he suggests such rejection is part of growing up an American male and a necessary prerequisite to entry into public life. As the increasing rate of publication on questions of masculinity attests, men are beginning to question whether such self-inflicted violence is necessary, and whether or not the cost is too high.

The emotional investment in Rodriguez's books rescues them from the stereotyping of gender roles on which they depend. Responding as a male academic myself, I value Rodriguez's books most for their relentless questioning of masculine myths of success. Rodriguez is involved in an unflinching cataloguing of the costs for himself of becoming a successful, "public" man. The elegiac tones of his autobiographies bespeak his sense of loss in his transformation. Rodriguez articulates the cost of being masculine in America.

Notes

1. Michael Herzfeld, *The Poetics of Manhood: Contest and Identity in a Cretan Mountain Village* (Princeton: Princeton University Press, 1985), 10. Hereafter cited parenthetically in text.
2. Jeff Hearn has argued that masculinity in the late nineteenth and

twentieth centuries is connected to a widening of the sphere of the "public man" and linked to organizations such as the state. See Jeff Hearn, *Men in the Public Eye: The Construction and Deconstruction of Public Men and Public Patriarchies* (New York: Routledge, 1992).

3. Richard Rodriguez, *Hunger of Memory: The Education of Richard Rodriguez* (New York: Bantam Books, 1983), 7. Hereafter cited parenthetically in text.

4. See Martin A. Danahay, "Breaking the Silence: Symbolic Violence and the Teaching of Contemporary 'Ethnic' Autobiography," *College Literature* 18, no. 3 (October 1991): 64-79; George Yuridice, "Marginality and the Ethics of Survival," in *Universal Abandon?: The Politics of Postmodernism* (Minneapolis: University of Minnesota Press, 1988); Michael M. J. Fischer, "Ethnicity and the Postmodern Arts of Memory," in *Writing Culture: The Poetics and Politics of Culture* (Berkeley: University of California Press, 1986); Werner Sollors, *Beyond Ethnicity: Consent and Descent in American Culture* (New York: Oxford University Press, 1986).

5. Rodriguez's attitude to silence shares some features with the role of silence in *Woman Warrior* and *I Know Why the Caged Bird Sings*; however, it also differs in the way Rodriguez links silence to his father, and speech to his mother. For analyses of silence in *Woman Warrior*, see King-Kok Cheung, "Don't Tell: Imposed Silence in *The Color Purple* and *The Woman Warrior*," *PMLA* 103, no. 2 (March 1988): 162-74; Elaine H. Kim, "Defining Asian American Realities through Literature," in *Cultural Critique* 6 (Spring 1987); Sally L. Kitch, "Gender and Language: Dialect, Silence and the Disruption of Discourse," *Women's Studies* 14, no. 1 (1987); and Sidonie Smith, *A Poetics of Women's Autobiography* (Bloomington: Indiana University Press, 1987).

6. In this Rodriguez parallels the account of masculine socialization in such studies as Nancy Chodorow's *The Reproduction of Mothering: Psychoanalysis and the Sociology of Gender* (Berkeley: University of California Press, 1978) and Arthur Brittan's *Masculinity and Power* (New York: Basil Blackwell, 1989). On pages 190–92, Brittan critiques the essentialist aspects of Chodorow's account, and argues that such gendered characteristics are socially constructed.

7. Andrew Tolson, *The Limits of Masculinity* (New York: Harper and Row, 1979), 48.

8. Jonathan Rutherford, *Men's Silences: Predicaments in Masculinity* (New York: Routledge, 1992), 78.

9. Richard Rodriguez, *Days of Obligation: An Argument with My Mexican Father* (New York: Viking Penguin, 1992), 2. Hereafter cited parenthetically in text.

10. Rodriguez's characterization of masculinity echoes analyses of male

attitudes toward emotion and intimacy by literary critics. For instance, Peter Middleton in *The Inward Gaze: Masculinity and Subjectivity in Modern Culture* (New York: Routledge, 1992) points out that "men in most Western cultures are not supposed to show any emotion in public other than anger . . . because anger is masculine power at its most impressive" (212). Hereafter cited parenthetically in text.

11. I am acutely aware that the same is true of my own analysis; although this article is motivated by strong personal interests, they do not appear overtly in the text. I am performing a "public" role here that relies upon the kind of separation of work and "private" life that Tolson describes in *The Limits of Masculinity*.

Contributors

David Bergman is the author of *Gaiety Transfigured: Gay Self-Representation in American Literature* (University of Wisconsin Press, 1991) and the winner of the George Elliston Poetry Prize for *Cracking the Code* (Ohio State University Press, 1985). He edited John Ashberry's *Reported Sightings: Art Chronicles 1957–87* (Knopf, 1989).

Miriam Cooke is Professor of Arabic at Duke University. In 1993 she edited, with Angela Woolacott, *Gendering War Talk* (Princeton University Press). Her anthology of Arab women's feminist writings in translation, *Opening the Gates: One Hundred Years of Arab Feminist Writing*, was published by Indiana University Press in the United States and by Virago in the United Kingdom. It has been translated into Dutch and German. Professor Cooke is the author of *The Anatomy of an Egyptian Intellectual: Yahya Haqqi* (Three Continents, 1984) and *War's Other Voices: Women Writers on the Lebanese Civil War* (Cambridge University Press, 1988). She has translated Haqqi's novel, *Good Morning! and Other Stories* (Three Continents, 1987).

Martin A. Danahay is a British, white, masculine middle-class subject and an Assistant Professor of English at Emory University, where he teaches courses on Victorian literature and the theory and practice of autobiography. He has published articles on ethnic autobiography, Victorian autobiography, and Victorian painting. His book, *A Community of One: Masculine Autobiography and Autonomy in Nineteenth-Century British Literature*, was published by the State University of New York Press in 1993.

309

Richard Dellamora, who recently completed a year as a Visiting Fellow in the department of English at Princeton University, lives in Toronto and teaches in the Departments of English and Cultural Studies at Trent University in Peterborough, Ontario. He is the author of *Masculine Desire: The Sexual Politics of Victorian Aestheticism,* (University of North Carolina Press, 1990) and *Apocalyptic Overtures: Sexual Politics and the Sense of an Ending* (forthcoming from Rutgers University Press 1994).

Leonard Duroche, whose major teaching and research areas are the literary representations of masculinity and the social construction of gender narratives, is an Associate Professor of German at the University of Minnesota. He is a former editorial board member of *Men's Studies Review,* is currently an associate editor of *The Journal of Men's Studies,* and is also editing an encyclopedia of men's studies. His publications include a book, *Aspects of Criticism* (Mouton, 1967), and articles on German, comparative literature, and male gender studies in various American and German scholarly journals. He is also a contributor to *Men, Masculinity and Social Theory,* edited by Jeff Hearn and David Morgan (Unwin and Hyman, 1990).

Jim Elledge has edited a collection of essays and reviews on Frank O'Hara, *Frank O'Hara: To Be True to a City* (University of Michigan Press, 1990). He wrote the article on O'Hara for the *Reader's Encyclopedia of American Literature* and published an essay on him, " 'Never Argue with the Movies': Love and the Cinema in Frank O'Hara's Poetry," in *Poet & Critic.* His critical essays have appeared in *Contemporary Poets* (4th and 5th eds.), *American Poetry, Tar River Poetry, Studies in Short Fiction,* among others. His books include *Weldon Kees: A Critical Introduction; Standing "Between the Dead and the Living": The Elegiac Technique of Wilfred Owen's War Poems; Various Envies: Poems; Nothing Nice: Poems;* and *Sweet Nothings: An Anthology of Rock and Roll in American Poetry.* He is an Associate Professor of English at Illinois State University and is the editor of *The Illinois Review.*

Alfred Habegger is a Professor of English at the University of Kansas. He is the author of *Gender, Fantasy and Realism in Ameri-*

can Literature (Columbia University Press, 1982) and *Henry James and the "Woman Business"* (Cambridge University Press, 1989). He has published in *PMLA, Novel, American Literature, New England Quarterly, Women's Studies,* and many other journals; his story, "A Little Spoon," appeared in *The New Yorker.* His current project, *The Father: A Life of Henry James, Sr.,* will be published by Farrar, Straus & Giroux.

Suzanne Kehde's article, "Voices from the Margin" appeared in *Feminism and Dialogics,* edited by Dale Bower and Susan Jaret McKinstry (SUNY Press, 1991); "Spivak, Bakhtin, Vygotsky and the Bag Lady" was published in *Perigraph* (Fall 1988); "Walter Van Tilburg Clark and the Withdrawal of Landscape" is forthcoming in *Western Landscape—Real and Imagined: Essays on Space and Place,* edited by Leonard Engel (University of New Mexico Press). Her play, *Everything You Always Wanted,* was produced at Wichita State University Theatre in November 1989. Kehde is a lecturer at California Polytechnic State University, San Luis Obispo.

David Leverenz is the author of *Manhood and the American Renaissance* (Cornell University Press, 1989), *The Language of Puritan Feeling* (Rutgers University Press, 1980), and various articles on American literature. He has also co-edited *Mindful Pleasures: Essays on Thomas Pynchon* (Little, Brown, 1976). From 1969 to 1985 he taught at Rutgers, where he chaired the Department of English at Livingston College for five years. He is now a Professor of English at the University of Florida.

Christopher Metress is an Assistant Professor of English at Samford University in Birmingham, Alabama. His work has appeared in *Essays in Literature, Studies in the Novel,* and *Studies in Short Fiction.* He is currently editing a collection of critical essays on Dashiell Hammet for Greenwood Press.

Peter F. Murphy is the Assistant Dean and an Assistant Professor of Cultural Studies at SUNY Empire State College. He has been a Fulbright Teaching Fellow at the Universidade Federal do Rio

Grande do Sul, in Porto Alegre, Brazil. His essay on John Hawkes, "The Woman Writer and Male Authority in *Virginie: Her Two Lives*" will be published in *Men Writing the Feminine: Literature, Theory, and the Question of Genders*, edited by Thaïs Morgan (SUNY Press, 1994). "Cultural Studies as Praxis" appeared in the June 1992 issue of *College Literature*.

Rafael Pérez-Torres is an Assistant Professor of English at the University of Pennsylvania. He teaches contemporary American literature for the Department of English and has published articles on the novels of Rudolpho Anaya, Luís Rafael Sánchez, and Toni Morrison. His most recent projects include *Against Myths, Against Margins—Movement in Chicano Poetry*, a book-length study of the course of Chicano poetic expression, and two forthcoming critical articles: "Nomads and Migrants—Negotiating a Multicultural Postmodernism" in *Cultural Critique* and "Feathering the Serpent: Chicano Mythic 'Memory,'" in *The Uses of Memory in Multi-Ethnic Literatures*, edited by Joseph Skerrett and Amritjit Singh. Pérez-Torres is also the academic coordinator for the Institute for Recruitment of Teachers, a program that encourages gifted college students of color to become teachers at the secondary and university level.

David Radavich is a poet, playwright, and literary critic. In addition to a play, *Nevertheless . . .* (Aran, 1988) and a collection of poems, *Slain Species* (Court Poetry, 1980), he has published a wide variety of poetry in the United States and abroad. His plays have been performed by the Charleston Alley Theatre, Mid-America Playwrights Theatre, and the Missouri Association of Playwrights, among others. He has also published academic articles on drama, poetry, and the contemporary writing scene. From 1979 to 1981 he taught as a Fulbright Junior Lecturer at the Universität Stuttgart, West Germany; currently he is Professor of English at Eastern Illinois University.

Peter Schwenger teaches English at St. Vincent University in Halifax, Nova Scotia. He is the author of *Phallic Critiques: Masculinity* *and Twentieth-Century Literature* and *Letter Bomb: Nuclear Holocaust and the Exploding Word.* The chapter included in this book was originally delivered as the keynote address for a conference on *Gender and the Curriculum* sponsored jointly by St. John's University and the College of St. Benedict in Minnesota.

Index